SPORT, EXERCISE AND SOCIAL THEORY

1 t

- Why are sport and exercise important?
- What can the study of sport and exercise tell us about wider society?
- Who holds the power in creating contemporary sport and exercise discourses?

It is impossible to properly understand the role that sport and exercise play in contemporary society without knowing a little social theory. It is social theory that provides the vocabulary for our study of society, that helps us ask the right critical questions, and that encourages us to look for the (real) story behind sport and exercise.

Sport, Exercise and Social Theory is a concise and engaging introduction to the key theories that underpin the study of sport, exercise, and society, including feminism, post-modernism, (Neo-)Marxism, and the sociological imagination. Using vivid examples and descriptions of sport-related events and exercise practices, the book explains why social theories are important and how to use them, giving students the tools to navigate with confidence through any course in the sociology of sport and exercise.

This book shows how theory can be used to debunk many of our traditional assumptions about sport and exercise and how they can be a useful window through which to observe wider society. Designed to be used by students who have never studied sociology before, and including an entire chapter on the practical application of social theory to their own study, it provides training in critical thinking and helps students to develop intellectual skills that will serve them throughout their professional and personal lives.

Gyozo Molnar is Senior Lecturer in Sport Studies in the Institute of Sport and Exercise Science at the University of Worcester, UK. His current publications and research revolve around migration, football, globalization, national identity, the Olympics, and sport-related role exit.

John Kelly is Lecturer in Sport and Recreation Business Management in the Moray House School of Education at Edinburgh University, UK. His research interests revolve around ethnicity, sectarianism, nationalism, militarism, and sport.

SPORT, EXERCISE AND SOCIAL THEORY

AN INTRODUCTION

GYOZO MOLNAR AND JOHN KELLY

Taylor & Francis Group

LONDON AND NEW YORK

First published 2013
by Routledge
2 Park Square, Milton Park, Abingdon, Oxon OX14 4RN

Simultaneously published in the USA and Canada
by Routledge
711 Third Avenue, New York, NY 10017

Routledge is an imprint of the Taylor & Francis Group, an informa business

British Library Cataloguing in Publication Data
A catalogue record for this book is available from the British Library

Library of Congress Cataloging in Publication Data
Molnár, Gyözö
Sport, exercise and social theory : an introduction / Gyozo Molnar,
John Kelly.
    p. cm.
    1. Sports – Sociological aspects. 2. Exercise – Sociological aspects.
I. Kelly, John. II. Title.
GV706.5.M65 2012
306.4´83–dc23   2012018407

ISBN: 978-0-415-67062-3 (hbk)
ISBN: 978-0-415-67063-0 (pbk)
ISBN: 978-0-203-13174-9 (ebk)

Typeset in Melior
by HWA Text and Data Management, London

MIX
Paper from
responsible sources
FSC
www.fsc.org   FSC® C013604

Printed and bound by CPI Group (UK) Ltd, Croydon, CR0 4YY

CONTENTS

ACKNOWLEDGEMENTS

We express our thanks to Routledge, especially to Simon Whitmore, who supported and helped develop the initial idea behind this book. We are also extremely grateful to Joshua Wells at Routledge for his unwavering support and much needed guidance during the production process. We also express our gratitude to our colleagues in our institutes at both Worcester and Edinburgh Universities for their support, encouragement, and helpful comments on early drafts of some of the chapters. And, last but not least, we thank all those students at both universities who took the time and effort to read and comment on various chapters of this book and made invaluable suggestions.

CHAPTER 1

INTRODUCTION

This book is first and foremost about sport and exercise, activities that are generally associated with fun, fair play, and the pursuit of healthy lifestyles, often viewed as separate from the challenges and toils of everyday life. It is no coincidence that the word *sport* emerges out of *disport*, meaning to indulge oneself in pleasure. Many of us who work within or study these spheres of activity already know the pleasure of playing, coaching, and watching sport and have been told of the benefits of engaging in regular bouts of exercise. Sport also provides many of us with a sense of belonging – most clearly witnessed perhaps during international sporting events that elicit the devotion of millions of strangers within the same country to form the 'imagined community' (Anderson, 1983) of the nation. Exercise, meanwhile, has become a major contributor to our sense of self, with health and fitness increasingly becoming our personal responsibility and marker of the responsible citizen. Yet, sport and exercise affect us in a multitude of ways that are often not obvious or clear and sometimes reveal surprising or even shocking aspects of their use and experience in our societies. We aim to shed light on some of these latent relationships for students, in tandem with helping them learn about social theory and how it can enable us to develop deeper understanding of sport and exercise and the societies in which they exist and, perhaps, flourish. Though our primary aim with this book is to enable students' greater understanding of sport and exercise in the twenty-first century, an implicitly connected aim is to develop their knowledge and ability to apply social theory, which we hope will improve their understanding of the complex and constant interplay between these activities and society.

Most sociologists (and, hopefully, historians too) would agree that society as a whole is socially constructed, and social habits are not set in stone. Social practices, values, and beliefs change and transform over time. What once was acceptable and cherished may now be frowned upon and uncouth or vice versa (see Chapter 7 for a more detailed discussion). For instance, our thoughts and perceptions about healthy lifestyle and the required amount and type of exercise have changed (for an historical account regarding men's exercise, diet, and grooming habits, see Luciano, 2001). Another example would be the gradually vanishing amateur ethos and associated values initially underpinning modern sports that have almost completely been replaced by hard-core professionalism (see Ingham and Loy, 1993). That is, sport and exercise have different meanings to different people in different places and in different time periods. The meaning(s) attached to them can diverge from society to society and from period to period, but so, too, can it differ at any one time in the same society. That is, sport and exercise always have multiple meanings.

Shifting social values and practices are not unique to sports and exercise. Other social structures undergo similar social processes, too. Education is one of the largest social structures affecting most of us during our life, and it also both enjoys and suffers the results of social change. One of these relatively recent changes that we have experienced is linked to widening participation in the higher education (HE) sector and, thereby, to the number and expectations of students entering university life (e.g. see Taylor, 2007). Therefore, it is safe to say that the landscape of British HE has significantly changed in the last decade and that it continues transforming (for a thought-provoking discussion of this, see Sparkes, 2007). In considering these socio-political currents, a primary rationale of this book is to respond to the rising changes in HE and to meet and cater for the emerging needs of current student cohorts.

Sociology, too, both as an academic discipline and everyday practice, has evolved greatly, and there is now a wide range of novel and recycled approaches and theories used and issues covered. The continuous transformation the sociology of sport and exercise has undergone is another rationale for writing this book and for providing a current outlook on the sub-discipline. However, despite the aforementioned changes, the basic purpose and nature of sociology and the sociology

2

of sport have remained relatively unaffected: That is, they focus on both the social (structures) and the personal (agency). On a personal (micro-) level, sociology is about helping us understand, decode, theorise, and interpret our own and others' behaviour in society (social structures). On a society-wide (macro-) level, sociology investigates the ways in which social structures operate and affect each other. We argue that today considering both the micro- and macro-aspects of society, supported by appropriate and sufficient empirical evidence, is essential for undertaking sociological studies to be able to unfold the multiple meanings that our fast-paced information societies (Feather, 2008) currently create and carry.

Due to its direct connection and sensitivity to past, present, and (hopefully) future social practices, sociology should not be considered an elusive abstraction invented and written about by secluded social scientists safely positioned in their ivory towers (although, sometimes, this might be the case). On the contrary, it is (and should be) a concerted effort and rigorous craft to reveal, interpret and, potentially, remedy social issues. The critical and inquisitive mind that can be developed and achieved through engagement with sociology (e.g. reading, debating, and writing about contrasting socio-political ideas) is, we would argue, an essential skill that is transferable across academic disciplines and everyday-life situations. We all have some degree of sociological imagination, and we all are, to varying extent, sociologists as we encounter, interpret, and negotiate a wide range of social situations on a daily basis. We also have the tendency to develop patterns and routines of thinking and acting and, thus, take specific aspects of our social practices and existence for granted. This is partly why when our students are first asked to provide examples of sport being used for political purposes, they highlight almost universally the Berlin Olympic Games of 1936 as the 'Hitler Games' or the 'Nazi Games'. Sometimes, they are able to point the 'political' finger at the ex-Communist bloc countries for their (ab)use of sports during the Cold War in their quest to demonstrate what they regarded as the moral superiority of communism over Western capitalism. Our students, therefore, pinpoint numerous examples of steroid use or extreme regimes for child athletes. Our students, however, seldom see 'our' own political use of sport. When we accept 'our' social norms and conform to the expectations and practices inherent in 'our' wider society, we may cease thinking deeply and critically about why we do what we do and how our acts, values, and practices may affect us and others. In other words, we allow society's norms and values to dictate the rules of our life and, in turn, transform our sociological awareness into meek acquiescence. To have our sociological imagination wither away is one of the outcomes of dominant ideologies – perhaps an aim of powerful people sympathetic to such ideologies – because in our somewhat subdued state, imprisoned by our own ready-made busy lives, we may forget (or not bother) to ask vital questions, even if we are aware that questions should be asked, which those with a critical mind might. For instance, by being acquiescent and believing in dominant narratives, we may never recognise that: hosting mega events such as the Olympics always has drawbacks; sports are not inherently or universally benevolent and good for wider society; being overweight may not be as dangerous to our health as being on a diet or as detrimental to our psychological well-being as the social stigma attached to being branded overweight; social class and our upbringing do have significant effects on our life chances; carrying out 'sex tests' on athletes may be viewed by some as assault and/or surveillance of the body gone too far; and we have not only the right but responsibility to express our disagreement with social structures such as government, education, and the corporate media, particularly when the decisions and values they make and promote around sport and exercise are done in *our* name.

To illustrate the complexity of roles sport and exercise play in our societies, please consider the following: Whilst writing this book, we were struck by the number and range of television news items around sport that appeared as mainstream news stories distinct from the usual separate 'sport section'. In a one-week period alone, these stories ranged from one of China's most famous athletes, Yao Ming, heading an anti-shark fin soup campaign to protect sharks from industrial killing, to a debate about eight-year-old children cage fighting in the north of England, to a major politician discussing the possibilities of 'Brand UK' on the back of the London 2012 Olympic Games. Within a short space of time, these stories had been joined by Dan Wheldon's fatal crash at the USA Indy Car event in Las Vegas; Marco Simocello's death at the Malaysian Grand Prix; England football captain John Terry's alleged racist remarks to an opponent; and the Scottish government's debate on a new law designed to prevent political expression at Scottish football matches. The field of exercise is just as contentious and is no stranger to the media, where our attention is often drawn to various news items that detail how much we should exercise and what physical activity we should carry out. With regular frequency, we are bombarded with 'expert' advice regarding what to wear, drink, and eat before, during, and after exercise and are informed that it will all make us healthy(ier), more attractive, and ergo, socially more acceptable.[1] In addition to being coerced into (not only doing but) consuming exercise, we are exposed to hyper-masculine male and hyper-thin female bodies that are portrayed as desirable, achievable, and associated with health and high social status. By fuelling our desire to be 'healthy' and possess the ideal body (for men: masculine and lean; for women: thin but shapely), various media messages and advertisements encourage us to buy the latest, state-of-the-art equipment, products, and nutritional supplements to achieve the physique that 'everyone wants'.

By revealing the centrality of sport and exercise in our lives in a number of competing and contradictory ways, the preceding examples provide another rationale for writing this book and discussing sport and exercise from sociological perspectives. Whether we are considering the use of sports stars for ideological purposes, questioning our drive for obtaining the ideal body, debating the fitness and moral arguments around schooling young boys in competitive combat, treating a nation-state as a brand, discussing the dangers of high-speed racing events, bemoaning the lack of role models in top-class sport, or alleging the widespread racism and bigotry in sport, one thing is certain: Sport and exercise are no mere *reflection* of society; they are at its kernel. Consequently, in line with the aim and promise of sociology and like many sociologists before, we persistently seek to find and, through this book, encourage students to continuously search for answers to respond to the question: 'Why do we do what we do in the field of sport and exercise?' In the next sections, we explain what we wish to achieve with this book and outline our main goals and the structure of this volume by providing a brief overview of the chapters that follow.

WHAT WE WISH TO ACHIEVE

We have been involved in HE for more than ten years and, during that time, we have taught a range of sociology of sport and exercise-related modules at various universities in the United Kingdom and the United States. The common denominator of our experience in HE has been the realisation that learning about sociology has the potential to be challenging, as the subject is frequently perceived by students as abstract and overly theoretical. Undergraduate sport and exercise sciences students, in particular, have often expressed their difficulty with learning sociology (i.e. understanding and applying theories), and they sometimes seem to prefer and cope better with other, more practical modules. However, the very essence of sociology (and, it could be argued, many other disciplines as well) is theoretical engagement through thinking with classic and modern (post-modern) conceptual frameworks to generate lucid summations of societies (or of a specific sub-section of a society), social values, social practices, and individuals' perceptions of society and themselves. So, to be sociological and critical, we must also be theoretical.

Our discussions with students and careful consideration of our students' feedback throughout the years have led us to write this introductory sociology book for mainly sports and exercise sciences students to help them get successfully acquainted with the discipline of sociology and, in so doing, further their knowledge and understanding of sport and exercise. That is, our main aim is to bridge the gap between students and social theories and to afford an informative and accessible textbook that practically explains and critiques a range of well-established and emerging sociological approaches and theories within the areas of sport and exercise. Even though chiefly aimed at sport and exercise students, we think that students outside of these areas but with an interest in sociology would benefit from reading this book to help them realise that both sports and exercise have a range of obvious and hidden social connotations.

Unfortunately, we do not have a magic wand and cannot dispense with the jargon of sociology, but we seek to be more sensitive than others before us to the needs, ability, and reality of many contemporary sports students having little or no prior learning experience of sociological theories.[2] Hence, we aim to provide clear accounts of sociological perspectives by explaining and critiquing them in the contemporary world and applying them to selected sport and exercise examples. We have sought to create an effective learning resource that students can use and reuse throughout their university studies to gain and reinforce

6

their sociology-related knowledge. In doing so, we endeavour to help students in building a solid conceptual foundation that will enable them to develop more informed and critical sociological accounts of their sports and exercise habits and general social surroundings.

In attempting this, we outline a selection of key sociological perspectives that have contemporary utility in aiding understanding of twenty-first-century sports worlds and exercise habits. These theoretical approaches are then applied to a number of selected sporting examples – historical and contemporary – and students are shown how these theories can help explain and debunk common claims and critically inform our understanding of the structural and individual power (or lack of it) particular groups/actors have in the world of sport and exercise. We believe that by embedding a selection of sporting examples within the theoretical chapters, students will more easily connect theory and evidence. This also demonstrates some of the ways theories, concepts, and related ideologies have been and can be used to manufacture consent (i.e. to make masses believe that sports are all-embracing, apolitical, and positive, benefiting society as a whole).

We can, thus, summarise our two main objectives: First, we make an attempt to facilitate the genuine application of sociological perspectives to sporting examples in ways that are not artificial or 'stuck on'. In our experience, too many students think in ways that result in their trying to 'fit' the sport example artificially into the theoretical framework. They resultantly misunderstand and/or misrepresent the sport or exercise example and the theoretical explanation, thereby creating a misfit between theory and evidence. This phenomenon probably derives from the fact that students often struggle to come to terms with the concept, meaning, and relevance of sociological theories, in fact with a range of sociological theories, which would be essential in properly conceptualising sport-related social issues. Thus, they automatically select the one that, for whatever reason, they find easiest to describe. By doing so, they limit themselves, curb their sociological imagination, and distort the sociological explanations of otherwise intriguing and relevant examples. In many instances, students with promising sociological observations and social examples to explore fail to demonstrate good levels of theoretical insight because of misinterpretations and/or selecting the only – but not necessarily relevant – theory they believe they understand. Consequently, and second, with this book, we also make an attempt to provide a potential remedy for such mono-theoretical thinking and application of sociology by making a range of theoretical approaches accessible to students. Whilst each chapter discusses a range of sporting examples, some examples are repeated across chapters to demonstrate to students how different perspectives can be used to explain the same sporting example in different ways. Of course, each reader should form her or his own opinion regarding which theoretical explanations are the most appropriate, insightful, and believable.

Whilst utilising mainly contemporary sociological theories, we aim to explain, wherever appropriate and necessary, their classical roots or historical links and to encourage students to develop their historical sensibility and understanding. Thus, each chapter provides a general overview of a selected theory and a biographic note of the central thinker(s) within that perspective. At the beginning of each chapter, we introduce a sport or exercise example, which we will refer back to in the chapter to explain and reiterate key concepts to help ease students' comprehension of sociology, its application, and the terminology surrounding it. These sport and exercise examples may occasionally draw wider links to other (sub-) disciplines (e.g. media studies and gender studies), showing an inter-disciplinary approach to understanding the complex nature and interconnectedness of sport and exercise in society. Occasionally, we draw wider links to other theories to illustrate how some explanations can benefit from combining more than one theory (e.g. see Chapters 5 and 6). We then examine specific concepts associated with that perspective and apply them to selected sport and exercise examples. The penultimate section of each chapter is a critical overview of the theoretical perspective covered. The main aim of this section is to demonstrate that no social theory is perfect and that we, sociologists, should always maintain an open and inquisitive mind, being critical of our own theoretical perceptions and limitations. Given the complexity of contemporary societies, we cannot (and should not) seriously claim that one theory can fully and perfectly explain every human action and cultural subtlety. With our investigations, we may try to achieve a reasonable account or reality-congruent explanation but, we would argue, that is as far as we can go. The last section of each chapter provides further readings whereby we direct students to classic and relevant sources

8

that, in practical terms, could be used by a wide range of students studying sport science/sport studies degrees.

We have also included a number of 'Reflection' boxes embedded in chapters. These boxes have many functions from providing brief definitions of selected concepts to detailing examples of engaging theory and evidence or serving as reminders and/or aids for understanding. In these boxes, we have featured a variety of 'Let's stop and think' questions to encourage critical reflection from students to practice and enhance their sociological imagination (see Chapter 2). We advise students to think about the examples and questions included in the chapters and discuss them among themselves and with their seminar tutors.

In this book and through the following chapters, we continuously argue against the tendency to artificially separate theory and evidence and society and sport, and we deploy an array of examples to demonstrate the socio-cultural embeddedness of sport and exercise. In doing so, we argue against the belief that sport is a social institution external to social actors and, thus, is a 'protuberance on society', transcending local – regional – global social issues or that sport simply mirrors society, assuming a passive, obsequious role within a great monolithic social entity. We encourage using sport and exercise as a window through which to gaze critically at society as we believe that each cannot be understood without the other.

STRUCTURE OF THE BOOK

In the second chapter, we unfold the meaning of sociological imagination by explaining what C. W. Mills means by this concept and what its key features are. After defining sociological imagination (SI), we turn our attention to the importance of differentiating between social issues and personal troubles and outlining the range of sensibilities that the active use of SI involves. We also provide a brief biographical note on Mills to illustrate his rebellious nature and achievements in sociology.

We begin the third chapter by looking at Emile Durkheim's work, in particular, his examination of the relationship between the individual and society. This involves looking at his concepts of the division of labour, mechanical and organic solidarity and his theory of suicide. We then discuss the post-1940s functionalist perspectives and how they can help us explain and understand sport, exercise and society, with reference to Talcott Parsons' work on social systems and social structure. We conclude with a functionalist analysis of sporting examples.

In the following chapter, we chart the (neo-)Marxist journey beginning with the works of Karl Marx, discussing his concepts of class, alienation, and ideology. We then turn to the Frankfurt School that became known for applying Marx's work in the modern age. With the help of Pierre Bourdieu's influential class analyses, we show that cultural forms such as sport and exercise join economic wealth as major conduits of class in the twenty-first century.

In the cultural studies chapter, we begin by showing how culture is viewed as contested terrain to be understood according to particular social and political contexts. The historical development of the perspective is then briefly outlined, including explaining its links to neo-Marxism. In the second part of the chapter, cultural symbols are shown to have multiple possible meanings, and these representations are explained as part of signifying systems that become normalised and/or conventional. This leads us into a discussion of the power to give meanings and values to cultural practices. This is where we consider the position of Antonio Gramsci's concept of hegemony to help explain how mass consent is achieved in stratified societies among competing class groups.

In the symbolic interaction chapter, we locate the approach's origins from its functionalist antecedents before charting its journey from George Herbert Mead's work on 'the self' and the subsequent establishment of symbolic interaction by his ex-student Herbert Blumer. We then turn attention to Blumer's ex-student Erving Goffman, whom we discuss in detail by outlining his famous symbolic interaction dramaturgy model before applying it to the world of sport and exercise.

In the chapter on process-sociology, we outline the significance of Norbert Elias, the first modern mainstream sociologist to pay extensive attention to sports, and some of the key concepts of process-sociology

10

such as the civilising process, social figurations, and sportisation process and how these have been and might be used to explain sports and exercise-related social practices over time. The chapter also devotes significant attention to the concept and phenomena of global sports and their interpretations through the notion of diminishing contrasts and increasing varieties.

In the feminisms chapter, we outline women's marginalisation in society and the ways in which the patriarchal social system has shaped sports and exercise. An exercise-related example is provided to explain and illustrate some of the major issues that women crossing gendered boundaries may face. Then we move on to discussing three specific rationales (aesthetic, biological, and social) that have been used to justify male dominance in both sport and exercise. Branches of feminism that frequently occur in academic discussions on sport and exercise, such as liberal, Marxist, radical, and post-modern, are also discussed.

In the chapter on post-modern perspectives, we discuss the socio-cultural shift from modernity to post-modernity, then turn our attention to some of those post-modernist concepts that have been used to explain sport and exercise-related issues. We consider two intellectual giants in the development and formation of post-modernity: Michel Foucault and Jean Baudrillard, whose work is gradually gathering momentum in sport and exercise. We explain sports and exercise-related social practices in late modernity and exclusively focus on disciplinary power (Foucault) and consumption and hyper-reality (Baudrillard).

In the final chapter, A guide to the craft of sociology, we provide practical advice for university students regarding their studies. In this chapter, we revisit C. W. Mills' 'On Intellectual Craftsmanship' chapter that appeared as the coda for *The Sociological Imagination*. Following the original chapter's outline, we give students tips on reading, writing, keeping a filing system, and recognising sociological and social connections. We then turn our attention to using personal experiences in studying and researching the social field and the relevance of balancing theory and evidence. We afford ample examples and suggestions that cut across a range of disciplines and, we hope, would make students' university studies more fruitful and enjoyable.

The book closes with an A-to-Z Glossary that is a broad list of definitions of key sociological concepts (e.g. class, status, hyperreality), enabling students to look up new and revisit/refresh notions already studied. Among many things, this feature will make the book relevant throughout students' university years. Whilst primarily aimed at undergraduates, we believe it will prove useful to postgraduates, too, especially for those mature students who return to education after many years of work and may have forgotten (or were never introduced to) the foundation of sociology but wish to embark on related studies.

CHAPTER 2

C. WRIGHT MILLS AND THE SOCIOLOGICAL IMAGINATION

Your sociological imagination (SI) has many uses, one of which is that the fields of sport and exercise can be viewed and interpreted through it. Specifically, by engaging your SI, you can see that there are numerous social reasons why you partake in certain sports and why you may never get involved or interested in others. For instance, your SI can help you explore and understand that if you are a man living in the United Kingdom, it is very likely that you might become involved in football (soccer) and/or rugby and that it is rather unlikely (but not impossible) to grow up to be a competitive skier. Or, you can see and interpret the social reasons behind American men getting predominantly involved in American football and baseball and Canadian men in ice hockey and other winter sports. By engaging your SI, you can also detect that most of these sport activities are gender-specific, geared toward a male clientele and, thus, women intending to partake or, in fact, partaking in them is often controversially received in contemporary Western societies. With the help of your SI, you can also observe that there are multiple reasons why you may decide to safeguard your health by taking up exercise, watching your diet, and quitting smoking. Alternatively, you can understand why you, along with others, may come to the conclusion that watching your diet and taking regular exercise are a waste of your time and so is listening to media-hyped health and dietary advice and campaigns often supported by health 'experts' and governments. In other words, you are going to be less likely to take social patterns, practices, and media messages for granted and more able to look behind the facade of everyday social occurrences and find/suggest truths alternative to the ones featured in dominant socio-political discourses.

Given that engaging your SI can help you – and, in fact, will encourage you – to become critical and, in turn, see the positive and the negative sides of everyday social practices and phenomena such as sport and exercise, it may be unsurprising that C. Wright Mills' work, extensively embedded in the use of SI, has often been controversially received. The reason for this is twofold: First, as we will describe in the Biographic Note, Mills' persona was controversial and, some might say, overly argumentative; second, he considered and critiqued social and sociological issues[1] with magnum force and which were of sensitive nature at the time of his academic career. Nevertheless, his book on and concept of sociological imagination has received extensive recognition and is still frequently used to help students get better acquainted with the nature, aim, and promise of sociology. We agree with Mills and also assert that SI is an essential concept in sociology because it encourages critical reflection and the practical application of sociology. When engaging your SI, it is vital that you question not only society per se but your position in it and the ways in which you investigate it. In other words, SI can help you achieve sociology's aim to and potential for identifying, understanding, and demystifying social issues. More important, SI connects you to sociology as a discipline whereby you learn to see yourself as a member of society and of a range of interest groups. By developing and engaging your SI, you will realise that seemingly distant and abstract social structures are, to varying extent, related to you and your immediate social milieu. It is worth quoting Mills (1959/2000: 3) to illustrate the connection between you/ us (agency) and external social forces (structures):

> The facts of contemporary history are also facts about the success and the failure of individual men and women. When a society is industrialised, a peasant becomes a worker; a feudal lord is liquidated or becomes a businessman. When classes rise or fall, a man is employed or unemployed; when the rate of investment goes up or down, a man takes new heart or goes broke.[2]

Mills explains that individuals and their life chances are greatly influenced by social structures and, when structures change, so do people's lives entangled in them. When structures shift, you have to move with them and, as a result, you may become redundant or forced into an unwanted position. 'When wars happen, an insurance salesman becomes a rocket launcher; a store clerk, a radar man' (Mills,

14

1959/2000: 3). Or, to provide a more contemporary example, you may become a personal trainer instead of working in the local shoe factory or a university student instead of looking for a real job. Using your SI can help you understand why you make certain choices or why you are being 'herded' to a specific direction. Willis provides a relevant example to demonstrate how external forces 'direct' individual choices.

> In difficult economic times, when jobs are difficult for everyone to secure, let alone for high school graduates, an understandable response by individual young people and their families has been to attempt to improve their chances in the job market by securing higher credentials. At the very least, by staying out of the job market for a few more years while getting a college education (what has been called 'warehousing the young'), a young person may see employment prospects improved.
>
> (Willis, 1996: 18)

The story, however, does not end here. 'Warehousing the young' has its consequences. There will be an increasing number of students attending universities, which might have an effect on the quality of education provided by those institutes. Universities may not have adequately prepared themselves for such increases in student numbers and, in turn, would have issues with finding appropriately large lecture rooms, with increased numbers of seminars, and with increased marking loads. Moreover, given that the growing unemployment is triggered by an economic decline and all public and private sectors are in the process of cutting costs, it is very likely that the staff already in position would have to deal with the increased workload, which would probably lead to them being exhausted and disenchanted with their job. These all have the potential to have an effect on the quality of education. In addition, with the increased number of university students and graduates, there comes the consequential inflation of university degrees. 'Jobs that were once done by high school graduates now require a college degree for entry' (Willis, 1996: 18–19). By virtue of the foregoing, one could argue that going to university because everyone does it and to enhance your life chances may not achieve what you might have initially thought.

We are not arguing against the relevance of education. On the contrary, we think that it is of great importance and, thus, should be done properly with teachers and lecturers who are knowledgeable and enthusiastic, with facilities that aid learning, and with skills in mind that will prepare you for life. Using your SI does not mean that you now must quit university and abandon your initial plans. Nor does it mean that life is and must be all gloom and doom as we are always at the mercy of social structures. Using your SI means that you can see more clearly what your life chances are, and then you can make more informed decisions as to how you want to capitalise on them. 'In many ways it is a terrible lesson; in many ways a magnificent one' (Mills, 1959/2000: 5). Engaging your SI is *magnificent* as it can show you the potentials you have in life and is *terrible* as it can reveal the obstacles you will have to face to achieve those potentials. For instance, if you realise that when you graduate there will be thousands of university graduates with similar qualifications applying for the same jobs, it is terrible news as you know that there will be fierce competition out there. Conversely, the early realisation of such competition would allow you to make necessary provisions so that you stand out. You would have time and opportunity to ensure that you have gained additional skills and experiences that would potentially give you the cutting edge. As Mills (1959/2000: 5) wrote: 'The sociological imagination enables its possessor to understand the larger historical scene in terms of its meaning for the inner life and the external career of a variety of individuals'.

As we said, the concept of SI is concerned with understanding your position and role(s) in society. Whatever degree of knowledge and understanding you have of your options, limitations, and roles in your immediate and more distant social milieux, by actively employing the concept of SI, your level of social and self-awareness can be

---

REFLECTION

Now relate what Mills states back to the example we outlined earlier by asking the following questions: What is the larger social/historical scene regarding higher education? What is the relevance of that in relation to you? In what ways have social structures (social/historical scene) had a bearing on your life choices? What can you do to maximise your potential given the current social scene?

significantly increased. 'The first fruit of this imagination... is the idea that the individual can understand his own experience and gauges his own fate' (Mills, 1959/2000: 5). The enhancement of self-awareness can be achieved by exploring a few fundamental sociological concepts and by adopting related self-reflective, self-investigative practices. This sociological self-discovery can be effectively used exploring the connections between personal troubles and social issues.

TROUBLES VERSUS ISSUES

Mills was genuinely concerned with people's lack of ability to distinguish and identify personal troubles and social issues and to recognise the historical and structural forces that have an effect upon their lives. He believed that most people 'do not possess the quality of mind essential to grasp the interplay of man and society, of biography and history, of self and world' (1959/2000: 4). Therefore, one of the salient aspects of SI is for us to recognise the necessity that although we need to differentiate between social issues (structure) and personal troubles (agency), these concepts are constantly interacting whereby they construct and reconstruct society and our situation within it. That is, social issues are connected to (our/your) personal troubles and vice versa.

Social issues are large-scale social problems and challenges that are faced by the majority of the population in a given era (e.g. obesity or unemployment). '*Issues* have to do with matters that transcend these local environments of the individual and the limited range of his life...An issue is a public matter: values cherished by publics felt to be threatened' (Mills, 1959/2000: 8, italics in original). Personal troubles, conversely, are difficulties individuals deal with on a personal level (e.g. loss of job or being overweight). '*Troubles* occur within the character of the individual and within the range of his immediate relations with others; they have to do with... those limited areas of social life of which he is directly and personally aware' (Mills, 1959/2000: 8, italics in original). 'A trouble is a private matter: values cherished by an individual are felt by him to be threatened' (Mills, 1963: 396). By engaging your SI, you can recognise the constant interplay between these two facets of society, which, when appropriately embraced, can lead to a fuller self-discovery. To illustrate the difference between

17

BIOGRAPHIC NOTE

If we had to describe C. Wright Mills in one word, *rebel* would be our choice.[3] This critical and iconoclastic thinker was born in 1916 in Waco, Texas to a conventional middle-class family. His father was an insurance broker and his mother a housewife. Mills began his university studies at Texas A & M University but, after one depressing year, he transferred to the University of Texas at Austin, where he completed his undergraduate and master's degrees in philosophy. In 1939, Mills moved to the University of Wisconsin to pursue his doctoral studies, which he carried out under the supervision of Hans H. Gerth, who facilitated Mills' acquaintance with the work of German sociologists. Prior to the completion of his PhD, Mills was offered his first post at the University of Maryland which he accepted but left in 1945. He relocated to Columbia University, where he remained for the rest of his life.

Wherever Mills studied or taught, he always ran into and/or created controversy. He constantly and tirelessly battled against anything and everything one could think of. 'One of the most striking things about Mills was his combativeness: he seemed to be constantly at war' (Ritzer, 1992: 211). Even as a child, he stood up against adults and challenged their views and authority. Mills was no different at university. As a graduate student, he heavily criticised established professors and, later, at Columbia University, his vitriolic comments regarding his fellow academics' work were not favourably received. Also, his vituperative views on Talcott Parsons' work, especially on his writing style, seemed never-ending. Mills was critical both of American social structures and academics trapped in them. Hence, he received support and camaraderie from only a handful of people. To illustrate Mills' fighting spirit, most books on him mention his invitation to the Soviet Union as he was severely critical of the American capitalist system. Whilst Mills accepted the invitation and the celebration, he used the opportunity to put a dent on Soviet political egos by critiquing the wide-spread state oppression in the country.

C. Wright Mills and the sociological imagination

Similar to his academic life, his private affairs were also controversial and full of activity. During his relatively short life, he married three times and had one child in each marriage. Ritzer (1992: 212) claims that Mills had 'a tumultuous life, characterised by many [sexual] affairs'. His demanding lifestyle and his ever-combatant attitude to sociology and social life eventually caught up with him, and Mills died at the young age of 45 of a heart attack.

In his short academic career, Mills produced thirteen controversial books in which he voiced his provocative and critical tone on a range of social issues. One of his well-known works is *White Collar: The American Middle Classes* (1951), in which he observes that the over-bureaucratisation of modern American society has robbed individuals of independent and creative thought and turned them into robots. However, these robots are cheerful as they are provided with a bearable existence that comes at the cost of being alienated from having an effect on larger social structures. Another noteworthy piece is *The Power Elite* (1956), in which Mills identifies three distinctive but interconnected groups of the elite – political, military, and financial – who collectively operate America. They perpetuate their own importance and existence by disallowing members of other social strata from entering their higher circles. These groups of the elite are in the position of power and can make decisions, which, in turn, supposes that the ordinary citizen is a relatively powerless subject of manipulation.[4] As you may have noticed, Mills paid a significant amount of attention to large social structures and their oppressive and exploitative power. It is little wonder that he was/is often associated with Marxism. This is no different in his, probably, most well-known book, *The Sociological Imagination* (1959). In this work, Mills made a powerful attempt to debunk the ways in which social structures can have an effect on social actors. He argued that the real power lies in the lack of recognition people have of their oppressors and them being oppressed, and only by recognising the difference between social issue and personal trouble and engaging and developing one's SI can one begin to fathom the degree of social oppression (cf. Chapter 5).

troubles and issues, Mills (1963: 396) provides an example on unemployment.

> When, in a city of 100,000, only one man is unemployed, that is his personal trouble, and for its relief we properly look to the character of this man, his skills and his immediate opportunities. But when in a nation of 50 million employees, 15 million are unemployed, that is an issue, and we may not hope to find its solution within the range of opportunities open to any one individual. The very structure of opportunities has collapsed.

Let's translate this connection and struggle between trouble and issue into sport by considering the influence of sport structures on athletes. Butt and Molnar (2009) investigated American varsity sport with regard to structurally induced failure. The authors argued that structural inducements to dropping out from sport are often overlooked and 'the fact that there are fewer and fewer places available the farther one works one's way up the feeder system of modern sport' is ignored (2009: 240). They identified six stages of the process of structurally induced failure in sport, during which athletes were carefully and strategically eliminated from their chosen sport by their coaches. All athletes interviewed had worked hard and had been under the impression that if they wanted to succeed, hard work and perseverance were the ticket to the Big Time. In the study, 'athletes discussed their hard work and effort at practice during the season and also the off-season as being an indicator of making a particular team. Athletes anticipated success based on their attendance at off-season practice sessions and summer camps' (Butt and Molnar, 2009: 251). Despite their anticipation of success, it later became gradually and painfully obvious to those athletes that they were going to be cut

---

REFLECTION

Think about whether you have experienced structurally induced failure in sport or exercise in your life. That is, ask the following questions: Have the social structures in place failed me in life, or have I failed social structures? This sort of failure you may have experienced as an athlete, coach, or exerciser and, by asking these questions, you link troubles and issues.

C. Wright Mills and the sociological imagination

from their sport. 'Motivation, commitment, effort and socialization are admirable qualities, but they are no direct guarantee of upward mobility in sport's occupational structure' (Butt and Molnar, 2009: 241). After structural elimination, 'athletes eventually show a tendency to blame themselves for getting cut from their primary sport. Specifically, a pattern of self-disappointment was apparent from the interview data' (Butt and Molnar, 2009: 251). Most of these athletes were slow to engage their SI and were conned by the feeder system of modern sport. If what is argued by Butt and Molnar (2009) concerns only a handful of athletes or a very small percent of the population of youngsters involved in sports, this may not be an issue but the personal trouble of those who have failed social structures. Conversely, if the number of athletes undergoing the process of structurally induced failure is significant[5] we cannot talk about personal troubles. We have a social issue at hand as structures failed athletes.

KEY ASPECTS OF SOCIOLOGICAL IMAGINATION

According to Loy and Booth (2004), SI consists of three strongly inter-related notions: craft, commitment, and sensibility (consciousness). We will not discuss commitment and the craft of sociology in this chapter, as we have devoted Chapter 10 to these aspects of SI where we outline a model for the practical application of SI and provide a 'how to' guide for you to establish and hone your sociological craft. (Note: We would recommend that you read Chapter 10 of this book after you have worked your way through this one.) We, however, pay appropriate heed to SI-associated sensibilities in the following sub-sections.

Sensibilities

When discussing SI, Giddens (1986: 13) notes that 'several related forms of sensibility [are] indispensable to sociological analysis' and lists *historical, anthropological,* and *critical.* Willis (1996) extends and slightly modifies Giddens's list by adding *cultural* and *structural* sensibilities (renaming *anthropological* as *cultural*). He writes, 'Applying the sociological imagination to understanding any social phenomenon involves considering four distinct [but interconnected] elements or components: *historical, cultural, structural,* and *critical*' (Willis, 1996: 7, italics added). More recently, Loy and Booth (2004) added another dimension – *corporeal* – to the previously listed sensibilities by recognising the relevance of the body in society and the growing sociological literature around it. Though acknowledging the importance of the body in society has its merits, singling out one particular aspect of society and adding that to the sensibilities associated with SI is not supported by us. We argue that, however relevant it might be, the body is only one part of the wider social spectrum across which sociologists find issues to investigate. If we decided to include the body, we would need to extend our list even further and enlist other social issues as sensibilities, for instance, gender, class, and race. This is not to say that it is not crucial to be mindful of social issues and consider them with great, critical care. However, we think that to clearly distinguish between approaches and issues is just as relevant. Acknowledging the presence of social issues around the body is especially important to those sociologists who are involved in the study of sport and exercise, but corporeality must remain a social issue, not an approach/ sensibility through which all social phenomena can be and must be investigated. In the following sub-sections (and chapters), we provide examples involving the body to illustrate arguments (e.g. see example of obesity at end of the section on *critical sensibility*), but we do not include corporeality into our list of key sensibilities. These examples are, just like the body, socially constructed labels, compartments, and issues that we as sociologists investigate but are not part of the tool kit with which we investigate them. Therefore, by combining Mills' original idea with the work of Giddens and Willis, the four sensibilities embedded in SI we will introduce to you here are *historical, cultural, structural,* and *critical.*

Historical

To understand our present, we must understand our past. It sounds like a cliché from one of the popular self-help books but, when it comes to sociology, this 'cliché' is significant. A great number of sociologists have alerted us to the importance of history in sociological analyses (see also the processual/historical thinking section of Chapter 7). Mills was certainly one who recognised the invaluable contribution of history to our understanding of contemporary society. 'The problems of our time...

cannot be stated adequately without consistent practice of the view that history is the shank of social study' (Mills, 1959/2000: 143). Willis (1996: 56) also observed that 'because history has an enormous effect on who we are as individuals and societies, it must be an integral part of the study of sociology'. Norbert Elias, whose work and contribution to the sociology of sport and exercise we discuss in Chapter 7, was also critical of those sociologists who retreated to the present and ignored the past in their explanations. Elias argued that contemporary society can adequately be understood only through long-term processual analyses involving the critical and multi-dimensional engagement of history. Consequently, 'the first effort of sociological imagination that has to be exercised by the analyst of the industrialised societies today is that of recovering our own immediate past – the 'world we have lost' (Giddens, 1986: 14). Only by doing so can we ensure that our sociological analyses 'attempt to come to terms with and understand the massive transformation in the social world (Willis, 1996: 57).

Let's look at, for instance, the so-called *sex test* in sport. To fully understand what it was and why it was implemented, we need to explore the historical reasons behind it, which cannot be done without enhancing our historical insight. Gender verification, or sex test, in sport was the result of Cold War paranoia. The rising concern of Western politicians, in general, and US politicians, in particular, toward the growing physical superiority of Soviet and Eastern European, especially their female athletes induced this practice of gender verification. As evidenced in debates around the so-called *muscle gap* (see De Oca, 2007), there was general concern in the United States that modern Western culture feminises its male citizens, and this was compounded by the masculine appearance of successful female athletes of the Eastern bloc. The effeminising impact of modern culture and the physical dominance of communist female athletes fundamentally shook Western gender stereotypes. It was commonly believed that some of the athletes of the Eastern bloc (e.g. Press sisters, ironically called the Press brothers) were men disguised as women. In an attempt to restore the traditional gender order and Western sport hegemony, a sex test for women taking part in international competitions was introduced and first carried out in 1966 at the European Athletic Championships (Bairner and Molnar, 2010). Gender verification was stopped in 1999, but there was an entire era when top female athletes had to endure the potentially psychologically scarring process due to political, ideological, and military tensions between the East and the West.

This example demonstrates the relevance of historical insight in developing an adequate sociological analysis and, given the cultural and ideological tension between the East and the West, it also points to the need for cultural sensibility.

Cultural

Cultural sensibility denotes the appreciation of culture as a key feature of societies and of socialisation and that there are, sometime vast, differences between cultures. 'Culture may be taken as constituting the "way of life" of an entire society, and this will include codes of manners, dress, language, rituals, norms of behaviour and systems of belief' (Jary and Jary, 2000:129). Cultural sensibility has two main aspects: 'to counter the conventionally held notion of a boundary between the natural and the social world, and to challenge notions that some cultures are superior to others' (Willis, 1996: 64). The first aspect of cultural sensibility is the age-old nature- (biological determinants) versus-nurture (social determinants) debate. This dispute revolves around the dilemma of the sole or more-dominant contributor to the development and formulation of human personality structures. Essentially, the chief question is: Are we *tabula rasa* (blank slate) or genetically pre-programmed/pre-determined individuals? It is not our aim here to take sides but to alert you to this aspect of cultural sensibility and to help you recognise that social phenomena cannot be adequately explained without considering cultural influences. As Mills (1959/2000: 132) puts it: 'What social sciences is properly about is the human [cultural] variety, which consists of the social worlds in which men have lived, are living, and might live'.

Cultural variety – human variety according to Mills – is relevant not only in regard to the socialisation and social development of agency but in terms of understanding how cultures are perceived by outsiders, representatives of other cultures. This leads us to the second aspect of cultural sensibility, which focuses on another tension that is between *ethnocentrism* and *cultural relativity*. Generally speaking, ethnocentrism is an old-fashioned way of perceiving and interpreting other peoples' culture. Ethnocentrism is usually judgemental and demeaning toward other cultural formations with the view to attribute superiority and more importance to one's own culture. Cultural relativism opposes this approach and offers a remedy to ethnocentrism by stating that cultures and social practices embedded in them should not be judged based on the values of another culture. Hence, each culture must be understood and interpreted on their own terms, not judged in relation to others. Giddens (1986: 20) observes that the anthropological (cultural) aspect of SI 'is important because it allows us to appreciate the diversity of modes of human existence which have been followed on this earth'.

Sports can be seen as a feature of Western ethnocentrism as they diffused predominantly from England to the rest of the globe. For

---

REFLECTION

There are two issues here you should consider regarding Western cultural dominance. First, Western countries should not be perceived as a unified, solid, and harmonious bloc of cultures united against the rest of the world. Jarvie (1991) debunked the myth of the integrity of Western nation states with regard to sports. He noted that British interventions in the Highlands are an exemplar for how centralising forces can give rise to dependency and cultural dominance with Western nation-states. This social dependency has obviously been influencing and forming the games and sports of the Highlands. The values of modern sport and capitalist British society through the processes of commercialisation, bureaucratisation, and commodification have been interacting with the indigenous sport culture and perhaps diminishing the original importance of the Highland Games. The second issue is that despite Western structural hegemony regarding sports and culture, local and regional entities have managed to preserve most of their local flavours and, as Bairner (2001: 12) aptly puts it: 'Global processes have not created a universe in which everyone drinks Coca-Cola and eats Big Macs with increasingly fewer dietary alternatives on offer'. Although social structures have not created a unified sporting culture, they are essential to be considered as one of the sensibilities associated with SI.

instance, consider the Olympics – a Western (re)invention – both the Summer and the Winter Games have for the most part been contested in Europe and North America. The Olympics have never taken place on the African continent. Although this Occidentalism seems to have eased off, given the 2008 Beijing Games, the 2010 FIFA World Cup in South Africa, and that in 2016 Rio de Janeiro will become the first South American city to host the Olympics, there can still be a Western structural dominance detected with regard to modern sports.

Structural

Structural sensibility unfolds the interplay between agency and structure (trouble and issue). 'We can think of both agency and structure as being important but neither as being solely responsible for a social phenomenon' (Willis, 1996: 76). That is, we need to question whether a specific event in history was the result of an agency or existing social structures or, perhaps, a combination of both. For instance, think about the foundation of the modern Olympics Games. Were they the sole achievement of Pierre de Coubertin or did social structures contribute as well. For another example, consider Jane Fonda's enormous success with selling exercise books and videos in the 1980s. Her first aerobics exercise video sold approximately 17 million copies and, in turn, became the most successful home video of all time. So, was it really Jane Fonda's personal qualities alone that led to this fruitful business venture or, perhaps, others factors also contributed? When we carefully examine both cases, we realise that there was interplay between agency and structures.

It would be foolish to deny de Coubertin's enormous personal contribution to the foundation and development of the modern Olympics. However, it would be equally foolish to say that he was solely responsible for the modern Games. 'The operation of particular historical agents, important though their personalities were, can be adequately understood only within a broader structural context' (Willis, 1996: 77). So, let's see some of the interactions between structure and agency.

Historical scene: After losing the French-Prussian war (1870–71) and the following disadvantageous Frankfurt peace treaty, the French aristocracy developed a genuine concern for the future of their nation and for the physical state of young men.

Cultural scene: During this climate of concern, de Coubertin believed that sport, and education through it, could reinvigorate his nation as he, too, lived under the impression that the French nation had been demoralised. During his extensive travels, de Coubertin encountered the Wenlock Games that gave him the idea that a quadrennially recurring international sporting event would help the reinvigoration of his nation.

Structural scene: He used his aristocratic national and international (structural capital combined with personal capital of agency) contacts to obtain support for his ideas. In 1894, he organised and held a conference at the Sorbonne, where the International Olympic Committee was created and the principles of Olympism were approved.

In a similar vein, Jane Fonda's success can be attributed to her personality and her physical appearance's adherence to the ideal of feminine beauty (personal capital of agency). The rapid spread of videocassette recorders also facilitated the wide spread of Fonda's exercise videos (historical scene). In addition, the ever-increasing modernisation and technologisation of life led to an ever-growing sedentary lifestyle for which Fonda's videos provided a remedy.

REFLECTION

As you may have noticed, clearly distinguishing between sensibilities is not always possible or necessary. What you consider historical may also be structural as well as cultural. For instance, in the example regarding Jane Fonda's exercise videos, the insecurities of modern women could be perceived as historical (modern women), structural (judging by the number of VHS tapes sold a large number of women experienced body-related insecurities) and cultural (buying exercise books and VHS tapes was a predominantly Western or Westernised phenomenon). We have separated these sensibilities out only for you to see how such analysis might be done.

Moreover, playing on the insecurities of modern women, Fonda's workout videos promised energy and attractiveness that cut across a range of social spheres from the household to the business office (structural/historical scene). In the case of both examples, you can see the interplay between agency and structure. De Coubertin's idea of reinventing the Olympics may have never taken off without his aristocratic links and a concern for the health of the French nation. Neither would have Jane Fonda's exercise videos become so extensively popular without an already existing demand for them and the accessibility of the videocassette recorder.

Critical

Another essential aspect of SI is critical sensibility. As criticality can easily be misconstrued, it is relevant to briefly explain what we mean by it. Being critical does not necessarily mean that you have to provide a negative view of whatever you are investigating. On the contrary, being critical means that you do not take things, ideas, and general assumptions for granted. To be critical, you have to become sceptical. This again does not mean that you are against or negative about an idea but that you are inclined to question it. It is possible that by the end of your process of questioning, the final outcome will be you agreeing with the original idea. Conversely, your process of critical inquiry my lead you to disagree with whatever you are investigating (for example, see our earlier discussion of Loy and Booth's (2004) idea of *corporeal sensibility* in the *sensibility* sub-section). What is important is that you question the original idea or issues and only after careful examination of it/them you decide to accept or reject it/them.

Generally speaking, the majority of people do not tend to perceive criticism very well and take it very personally. Moreover, critics have the tendency to be harsh and soul destroying and to forget that, as they are human beings, they can sometimes be wrong. Despite the difficulty of providing accurate, helpful, and balanced critiques, we simply cannot do without critical investigation in sociology (or, for that matter, in any other academic discipline) and, thus, we (should) make an attempt to provide constructive and well-informed criticisms, not soul-destroying vituperative recriminations.

Critical sensibility connects all other sensibilities associated with SI. The quest for debunking and demystifying social phenomena is (or should be) the starting point of any sociological enquiry. 'Applying critical sensibility means engaging in a systematic doubt about accounts of the social world, proceeding with scepticism about the claim of any statement to be valid' (Willis, 1996: 83). For Giddens (1986: 22) it has two aspects: critiquing 'the idea that sociology is like a natural science' and critiquing the existing forms of society in being aware of alternative futures. Critiquing the perceived similarities between sociology and natural sciences is necessary, as there is a clear and key difference between the subjects of investigation. In natural sciences, researchers investigate various features and components of nature that are, by and large, regulated by immutable laws (e.g. gravity). Whereas in sociology, we investigate various features and components of the social world that are socially constructed and, thus, change over time (see also Chapter 6). Johnson et al. (1992: 14, italics in original) clarify this dilemma as follows:

> When you *comply* with the laws of the state, there is no equivalence to the way in which a stone *complies* with the laws of gravity when it has been thrown into the air. This is not to suggest that you are free to disobey state law, while the stone cannot disobey gravity. It means you can *think* about whether to obey the state or not, and that in so doing you *interpret* what the law of the state is, and what the likely future consequences of that action might be... [Therefore] any attempt to explain human action in terms of existing material conditions loses sight of the ability of a human

29

being to act in terms of interpretations that do not even relate to the material present or past.

If we agree that social rules/structures are constructed by us and change over time and that they cannot be adequately investigated by mimicking techniques of natural sciences, we must also acknowledge that our future is not set in stone and that we have alternatives depending on the evidence we have and the ways in which the evidence is interpreted.

To accept alternative futures raises two further questions: How do we know what we know and how could it be otherwise? These questions essentially ponder upon the nature and interpretation of evidence. That is, what sort of evidence is collected, how is it collected, and how is it interpreted? Moreover, as social conditions change over time, these questions would have to be repeatedly asked, given the nature of what is being investigated. This aspect of criticality is concerned with some well-discussed fundamental philosophical issues that we do not detail here, given the introductory nature of this book. [6] We suggest that at the early stages of your studies, what you need to apply from the perspective of critical sensibility is that you should accept and reject ideas only after a careful and systematic examination. Let's take a look at an example here through which we demonstrate how to use and combine the SI-related sensibilities we have discussed so far.

Let's consider being overweight. How do you know that you are overweight? Being 'over something' usually means that there is a limit, a norm set against which you measure yourself. When it comes to your weight, you would check your body mass index (BMI), which is a calculation of the ratio between your height (centimetres) and weight (kilogram). When you calculate your BMI, you will have a score that determines whether you are underweight, normal, overweight, or obese (see http://www.bbc.co.uk/health/tools/bmi_calculator/bmi.shtml). Based on your BMI score and the medical and cultural normalisation of the body, your body will be classified as normal or pathological, healthy, or unhealthy (Tischner and Malson, 2011). If you are in the unhealthy category, you are put under structural pressure to become healthy. Tischner and Malson (2011: 90) argue that 'All adults are to a large extent held responsible for their health and well being'. General recommendation for 'fixing' (normalising) a body is through diet and exercise. For the sake of this example, let's say that being overweight equals unhealthiness and pathology, and it is a good idea to normalise our body. (Note that this statement has been critically received by many academics, e.g. Monaghan, 2008.) However, can the individual (agency) solely be held responsible for developing such a condition? We would argue that placing the blame on people who are considered overweight reflects naivety or hidden political agendas. To develop a more realistic argument, you must employ all the above-mentioned sensibilities. Monaghan (2008: 5) succinctly observes, 'In line with a sociological imaginative approach that views personal troubles and social issues as inextricably linked... studying men and the war on obesity furthers efforts to rethink various oppositional dualities...' such as agency – structure, healthy – unhealthy, fat – slim, and so on.

By using your critical sensibility, you should question whether it is indeed a personal trouble to be overweight. If you consider the statistics[7] available, you will see that we are dealing with a social issue as a significant percentage of our society (according to medically established norms) are considered overweight and obese. However, if we accept that obesity is a social issue, then, to use a quotation from Mills (1963: 396), 'we may not hope to find its solution within the range of opportunities open to any one individual'. Ergo, the individual cannot be solely held responsible. Gilman (2008: 3) contends that 'obesity is a [inter]national rather than an individual problem'. So by being critical and checking statistical evidence, you have established that obesity is a social issue and, thus, requires the examination of those social structures that might be considered instrumental in its emergence. As you may have already thought, the obesity epidemic (if we accept that there is one) has not appeared overnight, and the social perception of fat and being overweight varied from one historical era to another. 'Fat, however, is truly in the eye of the beholder. Each age, culture, and tradition has defined acceptable weight for itself' (Gilman, 2008: 3). This means that to understand obesity, you also have to engage your historical sensibility to see the long-term development of the phenomenon. When you engage the historical sensibility of your SI, you may even discover that being 'fat' or 'overweight' was not always associated with a negative social stigma (see Tischner and Malson, in press). Moreover, obesity is predominant in Western countries and, as such, would require investigation of the culture of those countries via your cultural sensibility. That is, you would need to look into sedentary lifestyle, development of technology, lack of exercise, dieting, and food availability and food choices (i.e. obesogenic environment).

As you can see, no social situation is simple and affected by only one factor. SI requires you to adopt a multi-perspective approach to whatever you are investigating by jointly engaging all the foregoing sensibilities. Therefore, you should be suspicious and sceptical of arguments that are mono-causal – attributing social change only to one factor (for another example of using SI in deconstructing obesity, see Monaghan, 2008: 7–13).

CRITIQUING MILLS AND THE SOCIOLOGICAL IMAGINATION

As Mills was disliked in almost all social circles, you can imagine that his work received criticism on a number of accounts and from many directions. He was often reprimanded for his populist style of writing in which he condensed pages and pages of conventional sociology texts into a few bite-size ideas (see the Chapter 2 of *The Sociological Imagination*). Hamilton (1983: 7) writes that 'As a maverick sociologist he also clearly irritated a number of his peers…in reducing, for example, much of Talcott Parsons's carefully argued analytical theory of the Social System to a few trivial commonsense points'. It is then understandable that authors of sociological texts written in line with the traditional style and by much jargon-driven precision were up in arms against Mills' claim that if you peel away the jargon of sociology, the emperor has no (or very few) clothes. We are sympathetic to Mills' initiative of eliminating unnecessary jargon from sociology and would not agree with his critics' accusations of Mills being overly simplistic or populist in his writings. Whilst we would not advocate meaning reduction of key sociological concepts and messages, the overuse of jargon and complicated writing styles have the tendency to miss our target audience and, thus, reduce the potential and impact of sociology.

As he was critical of both abstract empiricism and grand theory, Mills found himself, yet again, between a rock and a hard place. His attempt to develop a balance between theory and evidence was often rejected by academics in both camps. For instance, he had a long-term and vitriolic disagreement with Paul Lazarsfeld, a colleague at Columbia

C. Wright Mills and the sociological imagination

University. Mills (1959/2000: 63) described Lazarsfeld's work as the methodologist who reduces social 'realities into psychological variables'. To retaliate, Lazarsfeld accused Mills of 'advancing charlatanism not knowledge' (Eldridge, 1983: 29). This example demonstrates the sort of academic battles Mills fought and criticism his work generally received.

In addition, as Mills paid a great deal of attention to macro-social structures and the ways in which they operate and oppress individuals, he was/is often considered as a fundamentally Marxist sociologist. Although he rarely admitted to being a pure Marxist and seemed to have closer links to the sociology of Max Weber, his work often received critiques from this angle, pigeonholing him into a more vanguard leftist camp. Despite this, Mills' work received disapproval from many who disagreed with Marxian social analysis.[8] These accounts are along the lines that we outline in the penultimate section of Chapter 4 on Marxism.

Mills was also criticised for being 'gloomy' and pessimistic in his analyses of society. As he was critical of almost anything he sociologically considered, the general perception of his views was of negative social outlook. His description of the *cheerful robot* in the *White Collar* denotes exploitation, alienation, and passivity of the masses. Furthermore, in *The Power Elite*, he depicts another agonizing picture of exploitation and disenfranchisement of the lower classes, which is almost impossible to break, as the elite take great care in allowing only horizontal social mobility within their stratum, thereby eliminating members of other classes from social positions that hold significant power. Thus, it is not too difficult to see why Mills' sociology can be construed as pessimistic, as there is only a slim chance of escape from such oppression – through the active use of SI.

The practice of SI itself can be criticised for being overly reliant on personal experiences and, in turn, on the biography of the investigator to recognise and analyse social issues. One could argue that if we investigated exclusively those social issues we have personally experienced, we would be in danger of significantly reducing what we could sociologically scrutinise. In other words, we do not have to be a drug addict to investigate the steroid culture of bodybuilding or we did not have to be alive during the 1936 Olympics to find that a fascinating event is worthy of socio-historical investigation. Though we would not argue against the observation according to which we should not reduce our sociological investigation to our personal troubles, we would claim that perceiving SI as a tool through which only personal troubles and related social issues can be recognised and investigated is a distortion of Mills' idea. Without disregarding the importance of biography and personal experience, even Mills suggests that with the use of SI, a wide range of issues can be and should be studied. Once acquired and active, SI will shed light not only on social issues relevant to the individual researcher but on those that are, directly or indirectly, connected to them. In fact, Mills (1959/2000: 211) notes that 'the sociological imagination... in considerable part consists of the capacity to shift from one perspective to another, and in the process to build up an adequate view of a total society and of its components'. Should we solely focus on our personal troubles it would allow only a fragmented view of what is truly out there. However, when decoding societies and the way they operate, your SI can become your most powerful 'weapon'. Albert Einstein once said, 'Logic will get you from A to B. Imagination will take you everywhere'.

FURTHER READINGS

As we noted in Mills' brief biography, he was a prolific writer despite his short lifespan. So, if you wish to get better acquainted with Mills' work, we would recommend that you read *The Sociological Imagination* (1959) in original, along with *The Marxist* (1962) and *The Power Elite* (1956). The anthology of essays written by Mills and edited by Irving Louise Horowitz (1963) entitled *Power, Politics and People* is another valuable resource. In general sociology, Anthony Giddens, along with Evan Willis, often refer to SI as a useful investigative tool (e.g. Giddens, 1986; Willis, 1996). Steve Fuller's book entitled *The New Sociological Imagination* (2006) is another helpful source. In the area of sport and exercise, the following works should be considered: *Sport and the Sociological Imagination* (edited by Nancy Theberge and Peter Donelly, 2004), *Sport, Power and Culture* (by John Hargreaves, 1986) and *Class, Sports and Social Development* (by Richard Gruneau, 1999).

CHAPTER 3

FUNCTIONALIST PERSPECTIVES

We are often told that exercise is good for us, that it combats a host of health problems such as obesity, diabetes, and cardiovascular disease. Sport is often framed as 'getting kids off the streets' and providing fun and character-building activities. Sport and exercise, therefore, carry messages that become normalized and valued as providers of internal (sport and exercise specific) and external (society-wide) goods. Sport's and exercise's socialization process involves transferring the norms and values from the activities per se to wider society. For example, think about the Los Angeles cricket team, the Compton Cricket Club, set up by a homeless charity worker in one of Los Angeles's most violent neighbourhoods. Deviant behaviour becomes less appealing to local kids who can instead put their energies into the valuable activity of cricket and its associated moral goods such as fair play, teamwork, and rule adherence. BBC journalist Peter Bowes (cited in BBC news – see Bowes, 2011: 2), comments on the initiative: 'it was the start of what was to become a collaboration of former gangsters, homeless men and street kids, who now see cricket as a metaphor for living a purposeful and law-abiding life'. Also consider how some professional sportspeople assume special role-model status and how this status might be negatively affected by them engaging in the very type of misbehaviour or deviance these homeless cricketers are trying to avoid by playing sport. For example, England and Harlequins rugby union player Danny Care was dropped from the England Six Nations squad after being arrested on drunk driving charges having been arrested a week previously for being drunk and disorderly.

Sport is also used to foster group identities such as national identity. For example, during the Vietnam war, Spiro Agnew, the vice president of the United States, noted sport was one of the few bits of social glue holding the country together (see Jarvie and Maguire, 1994). More recently, during the pre-London 2012 Olympic torch tour of the United Kingdom, Britons were told that the flame would travel within ten miles of everyone in the country. This was presumably to foster a sense of nation-wide inclusion and involvement in an event deemed to be of national (and global) significance.

Modern functionalist perspectives (sometimes called *structural-functionalism*) are closely associated with the work of American sociologist Talcott Parsons (1902–1979) and his graduate student, Robert Merton (1910–2003), and the theory first gained momentum in the inter-war years largely due to their work. Like most perspectives, however, it is heavily influenced by the work of the classical sociological traditions, most notably that of Emile Durkheim (1858–1917). Therefore we begin this chapter by looking at Durkheim's work, in particular his examination of the relationship between the individual and society.

Functionalist perspectives are based on viewing society as made up of a set of interconnected and mutually dependent parts, each of which functions according to widely shared sets of values, expectations, and obligations in ways that support the overall interests of society and, by doing so, help hold society together. Broadly speaking, these parts are made up of organisations and institutions but are supported by the accompanying roles that people perform within these organisations and institutions. The institutions include sport, education, religion, family, media, the economy, and the like, and they each develop norms and values that become crystallised. These norms develop from the expectations and obligations that emerge over time to become widely accepted and mutually reinforced (value consensus). Individuals learn these norms through the process of socialization. Balance occurs,

36

functionalists would argue, by disparate groups sharing broadly the same *core* values and viewing them to be in the best interests of society as a whole. Some individuals and groups within the overall system may not share all core values. They may, therefore, rebel against or act illegally toward those values they oppose. Consensus is still maintained by the system's support mechanisms though such as group norms and the justice system (police, law courts, and prisons) that combine to help maintain order. Thus, high levels of conformity are key features of functionalist theory. As a consequence, those who transgress the shared codes (laws, rules, values) must face what are deemed to be proportionate sanctions to punish and prevent them and others from repeating such transgressions in future. Hence, strong punitive measures for rule breakers are usually a major and necessary feature of society for functionalists.

Functionalist perspective is a consensus theory. It stresses that successful societies[1] are based on social solidarity rather than conflict, and this is illustrated in its assertion that societies are made up of interrelated parts that combine to serve the needs of the whole, rather than the interests of *every* individual. Functionalists, therefore, acknowledge some people's interests will not be served but view this as an inevitable outcome of satisfying the majority and, as such, a necessary condition of a successfully functioning society. Given that some people's interests will not be met, this makes the successful integration and promotion of the majority groups' values critical in maintaining social and political equilibrium and preventing mass dissent such as rioting or major institutional disputes such as strikes. Therefore, in addition to strong punitive measures for rule breakers, a major aspect of functionalist theory is devoted to explaining how the dominant cultural values and institutional systems become normalized, valued, and part of a shared consensus illustrated by disparate groups broadly sharing the same beliefs and values.

When thinking about functionalist perspectives, we often make the analogy between society and an organic system (such as the human body) whereby a set of interdependent (sub)systems are necessary and must work effectively to ensure the successful functioning of the overall system (society). So, just as a healthy person requires her or his heart and lungs to operate the cardiovascular system, allowing him or her to breathe and transport blood between the heart and the rest of the body (for example), a successful society has a number of functional requirements necessary to meet its demands, or the entire system may fail. And just as the human body adapts to its changing conditions – breathing faster and increasing its heart rate when exercising for example – sub-systems within society also adapt to dynamic societal conditions to ensure society's successful continuation. For example, in response to the 9/11 terrorist attacks in the United States, the American sub-system of government reacted by implementing new legislation[2] designed to prevent future terrorist attacks.

Though there is a popular belief that sport has been overwhelmingly analysed in functionalist terms, recently sociologists of sport have not been as keen to use the theory as some may think. However, individuals, politicians, and popular media contributors often present sport and exercise in highly functionalist terms – viewing them as contributing positively to a host of local, national, and international causes. Additionally, they are often viewed in functionalist terms as useful tools to tackle social problems such as drug abuse, unemployment, poor health, and general delinquency. Many everyday assumptions about sport and exercise are functionalist in that they are overwhelmingly presented as having positive functions that are beneficial for society's overall well-being. Whether it is the fight against childhood obesity or initiatives to prevent antisocial behaviour among teenagers in poverty-stricken neighbourhoods, sport and exercise are commonly presented as social control mechanisms to alleviate societal problems. To begin to understand the origins of such assumptions and the perspective per se more fully, we turn to its origins and to the work of Emile Durkheim.

CLASSICAL THEORY

For Durkheim, society provides the conditions for individuals to develop norms, values, and societal characteristics as opposed to individuals having complete autonomy to act. Durkheim rejected any notion of society being merely the aggregate of individuals. He claimed that collective representations (sometimes called *social facts*) had their 'own type' and were distinctive or, to use the Latin term Durkheim employed, *sui generis*. These distinctive types include religious doctrine, legal rules, and family relations, and they could be

BIOGRAPHIC NOTE

Emile Durkheim (1858–1917) was born in Epinal, France, where he studied philosophy at the Ecol Normale Superieure in Paris. He taught at Bordeaux for five years before earning a professorship at the Sorbonne in Paris in 1902. He studied the work of the positivist thinker Auguste Comte and was influenced sufficiently to attempt to understand society by applying a set of scientific rules and replacing preconceptions and ideology with empirically sound social facts. Throughout his life, he produced a number of important works that helped shape the future of sociology and social theory more generally. These works include *The Division of Labour in Society (1893)*, *The Rules of the Sociological Method (1895)*, *Suicide: A Study in Sociology (1897)*, and *The Elementary Forms of the Religious Life (1912)*. Many important theoretical developments in sociology can be traced back to the work of Durkheim. For example, besides influencing functionalists from the twentieth century onward, there are close connections between Durkheim's work and the development of symbolic interactionism (see Chapter 6). Durkheim lived in a period in which sociology was just emerging, and he focused much attention on legitimizing the study of society and showing it to be a rigorous and scientific pursuit that was worthy of study. He viewed society as being made up of social facts that, although difficult to observe, could be evidenced in their effects and, therefore, explained with theories. These facts 'consist of manners of acting, thinking and feeling external to the individual, which are vested with a coercive power by virtue of which they exercise control over him' (Durkheim, 1895/1982:52). These facts were to be distinguished from those that already had academic and scientific legitimacy such as biology (organic facts) and psychology (individual consciousness facts). Durkheim lost his son in the First World War, and soon after he suffered a stroke and died some months afterward in November 1917.

both enabling and constraining on our behaviour. We are free to act, yet this freedom is not limitless but is constrained by the status and position we come to occupy in the church or mosque or as a lawyer or defendant or as a mother or eldest son. An example of societies conditioning individuals is illustrated in what Durkheim called 'status roles', what we would now call *social roles*. He argued there are certain ways of acting – manner, behaviour, and dress – associated with particular roles we occupy in society and rather than being matters of individual choice or consciousness, these roles become established collective conventions. We become obligated to be a good wife or husband, a loving mother or father, an obedient child, and even though we may believe we are acting with complete autonomy and free will, we have acquired these 'choices' and their associated values through socialization and the conventions and obligations of the society in which we live. Though individuals influence these roles and may affect some changes to them, the general norms and values associated with each role travel from generation to generation, embedding themselves deeper into our consciousness.

Part of this system of status roles involves formal and informal rules/ expectations that emerge in most areas of everyday life. For example, the police may not always act according to the letter of the law when merely warning the drunk person on New Year's morning for breaching the peace at 3 a.m. in a residential area by singing loudly. Here, the police have acted according to informal rules (that a certain degree of disruption or revelry is to be expected on New Year's morning) rather than the letter of the law. In sport, it is often the opposite issue that arises, with the referee who acts according to the letter of the law (within the sport's rules) and punishes a player for a transgression others may view as soft, such as when a footballer gets penalised for shirt pulling in the box when defending a corner kick. Hence, the referee may get criticized for not acting according to the *spirit of the game* in which the dominant norms and values have existed (in this case, that some informally acceptable level of shirt pulling is part of the game and that if the game stopped every time this occurred, there would be multiple disruptions to the flow of the match). In both cases, however, the rules and expectations of the sub-systems (law enforcement in wider society and sport) are products of convention *and* individual choice rather than choice alone.

Central to Durkheim's work are the developmental shifts in the relationship between individual and society. He charted these by discussing *the division of labour.* The division of labour for Durkheim represented the shifting structure of people's occupations within their

Status roles (these will be further discussed in Chapter 6) are roles people occupy and, by occupying, reinforce to themselves and others how they *should* behave in these roles. In other words, the structural position (status) one occupies within the social system combines with the behaviour of an individual (role) holding such status to mutually reinforce one another. Think about what we expect of doctors and law enforcement officials and how this may affect their behaviour in fulfilling the expected roles to the general public. Though there will be degrees of specificity across roles – with doctors, rather than judges or policewomen expected to wear white coats and be sympathetic to our health concerns – there is, nevertheless, a broad consistent pattern of behaviour that transcends individual cases with all these roles expected to be performed by highly trained, dedicated, and professional individuals. In other words, general patterns of behaviour will be similarly experienced across a range of social situations – in these cases, authority positions acting in accordance with professional training, rules, laws, guidelines, and the like. This all gives rise to values that become institutionalised, reinforcing and normalizing beliefs about how elements of society are and should be. Think about our attitudes to work. A job is respected and, even if one does not have one, one shows her- or himself to be a good citizen by displaying the desire to get one and conversely a bad/questionable citizen by avoiding work or employment. Considering this a little further, we could note the influences of the historical value that hard work has on our Western capitalist societies, impressing on us the value of effort and achievement ranging from settings such as the classroom, the sports arena, family life and, of course, the office, factory, or shop floor. Hard work is valued, and quitting is viewed as failure. Another example might be seen in being on the right side of the law, which marks off the 'good citizen' from the bad citizen. Durkheim viewed this collective conscience as widely shared beliefs and values within the community-society.

society. These were illustrated by the transformation from pre-modern and pre-industrial societies and their undifferentiated communal jobs to industrial society and their specialized, highly organized jobs. As societies grew in size and developed socially, politically, and technologically, they acquired increased differentiation that, in turn, required more interdependent and complementary cooperation between increasingly disparate groups in ways that pre-modern village life did not. Durkheim described this division of labour as being characterized by levels of group solidarity that were essential for the successful continuation of society. Most pre-industrial societies experienced *mechanical solidarity* whereby conformity was maintained through an uncomplicated and localised shared belief system such as those commonly found within the indigenous tribes of North America or Australia. In such groups, life was arranged and experienced in rather basic, close-knit relationships where there were few roles among the group (and those were shared by many within the group). As societies developed and became more complex, with more numerous and varied roles, solidarity shifted toward what Durkheim labelled *organic solidarity* whereby increased cooperation on numerous levels of interaction between varied groups with growingly diverse interests in a multi-faceted society occurred. An essential feature of these societies was the development of group norms that helped to regulate each new layer of activity.

A fundamental point in Durkheim's notion of solidarity is that it must involve high degrees of interdependency and, by extension, a sense of mutually beneficial outcomes as a result of the forms of human interaction. A major feature of Durkheim's work, therefore, focused on the processes by which highly organized and structurally complex societies continued to reinforce values and generate cultural norms that were seen to benefit society as a whole. This is where his work on religion generally and on the sacred and profane more specifically is helpful. Durkheim viewed religion as connected to the 'sacred' rather than exclusively to a deity (e.g. God, Allah, and other divinity). Therefore in highly developed and complex societies, the sacred was often not associated with religious gods but rather represented by a totem. Totems were viewed by their worshippers as sacred, but the crucial factor Durkheim argued was less to do with the totems being sacred but rather being the symbolic representation of what *society* deemed sacred. In our society, we may think of the nation-state's flag and national anthem as totemic symbols that elicit devotion, worship, and deference. The flag and anthem in themselves are pretty meaningless on one level but, at an important cultural level, they represent 'us', 'our past struggles and glories' and allow 'us' to continually re-invoke collective memories formed from past heroes, victories, trials, and tribulations in ways that enable the 'nation' to become real, shared, and timeless. Here we see Durkheim's crucial distinction between worshipping the totem itself and what it represents or symbolises. Moreover, totems are the symbolic representations of society holding up a mirror to itself and, rather than worshipping a sacred spirit, actually represent society worshipping itself. Durkheim argued that over long periods of time, feelings toward the cherished or sacred elements of society were likely to diminish and that, unless these feelings were reinvigorated, they may disappear. Therefore, individuals within society need to be periodically reminded of their own sacred elements, and one such way to do this is to continue to worship totems in the name and benefit of our own society.

A central feature of Durkheim's analysis of religion is the way he positions the sacred against the profane. Accordingly, if national flags, national heroes, and other symbols are seen as sacred in this way, to mistreat these symbols or to treat them as ordinary becomes profane (when the majority view them as sacred). So, if a level of profanity occurs against the sacred, a certain level of disdain manifests toward the profane actor, and all the time the sacred status of the totem is further reinforced. Obvious examples include national anthems, national ceremonies such as Canada Day, Thanksgiving Day, Veterans' Day, Remembrance Sunday, and other such occasions that allow society to worship itself. This sacred and profane relationship also works at a more localized level with everyday interaction. Thus, racist or criminal behaviour precipitates individuals' disgust or outrage whilst connecting us more closely to those who share our non-racist, lawful values. This collective sharing of values reinforces their validity and strengthens our social and cultural connections to others who share our experiences whilst further cementing the common values deemed beneficial for society to function.

DURKHEIM'S EXPLANATION OF SUICIDE

Besides explaining group behaviour as the result of collective norms and values emerging in wider society, Durkheim famously showed

As a major site of collective emotion, sport is often incorporated into these totemic acts of collective renewal. Thus, let us consider two related sacred elements of UK society that often accompany one another in discourse around the United Kingdom: the 'nation' and the Royal Family. In his 2012 New Year speech, the UK Prime Minister, David Cameron, focused on two events occurring in the United Kingdom later that year: the London Olympics and the Queen's golden jubilee. He enthusiastically informed the collective nation these events allow 'us' to 'show the world what Britain is all about'. He added, 'We honour our Queen and all that is great about Britain … and let us use these things [Olympics and Jubilee] too as a mirror of ourselves, a mirror of the nation' (David Cameron's New Year speech 1/1/12). He, therefore, was reminding British citizens what we are all about and invoking us to view this version of ourselves in the Olympics and golden jubilee. Here we also see this self-worship and celebration of Britishness and monarchy (totems) that requires periodic stimulation to prevent the undesired erosion that Durkheim noted was likely. To help us understand this further, when thinking about the nation-state, let us think about the UK New Year Honours system that, like the Olympics and golden jubilee, offer British individuals the opportunity to worship themselves through the totem of honours given to celebrities, sports stars, and various other apparent good citizens – the mirror of themselves. Consider the four nations the United Kingdom is made up of: England, Scotland, Wales, and Northern Ireland. In functionalist terms, equilibrium is aided by reminding members from within these separate nations of their shared values and norms and their greater unity as collective parts of a *United* Kingdom. Being an important unit within the wider system of society, sport plays a central role here and allows us to see how sport (and the honours system) can be viewed in functionalist terms. The 2012 New Year Honours' list included Northern Irish golfers Rory McIlroy and Darren Clarke, Scottish rugby union player Chris Paterson, English rugby league player Jamie Peacock, and Welsh rugby union player Martyn Williams. This snapshot illustrates that all four parts of the United Kingdom were selected to 'honour'. Honours, viewed in this functionalist light, are totems symbolizing 'our' support for (if not dependence on) the shared norms and values of wider UK society and every year are celebrated, thus reducing any possibility of Durkheim's fear that 'our' appreciation and devotion would diminish.

Think about wars, natural disasters, coronations, royal weddings, and national sporting achievements. These can elicit nation-wide emotions of shared experience. Or consider smaller group attachments in which you have been present among like-minded people; events such as music concerts, festivals, raves, comedy shows and, of course, sporting fixtures among your 'own fans'. Think about the feeling of kinship, of belonging, the common bonds shared by so many others who witnessed the same event as you and who feel the same way about it as you. The excitement is intensified by virtue of its shared experience, and the sense of collective identity is reinforced in terms of feeling connected to your fellow group members. Of course, one's sense of difference from (if not hostility toward) any outside group that does not share your group attachment and your norms and values may also be intensified in such situations as we often see in sporting settings, with opposing sets of supporters emitting heightened emotional behaviours when confronted by their major rivals. Bonding of this nature represents a form of *collective effervescence* that strengthens feelings toward the totem and influences others in the same environment. 'Collective effervescence' describes those shared emotions that involve intense feelings and expressions within a society that often end up enhancing the original high emotions still further. Some extreme examples are used here to illustrate the term clearly. Think about the aftermath of Princess Diana's tragic death in a car accident in 1997. The extraordinary outpouring of grief resulted in a classic example of collective effervescence in which individuals who had never met nor known the Princess felt overwhelmed with grief and felt the need to act upon it by public and collective mourning that seemed to spread across London and other parts of the United Kingdom. More recently, after the death of North Korea's 'Dear Leader' in December 2011, the world's media were dominated by images of thousands of North Korean citizens collectively and hysterically crying and mourning despite never having met nor individually known the man. Of course, given the totalitarian nature of North Korea, there are likely additional reasons for this apparent outpouring of grief, but the point remains and may indeed strengthen further the view that, irrespective of whether it is spontaneous or manufactured coercively, collective effervescence and continual stimulation of totem worshipping is required to maintain adequate levels of consensus for the successful continuation of each particular society.

how even the most apparently personal and individual acts are connected to collective norms and values. One of Durkheim's most famous books is *Suicide* (1897/1952), in which he argued that the apparently individual act of taking one's own life was, on closer inspection, intimately linked to wider societal factors such as levels of social integration, family commitment, and religious attachments. Durkheim argued that religion helped society foster a better sense of togetherness, community spirit, and solidarity. He concluded that low levels of religious observance resulted in reduced levels of solidarity in society, whereas higher levels of religious observance were more likely to foster higher levels of society-wide solidarity. He found that religion and family relationships, for example, were clear indicators of differing patterns of suicide rates among Protestants and Catholics and married and single people, respectively. For instance Catholics and married people were less likely than Protestants and single people to commit suicide because Catholics and married people were more likely to have higher levels of social solidarity compared to Protestants and single people, who were shown to have less binding connections. Weak integration resulted in isolation, individualism, and an over-emphasis on the self or ego, resulting in *egoistic suicide*. Another type of suicide Durkheim called *anomic*, and this was associated with a severe disruption within society, leading to a sense of imbalance, lack of shared norms, and general frustration. Though there are two further types (*altruistic* and *fatalistic*), the former two demonstrate that separateness and hopelessness were major factors in the breakdown of the human condition. Thus, it becomes clear why functionalist theory emphasises social integration and regulation (pattern maintenance) through the reinforcing of shared values and norms, and this forms a key theme in the modern varieties of functionalism.

REFLECTION

Bearing in mind the preceding discussion on various forms of suicide, consider the tragic suicide of Welsh national football team manager, Gary Speed, on 26 November 2011. By employing Durkheim's observations on suicide, discuss why he might have committed suicide.

46

MODERN THEORY

Like other perspectives, modern functionalism should not be viewed as completely uniform across all of its adherents. There are notable differences between some of its proponents and forms. For example, two of its key figures, Talcott Parsons and Robert Merton, had some major differences in their approach to explaining conflict. For our purposes, we focus mainly on the work of Parsons and the most common form 'societal functionalism' (see Loy and Booth, 2000 for in-depth discussion of the forms of functionalism). Societal functionalism is primarily helpful for analyses of the large-scale institutions and their enabling and constraining functions on society. That is, what functions do major structural institutions like schools and universities, banks, the media industry, and sport provide for one another?

BIOGRAPHIC NOTE

Talcott Parsons (1902–1979) was born in Colorado and was the son of a clergyman. He studied economics and biology at Amherst College before postgraduate study at the London School of Economics where he took two classes with the famous structural anthropologist, Bronislaw Malinowski. This most certainly influenced his later turn toward sociology, which occurred at Harvard in 1930 when he moved from teaching economics to sociology after the department of sociology was founded there. Parsons's first major publication, *The Structure of Social Action*, was published in 1937 and, in 1939, he received tenure at Harvard. He became chair of the Harvard sociology department in 1944 and, in 1946, he founded the Program in Social Relations that was his attempt to outline a scientific and systematic study of social sciences. This grand aim emerged further with his next major works, *Social System*, published in 1951, and a collaborative work published the same year, *Toward a General Theory of Action*, which was an attempt to outline a theoretical framework for the social sciences. Throughout his life, Parsons aimed to create a general theory of society that would explain its operation in sociological terms. He died of heart failure whilst in Germany in 1979.

47

Parsons (1951) described society as a system consisting of three main elements, each requiring high levels of integration for successful societies to exist. These were the social system (structure), culture, and personalities (agency). For social order to exist, personalities had to be satisfied for, if widespread individual dissatisfaction (alienation) existed, society would break down. Parsons argued that culture is institutionalized by the social system. Individuals internalize the values and norms of wider society, and they become embedded into the dominant cultural practices and values. In other words, rules and rule adherence (social system) form behaviour and, over time, this becomes crystallised as culture. He recognized that this process was neither automatic nor guaranteed and that some degree of disenchantment was likely; hence the reason why rules, norms, and punishments help to balance out the system. Parsons argued that the 'social system' and 'personality' are connected by 'internalisation'. This is when the requirements of people's positions in society become integral to their personality and links to Durkheim's previously mentioned status-roles. This can be seen in the extreme example of the master-servant relationship whereby both parties play their different parts accordingly to maintain the overall system. Both know their place and internalize the norms and values associated with these places. The master feels it is her or his entitlement to be waited on whereas the servant acts with subservience, outwardly thankful for having such a patient master, thus acting in accord with his or her rightful place in the household hierarchy. Closer to modern day illustrations, we might compare the meaning behind the oft-repeated phrase, 'the customer is always right'. The customer expects a certain level of service from the sales assistant, and the sales assistant expects to be of service to satisfy both parties' expectations of the situation. So, when the rules (of the household, society, or these other smaller interactions within society) are broken, we feel personally insulted by such acts. Imagine if you asked a shop assistant for help and were told to do it yourself. Going against the system is tantamount to going against the culture, which is itself formed in tandem with personalities that occupy particular internalized roles.

Social roles become institutionalized and standardised to a degree that, without prior knowledge of and agreement with them, social life would be overly complex. For example, consider if each time you entered a new social situation you and others present had to continually work out each others' roles and expectations. Parsons argues that we are socialized into understanding these roles and expectations (norms). High levels of social order are possible because of social understanding of norms. Important to note here is that for Parsons, these roles and expectations acquire *moral* elements for we expect and demand appropriate behaviour and, if we do not get it, there are punitive actions we and others can take – from official rule and law enforcement and financial rewards or constraints to the more informal sanctions such as ignoring, shunning, avoiding, and chastising. Control can be ideological or direct intervention (force). Berger (1966) identified eight sources of social control: economics rewards/punishment; ridicule/gossip; ostracism; fraud/deception; belief systems/ideology; sphere of intimates/peer pressure; and the contract/formal agreements. Consider the teammate who refuses to obey the instructions of the team captain or even the coach him- or herself? Even when we enter a new team for the first time, we know the 'normal' expectations of players, captains, officials, coaches, and spectators, given that we have already been involved in a sporting environment or, at the least, are familiar with such environments. These expectations help maintain order when some people may act against the overall system. When laws are broken, we expect the legal system to deal with this through the courts and penal system. Moreover, we develop behaviour patterns around how to react in these instances – so, for example, when a heinous murder occurs, many commentators demand life imprisonment or the death penalty. Furthermore, if this occurs in a 'quiet neighbourhood', we often witness media interviews of neighbours stressing their disbelief about how this could happen in such a 'normal' street and in 'our town' and that the deceased was such a nice person. These reactions fit the rules and requirements that have become normalized in such situations and, as Durkheim had previously shown, this shocked or outraged reaction reinforces our common values with others and reminds them and us of our devotion to society's rules, in this case its laws.

Parsons draws on Durkheim's claims of collectively held beliefs/values being a 'social glue' creating cohesiveness and order. In his first book, Parsons (1937) rejected the notion that people acted solely out of self-interest as this, he claimed, takes for granted society's orderliness. Group values and norms help create the social glue that holds society together – so rather than self-interest, we have group cooperation (and punishment and ostracism for rule breakers). Central to Parsons's

In sporting terms, consider our earlier example of England and Harlequins rugby union player Danny Care, who was dropped from England's Six nations squad after being arrested on drink driving charges three weeks after being arrested for being drunk and disorderly. Why would he be dropped from a sporting team based on his behaviour in his personal life? In functionalist terms, the social system (consisting of totem, rules, and status roles) becomes internalised by individuals, and an international rugby player symbolises a national role model who comes to represent England rather than merely Danny Care. When these roles and the system itself are transgressed (rule breaking), people feel personally affronted, and the system requires this to be redressed appropriately.

functionalism, then, are the overlapping elements of consensus, cooperation, and legitimacy of power.

Parsons's student, Robert Merton, was concerned less with Parson-like grand theorizing and grappled more with strain and conflict, offering a less conformist version of functionalist theory. He outlined a more agency-centred and less-determined version of functionalism that accounted for social inequality more than previous functionalist traditions. He rejected the view that all elements within society provided positive functions, introducing us to *dysfunctions* (negative outcomes). That is, institutions and structures can help maintain the social system, but they can also hinder it. The housing market, for example, may help maintain an economic system when it is riding high but does so at the expense of first-time buyers or poorer individuals unable to afford the ever-increasing cost of a mortgage. Conversely, when the market crashes and house prices drop, poorer people may be able to afford mortgages, but existing owners find they are in negative equity and/or cannot sell their existing property. Thus, here we see examples of functions (positive outcomes) and dysfunctions (negative outcomes). Layder (2006: 29) summarises Merton's position:

> Merton offers a vision of social activity as the product of the creative and adaptive responses of people to the social circumstances in

50

which they find themselves. In this sense, Merton's version of functionalist sociology escapes from the extreme determinism of Parsons's framework as well as taking into account some fundamental dimensions of social inequality.

Merton viewed society as having varying degrees of successful integration, arguing that equilibrium was best maintained when institutionalized goals and the means to achieve these were balanced out: Of course, how this occurs is the main question. Anomie and deviance appears, Merton noted, when people's choices do not match the institutionalised goals and means. So, some who reject the norms and values of mainstream society drop out, favouring alternative behaviour, and this often results in this behaviour being branded deviant according to established social structures and, subsequently, culturally frowned upon or made illegal. Deviance was more likely to happen for Merton when social stratification occurred as some people's goals were unattainable.

THE AGIL SYSTEM

Though in some respects Merton offers an alternative functionalist approach, many functionalist accounts of sport and society can be explained with reference to Parsons's four functional prerequisites. These stages are called *adaptation, goal attainment, integration*, and *latency* (sometimes called *pattern maintenance*). Often abbreviated to the AGIL system, the four functions represent a goal-oriented system of stages or sequences that need to be met for successful societies to exist. As functionalists argue that society is geared toward achieving specific functional ends (goals), the attainment of goals first requires preparation of the means by which to successfully achieve these (and maintain a successful society). This involves adapting within the environment to ensure the conditions are met to enable further goal attainment. So, just as we noted for human bodies, the cardiovascular system adapts to exercise, in sporting systems more broadly, this adaptation stage may include the forming of new sports leagues and new sponsorship deals that are viewed within the wider system as helping to lay the groundwork for further shared goal attainment such as making more money, producing better players, or even developing more exciting competitions. It also explains how hindsight of experience may lead to further adaptation of the system. For example, in European football in the 1980s, the controlling authorities decided it would be a functional benefit to encourage all-seater stadia to reduce antisocial and violent fan behaviour, thus enabling the attainment of their goals of family-centred, safe, and fun sporting stadiums. In more recent times, the events of 9/11 have resulted in increased fears of terrorist attacks at events such as the Olympics and the Super Bowl. Further adaptation occurs with tighter security (CCTV, bag searches, undercover surveillance) around major sporting events (and wider society) in the post-9/11 era of perceived threats from terrorists.

Goal attainment is the next stage in the AGIL system and is a collective affair, with political and cultural influences helping to foster common pursuits deemed worthy of society as a whole. For example, tackling obesity is often held up as a universally beneficial goal worthy of wider society's support. Specific goal-oriented exercise, fitness, and sport programmes, therefore, become key resources in our society, gaining support at the social, political, and cultural levels and illustrated by common everyday attitudes toward food and the body, tax-funded initiatives in schools and after school clubs, and in media reporting. Another primary goal in many societies is to foster leadership skills and volunteerism in young adults and teenagers. We can see functionalist reasons, then, for the development, support, and promotion of programmes such as the Duke of Edinburgh Award in the United Kingdom and camp counselling in North America. Given that functionalists view the system as striving toward a common good, maintaining minority groups within the system also becomes a goal, and this is where we see minority sport and exercise initiatives – such as fitness classes specifically for females or young mothers. Or consider walking clubs for the elderly, which help achieve the dual goal of maintaining fitness and developing social contact for some of society's most vulnerable and isolated groups. In sport, more specifically, trying to secure a place on a team, gain the captaincy, achieve a personal best, win the playoffs, and accumulate medals all become clear and popular goals for many sportspeople, and these happen to dovetail with wider goals within capitalist society, mutually reinforcing both. These also include the goals to be the best you can be, be competitive, work hard, collect accolades, and measure success in quantitative terms.

The next prerequisite is integration. The success of society or any system within it requires group cohesion and togetherness. Thus, the integration of people and organisations with competing interests must be ensured. Individuals and groups, then, need avenues and mechanisms to ensure that successful integration occurs. Locally, different neighbourhoods might be involved in dual initiatives to foster community relations, or inner-city kids from different gangs might become active in special street sport initiatives such as midnight basketball or football (soccer). Nationally, ethnic groups might be involved in cross-community initiatives and international major sporting ceremonies, with national anthems and flags inculcating this integration. Cathy Freeman, an Aboriginal athlete, was chosen to light the Olympic flame during the opening ceremony of the 2000 Sydney Games, demonstrating to some that Aborigines were patriotic and fully integrated into the modern nation-state of Australia. Likewise, the aforementioned London 2012 torch relay of the United Kingdom seeks to involve most culturally disparate groups in the United Kingdom to view London's Games as a UK-wide festival for everyone in the country.

To maintain a society consisting of different individuals occupying different positions – and with lower- or higher-valued status – individuals from *all* stratified groups need to value the overall system, and this stage is called (latent) pattern maintenance. Therefore, the socializing of dominant cultural norms and values become central to the success of the functioning system. The constant renewal of motivation for individuals and groups to work and gain success within the system is key. For example, in the workplace, gaining promotion or moving up the corporate ladder is highly valued and encouraged. In sport (and society), a dominant narrative is the success story of 'escaping the ghetto', and this is presented as both possible and desirable. Sport offers a rich environment for such social reinforcement. We are all familiar with the Rocky-type story of immigrant working-class poor kid 'makes good' by boxing his way out of the ghetto. Pattern maintenance also involves fostering strong group attachments and viewing oneself as part of a larger whole, a team. Thus, self-sacrifice becomes valued as evidenced in 'taking one for the team'. This is also where the singing of team songs or national anthems and even minute silences at sports events can be viewed as latent pattern maintenance.

Consider team initiations as an example of fostering team cohesion. Have you been involved in a college or university team and been encouraged to take part in team initiations? Of course, occasionally these can result in tragic outcomes. In 2011, Florida Agricultural & Mechanical University experienced extreme hazing (bullying and initiation) resulting in the death of student band member Robert Champion.

If we consider these four stages more generally, we see that sport and exercise activities are often promoted as functional benefits to wider society in general. This occurs largely in two overlapping ways. First, sport and exercise can be viewed as mere parts of a larger social system. As Parsons's four prerequisites show, sport provides functional activities to help wider society function. For instance, building leisure, fitness, and sports centres in inner-city areas is often promoted as an inherent social good in the belief that it helps provide services for numerous groups thought to benefit such as the unemployed and teenagers. However, sport and exercise can also be thought of as (sub)systems themselves consisting of smaller functional elements, whereby they are infused with functionalist values. For example, sport and exercise can be used to teach important lessons that are viewed as valuable both in sport and exercise and also in 'real' life. These lessons include teamwork, hard work, sacrifice, taking and giving instructions, leadership, prize-giving, and competitiveness. An excellent illustration of both levels of functional analysis occurs in the previously introduced example of the Los Angeles cricket club. The BBC reporting of it leaves us in little doubt about the functional benefits of the club with its headline: *LA cricket: club helps tame Compton's mean streets* (see Bowes, 2011). Teaching cricket to homeless people and gang members has the aim of diverting them from potentially damaging street activities in becoming criminal or deviant – often described in functionalist terms as 'getting kids off the street' – by encouraging them to engage in socially acceptable and productive activities. However, it also teaches these vulnerable individuals lessons about valuing the society in which they live. For example, Katy Haber, one of the organisers, notes, 'We were so successful at teaching the homeless guys civility through the game that we lost a lot of players' who got jobs and permanent homes with their help (cited in BBC news – see Bowes, 2011). Here we see sport inculcating functionally positive values and preparing individuals for functional integration into wider society.

When applying functionalist theory to sport and exercise, we can highlight the following broad arguments:

- Sport teaches people valuable lessons about life in society.

- Sport can help motivate workers and is necessary in industrialised societies.

- Sport can unify disparate units of society.

- Sport reflects common values, social norms, and objectives of its major members and subgroups.

- Sport reflects existing values – fair play and healthy lifestyle.

- Sport aids pattern maintenance and tension management.

- Sport is a source of inspiration – facilitates transmitting of societal values – teamwork, hard work, industriousness, nationalism, camaraderie, community spirit.

- Sport aids social control.

- Sport acts as national unifier.

CRITIQUING FUNCTIONALIST THEORY

Parsons was accused of being abstract and not dealing with real life (interaction and agency). So symbolic interactionists (and indeed Merton) objected to the abstract nature of his theory and its generality (as opposed to its specificity). Giddens (1979) suggested that we should understand individuals within society as more active in reproducing *practices* rather than roles, as practice, unlike roles, leaves room for human agency to create and recreate behaviour and shape society's norms and values. Parsons's view reduced individuals' ability to act independently. He was also criticized for overlooking change and conflict. He did not overlook them exactly but viewed them over the long term, considering them as largely compatible parts of the system rather than features of particular individuals or groups. He was also criticised for his excessively technical writing style (see also Chapter 10).

Functionalist analyses more generally assume an apolitical stance despite often being inherently conservative, overlooking history and conflict. Though care needs to be taken not to tar all functionalist work with this conservative brush. Merton recognized that some structures were dysfunctional or irrelevant to the successful functioning of the overall system, thus enabling functionalists to seek social change and overcome accusations of conservativism. Harry Edwards, a social activist, used a broadly functionalist framework in his *Sociology of Sport* (1973) book and, perhaps partly due to his activism and the alleged inherent conservativism of functionalist theory, he is seldom viewed as a functionalist. The fact that the theory is devoted to analysing how the system is perpetuated rather than challenged contributes to functionalist perspectives being accused of reinforcing rather than challenging the current status quo. Therefore, those using functionalist theory often adopt a default position of viewing the needs of the system (society), which often happen to be the desires of its most powerful members, as the *correct* needs. Therefore, there is still a criticism that functionalist analyses reinforce and normalize the privileged and powerful groups within society. For example, functionalism legitimises high levels of stratification and polarized salaries and wealth based on the assertion that the most valuable positions within society need the most valuable (motivated, bright, educated, and innovative) individuals and, therefore, these individuals require exorbitant salaries. Not only are these people richly rewarded; society is told that it is in its interests to do so to attract the best and brightest for its own good. However, are tennis players, Formula 1 drivers, golfers, football, baseball, basketball, and hockey players more valuable to the functioning of society than a nurse, a care worker for the elderly, or a school cleaner? Or let's consider sport on its own. Is it really necessary to pay a tiny percentage of top players (often males in baseball, football, soccer, golf, tennis, and so on) millions of pounds per year when many more players are left with far inferior

56

salaries? Would it not be more functional to share the wealth a little more evenly and to reward more sports people farther down the ladder and across the sexes rather than the elite few at the top? Would the top-class players be able to succeed if it were not for the rest of the players, teams, competitions, governing bodies? Would they be unlikely to strive to the top if the financial rewards were a little less than they currently are?

Functionalism often overlooks the coercive and contested nature of power. Parsons emphasises power's enabling effects but ignores its constraining effects and fails to recognise how power was achieved in the first place. Layder (2006: 30) notes: 'it is because Parsons defines power itself as part of the legitimate and overt authority structure of society that he tends to overlook these aspects'. Thus, power appears to many functionalists as already legitimate – due to it being viewed as merely the democratic will of the people given over to power-holders on our behalf. This overlooks the Marxist conceptualisation of ideology – where power may be manipulative, hidden, unequal, or exploitative (see Chapter 4). This inability to deal with conflict and power relations is based on the assumption that all groups in society broadly share the same values and goals whilst overlooking power differences. This is referred to by Loy and Booth (2000) as the *consensus bias*; the exaggeration of society's harmony and unity and the minimization of conflict and disagreement. Despite recognizing that there are conflicts, Parsons still overlooked the material inequalities that likely affected the institutionalizing of values and norms. Key to functionalist views of conflict and change is that though both are inevitable, even in highly functioning societies, they occur *in* the system, not *against* it. In other words, the conflict and change are viewed within the parameters of the system, and change is sought within those parameters, which are compatible *with* the system, thus reinforcing the very system itself. As you will see in the Marxist and Cultural Studies chapters, conflict theories challenge this view of the functioning society, sometimes perceiving the system itself as part of the problem and thus, central to these theories, altering the system is often viewed as a potential solution.

There is a paradox partly visible in the criticism directed toward Durkheim as being conservative (despite his reputation as a socialist and radical), and it applies to critics of Parsons' functionalism, too.

This links to a misunderstanding centred on functionalism's status as a consensus perspective that is concerned with social solidarity and linked to Durkheim's rejection of individualism. When first introduced to functionalism and when learning of its concern for social solidarity (and rejection of individualism), some students mistake this for a socialist-type perspective. The problem with this is that just as Durkheim was not himself a conservative but merely a theorist who showed how Anglo-American society was organized and experienced along conservative principles, functionalism's emphasis on social solidarity should be understood in its specific context of defending and reinforcing solidarity within Western capitalist societies. So, whilst other theoretical perspectives (such as Marxist and cultural studies) would agree with the functional position that successful societies require high levels of social solidarity, those applying these other theories would argue that this social solidarity often becomes possible only through struggle among and between conflicting groups with incompatible desires that are often contrary to those in positions of power. This is the reason why Marxist and cultural studies perspectives are called *conflict theories*. Indeed, Cohen (1978) proposed that Marx's core theory actually used a functionalist analysis. In other words, Marx did recognize that parts of society functioned in ways that contributed to the maintenance of the whole. However, as you will see in the next chapter, he did so in ways that markedly differed from functionalists.

FURTHER READING

It is true to state that despite sport and exercise often being thought of in functionalist terms, over the relatively short period of time in which the sociology of sport has been a sub-discipline, few analyses of sport and exercise have used a functionalist approach. However, a good starting point is Harry Edwards' classic (1973) book *Sociology of Sport*. Nitsch (1985) and Luschen (1990) are partly influenced by functionalist theory when discussing sport. Meanwhile, Puig and Vilanova (2011) explicitly apply a functionalist perspective to their study of men's involvement in outdoor sports, along with Taylor (1988), who discusses sport and international politics looking at international sporting bodies from a functionalist perspective. Lewandowski (2007) attempts to overcome some of the flaws in functionalism by applying what he terms 'a constraint theory of sport to boxing'. Beyond the sport and exercise world, Abrahamson (1978) provides a threefold typology, of individualistic, interpersonal, and societal functionalism, and Davis and Moore's well-known paper (1945) discusses at length their social stratification theory, which became a major point of discussion for Merton. Munch (1987) provides an account of how Parsonian functionalism can be applied in more modern times.

CHAPTER 4

MARXIST PERSPECTIVES

Let us think back to 2008, to the start of the banking debts crisis, which considerably contributed to the world-wide recession. That same year, a UEFA-commissioned report found that despite the combined debt of eighteen English Premiership football clubs[1] being £3.5 billion, the average salary for one player totalled £1.46 million (see *The Telegraph*, 28/3/10 and sportingintelligence.com). During this same period, the total paid to agents for 'fees' was £70.6 million (see *The Independent*, 1/12/09). The Royal Bank of Scotland recorded the largest corporate loss in UK history that year, £24.1 billion. Yet its CEO, Fred Goodwin, retired on 1 January, 2009 with a £16 million pension package. The cost of the 2012 Olympic Games in London was around £24 billion, with a reported £12 billion coming directly from the British taxpayers (see Oliver, 2012). The children's charity Barnardo's estimates that one in three (3.8 million) UK children are currently living in poverty. As a student of sport and exercise, think of these facts; consider the reality of football clubs who are billions of pounds in debt yet pay millions of pounds to players and agents; how are banking debts and recessions linked to professional sports and their financial arrangements? How important is it for taxpayers to fund an elite mega sporting event whilst the country is in recession, unemployment is rising, and the cost of living has spiralled sharply (UK inflation rates in 2011 averaged 5 percent)? Are new sports stadia, and roads to ease travel to these facilities, more important to fund than programmes to tackle child poverty or improve health care or higher education?

Marxist analyses of sport and exercise often focus on economic power and inequality, with particular emphasis placed on the extent to which sport and exercise are implicated in the (alleged) unequal distribution of economic power. Marxists argue that sport and exercise are often (wrongly) viewed as somehow separate from serious things in life, transcending the worlds of politics, nationalism, identity, and the economy. Perceived in this light, sport and exercise can be thought of simplistically as play, fun, free time, and fantasy and, therefore, mere extensions of the leisure market as opposed to highly structured, regulated, politicised, mediated, and capitalist activities. Thus, as you have seen in the book's introduction, it is unsurprising to learn that sport originates from the word *disport*, which means to enjoy oneself. This view reduces sport and exercise to non-serious activities and part of the leisure industry whereby they become commodities available in the market place where the selling of those products occurs that simply satisfy the market's needs or desires. Given that the market per se has no needs or desires – people have needs and desires – Marxists argue that only some people's needs and desires are satisfied at the expense of the needs and desires of others and that sport is one of many elements within society that helps reinforce and reproduce these uneven and unfair practices. The capitalist practice of producing *things* to satisfy consumer desires (often claimed to be needs) encourages competition between producers to make the best product at the best price or face being beaten by a competitor who makes a superior alternative. This may involve making a cheaper, more functional product or an expensive, exclusive, and more desirable one to overtake competition and maximise profit. Given sport's and exercise's deep-seated and oft-assumed natural competitive qualities, which usually involve outperforming the opposition (or one's own personal best), we should not be too surprised to find that sport and exercise provide fertile environments to recreate and reinforce the capitalist values and win-at-all-cost philosophy that Marxists allege reproduce capitalist ideologies by permeating non-economic spheres of life within capitalist societies. Harry Cleaver makes this connection explicit in his foreword to Carrington and McDonald's (2009: xxii) collection on *Marxism, Cultural Studies and Sport*, where he bemoans state education's competitive, elitist, and hierarchical structure often seen as central elements of capitalism:

> In high school I also became as hostile to competition in the classroom as I had become towards competition in sports. Like coaches, teachers and administrators encouraged competition, systematically pitted student against student and rank ordered us in a grade hierarchy.

To enable us to think about sport and exercise from a Marxist perspective, (sometimes called conflict theory),[2] we begin by outlining orthodox Marxism (also called classical Marxism), which derives from the original writings of Karl Marx and Frederick Engels. The historical origins, major concepts, and strengths and weaknesses associated with Marxism are highlighted. We look at the Marxist-inspired concepts of class, alienation, and ideology. This leads into the second part of the chapter that discusses neo-Marxist perspectives and its more subtle approach to explaining the dynamics of power, with reference to the Marxist-inspired Frankfurt School before discussing the work of Pierre Bourdieu and concluding with a neo-Marxist analysis of sporting examples and critiques of the theory. This chapter should be read in conjunction with the following chapter (Cultural Studies), as it is from the neo-Marxist tradition that cultural studies developed, and both share important elements that allow us to appreciate the position of sport and exercise both historically and contemporarily and each perspective more fully. In unfolding Marxism as a social theory, we turn our attention to orthodox Marxism and its origins.

ORTHODOX MARXISM

Like most theoretical positions in sociology, Marxist analyses recognise the importance of historical developments. In particular, this perspective focuses on the links between the emergence of the Industrial Revolution (industrialisation and urbanisation) and the development of modern-day social structures and relationships. Technological advancements, such as the steam engine and electric power along with newly developed machinery contributed to new industries emerging around mechanized forms of labour and, in turn, these contributed to changing working conditions in the new factories. Additionally, living conditions changed from rural settings to the newly emerging urban towns and cities. In the United Kingdom, a new national railway network developed from 1825, allowing rapid movement of people and goods across the country and making many people mobile for the first time. These factors all combined to enable capitalism and social classes (and economic conflict) in the modern era to arise. With regard to work relations in particular, large-scale investors who had paid for the new factories and raw materials of industry wanted the most out of their high-cost machinery, and this required new forms of discipline and rationality to be instilled into a rapidly growing and new type of workforce.

These new conditions and the relationships between the workers (or as Marx labelled them, the *proletariat*) and owners of the means of production (the bosses, or as Marx labelled them, the *bourgeoisie*), formed and sustained through capitalism, led to a new phase in history where the masses began appropriating things (goods and services) beyond their basic needs of food, water, and shelter on a new scale. Thus, humans further extended the scope from meeting their essential needs to creating and servicing desires and to accumulating more money to own more goods, services, and property beyond what was essential for survival. Marxists argue that these practices and their associated values decreased human creativity and freedom by reducing relationships to capitalist relations of competition, wealth accumulation, and division of people based on their class position. The bosses own central elements of production including the labour power of the worker, the machinery, the factory, and the raw materials required to manufacture products. Marx termed this 'the means of production'. Under capitalism, the owners of the means of production and the workers enter a relationship whereby the workers are allowed access to the means of production to produce for the boss/owner and in return are paid what Marx called a 'subsistence wage', usually as little as the boss can get away with. Marx believed this resulted in exploitation, with the bosses benefiting from the monetary difference (surplus value) between the cost of producing the goods and the sale of the products. This surplus value (profit) goes (unfairly, according to Marx) to the bosses rather than to the workers who produced it in the first place.

Marx argued that under capitalism, people's activities were conditioned for them by the relations of production – their need to produce for the benefit of owners (capitalists) was essentially conditioned under circumstances directed by the owners, and this reduced human potential and freedom, leading to what Marx called *alienation*. Alienation resulted from humans being prevented from reaching their full potential (as defined by Marx). Marx claimed that under capitalism, physical labour was not freely engaged – so though the industrial worker was legally freer than the peasant or slave from earlier epochs, they were still not truly free. Second, Marx argued that

BIOGRAPHIC NOTE

Karl Marx (1818–1883) was one of the most significant thinkers of the nineteenth century, whose intellectual heritage still bears relevance today. He was born in Trier, Germany into a German-Jewish family who had converted to Christianity. He studied at the universities of Bonn and Berlin. After graduating from Berlin, Marx started a career as a radical journalist and, within a year, became editor-in-chief of his Cologne-based newspaper but, due to government suppression, he fled to Paris in 1843 and then moved on to Brussels in 1845. He made a brief return to Germany in 1848, taking part in an unsuccessful democratic revolution before moving to London in 1849, where he spent the rest of his life and where he is buried in Highgate Cemetery. Marx worked on a number of philosophical and economic books and spent his life engaging in radical politics, publishing works in newspapers and periodicals. He found it difficult to complete books, and a number of his works were published after his death as a result of editorial work by his long-time friend and collaborator Friedrich Engels (1820–1895). He and Engels collaborated on a number of projects, including the *Communist Manifesto* (1848). One of his most important works, *The Economic and Philosophical Manuscripts* (1844), outlines his theory of 'alienation'. In 1867, the first volume of his great study of economic theory and the economic basis of society, *Capital* (*Das Kapital*), was published. Some suggest that the young Marx (1840s) was naïve and immature compared to his later (1860s) works, and *Grundrisse* (1858), a collection of diverse notes on alienation, capitalism, technology, distribution, exchange, and use values, is sometimes viewed as a key bridge between young and mature Marx. Marx was a political activist and a social theorist and, indeed, viewed the two as inextricably linked. Thus, even today, genuine Marxist thinkers desire not simply to understand the world but to change it. His overarching theory critiques Georg Hegel's idealist philosophy – rejecting abstract philosophies in favour of a historical process of material relations, and this became known as *historical materialism*.

Think about paid athletes and their 'owners' who may consist of some or all of the following: the governing body, the sports club, the millionaire owner. Think about the sport-labour relations. To what extent are these 'workers' exploited and/or alienated from the fruits of their labour or from their true human potential? For example, is the paid athlete earning £20,000 per week or winner of Wimbledon who gets £1.1 million really exploited in the way workers were according to Marx? Or perhaps they are alienated by having little power to decide on crucial aspects of their sporting life – surrendering this to a governing body, sponsors, a team coach, or agent? Alienation can occur when workers do not choose what they produce or how their product is used/marketed or when the worker does not own the actual product. Do the drivers of Formula 1 or the players on the LTA circuit have a say about the running of their sports, the dates, the venues, the public relations work that they are duty bound to engage in for sponsors? Or consider the 2004 National Hockey League (Canada) and 2011 National Basketball Association (USA) lockout disputes over collective bargaining agreements between players and owners? How could a Marxist analysis explain these? Or what about the producers of the sports goods manufactured by global companies exploiting cheap labour in developing countries? Are these workers alienated?

those who did not labour were denied a vital element of their human essence, their expressive and creative capacities and, thus, were also not free. We must remember that new industries and working practices and living conditions are always dynamic and, therefore, able to continue shaping and influencing social classes and their relationships but, as you will see here and in Chapter 5, sometimes in less obvious ways than in Marx's time.

Though critical of prominent philosopher Georg Hegel (1770–1831), Marx was influenced by his work – particularly by his *dialectical mode of logic*,[3] which viewed history as a progressive development based on conflict inevitably being resolved by resolution. Hegel argued that increasing levels of conflict were essential developments in human progress, as they would ultimately lead to positive change, thus increased civilising stages in human development. Whilst Hegel focused on ideas, viewing philosophical knowledge and intellectualising as the highest forms of development, Marx applied this to social relations and the material world. For example, over time feudalism's slavery and gross inequalities were replaced by wage labour and private property (constituents of capitalism). However, Marx thought that something better still would develop out of capitalism, too, once the workers realised their true position and potential. Marx adopted much from Hegel's method and sought to provide a *grand narrative* of the history of society. However, Marx believed that Hegel's idealist philosophy provided the illusion that human inequalities were *natural* actualities of history grounded in consciousness rather than *products of material conditions* giving rise to economic inequalities. 'For Marx, the real history of human development could not be a history solely of thoughts or ideas; it would have to be a history of human life in the real world, i.e. the world of economic and political being' (Cuff et al., 1998: 15). Therefore, rather than ideas coming first, as Hegelians believed, Marx posited that ideas were the historical outcomes of economic activities. A necessary and central condition of Marx's entire belief system was that the aim of theory was not merely to interpret history but to change it (Marx and Engels, 1947). As Calhoun et al. (2002: 21) explain further:

> For Marx ... ideas cannot be understood in isolation, but rather only in direct relation to the social context within which they were born ... it is not ideas that determine the material world, but rather the other way around. Marx called this 'turning Hegel over on his head'.

Marx stressed that this *turning reality upside down* in understanding human existence only as ideas and thoughts was to distort the realities of human experience. Clearly this has implications for students of sport and exercise – as you will discover later in the chapter – whereby any true Marxist analysis is preconditioned to seek change and/or to develop human action (Figure 4.1).

Though orthodox Marxism is often portrayed as diametrically opposed to functionalism, both are *structural, macro theories* (see Chapter 3). In other words, they place emphasis on how large structural systems such as law, education, the media, culture, and industries affect our individual actions and attitudes (agency). This is illustrated by Marx's

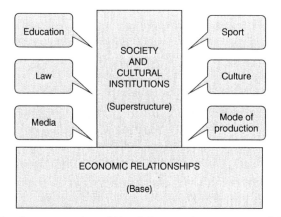

Figure 4.1 Visual representation of Marx's base–superstructure model

base-superstructure model (see Figure 4.1). Orthodox Marxism is concerned with the role of cultural institutions in analysing industrial societies. For Marx, economic relationships form the base upon which institutions and the ideas generated within them are balanced. Thus, in Marxism, the material reality of producing the basic human needs of food and shelter under capitalist conditions influences (or, in fact, governs) the social activities of a society. Furthermore, these activities themselves come to reproduce core capitalist values and practices. Figure 4.1 illustrates the societal representations of the base-superstructure model, demonstrating Marx's genius as a social analyst and the limitations of his economic determinism. Despite viewing society from an economic vantage point, Marx did pay a great deal of attention to the creation and use of social values and ideology.

IDEOLOGY AND MARXISM

Whilst Marxism and functionalism may both be structural macro-theories, major differences exist between them. For example, Gruneau (1999: xxiii) notes that Marxists often view functionalism as 'ideologically neutered', perceiving it as being 'little more than a handmaiden of the status quo'. In other words, functionalists (see Chapter 3) were accused of presenting societal values and norms as emerging from an apolitical or neutral will of the people, a *general consensus*. This opened up the debate to consider more carefully one of Marxism's central concepts: the position of 'ideology'. Marx believed norms and values to be ideological products that represent the desires and interests of dominant groups in society. Marx's analysis of ideology advances his previous notion that reality is turned on its head, as Morrison (1995: 46–47) explains:

> In ideology, everything appears upside down and actively turns things upside down in imagination. This active turning of reality upside down in perception is directly linked to the fact that dominant conceptions always reflect the dominant material relationships, and this happens, Marx thought, when the ideas and beliefs reflect only the wills, intentions and interests of the dominant classes.

Ideas 'take on the form of universality', allowing the dominant classes to represent their interests as the common interest and 'the only universally valid ideas' (Marx, 1970: 39, 41). That is, the dominant class's way of doing things becomes *the way* of doing things. Morrison (1995: 49) adds: 'in this sense, ideology legitimates and justifies the reality of one class'.

REFLECTION

One such example of these dominant class ideas assuming universal validity is that high salaries are required for some specialist jobs to secure the best and brightest employees. Thus, consider the high-earning athlete whose agent justifies his – and it usually is a male's – exorbitant salary demands by claiming his or her client is one of the top attractions and, as such, needs to be paid the equivalent of other 'top' athletes. In management circles, this is called *benchmarking*. Or away from sport, consider the ubiquitous claim that top-earning bankers and executives are the wealth creators and, as such, require exorbitant salaries to attract and keep them in position. Marxists would argue that it is the masses of workers rather than the individual banking executives, and the paying fans rather than the top-class athlete who are the primary creators of wealth – as without them there would be no product or consumption. However, despite this, many accept the underlying premise that some workers – usually those in senior and specialised positions – require and deserve hugely inflated salaries in comparison to those carrying out the menial, less-valued jobs.

68

The power of the dominant ideology results in many sports fans (and victims of collapsed banks) still extolling such benchmarking practices as beneficial. Think of the English Premiership football fan or North American baseball fan who defends the rapidly increasing ticket and replica shirt prices by saying 'but we need to pay this so we can get the best players and compete against the best teams'. They accept the underlying definition of the situation – that to compete against the best requires paying the most to ensure higher income streams for your club. Yet Marxists would challenge this ideological premise and suggest that rewarding teams and players with exorbitant financial payments is in itself part of the problem facing sports teams and fans in the twenty-first century. Instead, however, those who question these practices often end up being viewed as the problem for discouraging 'enterprise' or rewards for achievement.

Though Coakley and Pike (2009: 41) are correct to suggest that Marxist theory 'focuses on the ways that sports are shaped by economic forces and used by economically powerful people to increase their wealth and influence', we would further extend this definition and suggest that the full power of Marxist analyses are their ability to reveal how sports and exercise can be shaped and used to benefit wealthy and influential groups *by exploiting the general population* in ways that involve subtle forms of manufacturing consent. For instance, as we have just seen with sports fans accepting the underlying definition of the situation (i.e. paying more is necessary for more club income and increased ability to compete with the best), Marx argued that often neither person was aware of their role as exploiter/exploited, and this has become known as *false consciousness*.

To use Marx's original terminology, the workers may feel they are rewarded by a fair day's work, and the bosses may think they are masters of a fair and open system ('the free market'); thus, both contribute to what is for Marxists an unfair system of relations characterised by domination and subordination. Furthermore, besides economic factors, Marxist accounts of sport and exercise seek to analyse the struggle over the definitions of dominant meanings of sport and the legitimate uses of time and the body itself.

Marx argued that without this awareness (i.e. class consciousness), revolution and change were impossible. The material reality of our

Some alternative sports started off as counter-cultural activities, often with counter-cultural lifestyles accompanying them. From surfing in 1950s southern California to Parkour (free running) in modern day France, a number of sport and exercise practices have emerged as alternative activities with corresponding sporting frameworks – often rejecting competition, sexual division, sponsorship, commodification, overt expressions of nationalism, and other such mainstream sporting values. Yet, despite starting out as an on-the-surface challenge to the mainstream, rather than meaningfully subvert the dominant ideological frameworks, they often become incorporated into them. Think about the development of competitions, governing bodies, and spatial artificialisation (the creation of special locations restricted to this activity). Before too long, what was once counter-cultural has become another mainstream activity contributing to the status quo rather than challenging it. So, as Beal (1995) discovered with skateboarders, what was once viewed as counter-cultural can be transformed into official competitions and professional competitors competing for sponsorship, fame, and glory. Thus, an ideological distortion of thought occurs whereby the original subversive intention becomes transformed into the dominant framework. This works on two levels; first, it deflects genuine challenges to the dominant way of doing things by incorporating counter-cultural activities into a contained environment characterised by mainstream practices and values; second, it reinforces the power of the mainstream culture further whilst appearing to 'allow' radicals to exercise their counter-culture. As Beal's (1995) work highlighted, some of the skateboarders who remain motivated by the counter-cultural values of their sport refer to the professionals as 'rats'; thus, they would appear, at least, to retain a true sense of consciousness (according to Marxist analyses).

lived conditions acts as conduits for our experiences, meaning that 'our apprehension of reality is conditioned by our location in a social class' (Morrison, 1995: 48). Therefore, our internalised experiences, which themselves are contoured by material conditions such as

Let's pause for a moment and think of your own class background and its relationship to sport and exercise and other spheres: How would you feel if you were to accompany a new boyfriend or girlfriend to his or her father's yacht club charity ball and enjoy a five-course meal? Would you have an appropriate dress or suit or shoes? Would you look 'right'? Would you feel out of place or right at home? Alternatively, how would you feel if you were at a twenty-first birthday bash in the upstairs lounge of a local pub complete with finger buffet, balloons, local DJ, and drinking games? What sport and exercise activities does your family value and participate in (if at all)? What kind of house do you live in, and what kind of school did you attend? What sport and exercise activities do other families who live in other types of houses and whose children attend other types of school from you participate in? Are the activities you and your siblings do the same as your parents or grandparents?

family life, education, work, leisure, life histories, and biographies, influence our values, beliefs, and potential behaviours, helping to shape future opinions, views, and relationships (to people and to situations; see also Chapter 2). Yet, class is not fixed – to place or time – but the potential for class movement (social mobility) remains limited as a result of our *location in a social class* and, more precisely, how this location has impacted on our past and impacts on current experiences, values, practices, and beliefs. Hence, the common working class feeling of 'not belonging' in many a middle-/upper-class space and vice versa.

Despite Marxism having shortcomings – notably, its economic determinism – its ubiquitous impression on contemporary sociology is unquestionable. As Mills (1962: 27) puts it: 'No one who does not come to grips with the ideas of Marxism can be an adequate social scientist; no one who believes that Marxism is the last words can be either'. In seeking explanations for its economic determinism, Marxists themselves developed more advanced interpretations, referred to as neo-Marxist accounts. It is to some of these we now turn.

71

NEO-MARXISM

Those who continued clinging to over-determined accounts of Marxism were heavily influenced by Althusser's (1971) essay, *Ideological State Apparatuses*,[4] which presented an overly pessimistic and simplistic view of society being shaped by those in powerful positions using the state to repressively maintain their ideology through institutions such as education, law, and sport. In other words, Marxists, sympathetic to Althusser's ideas, argued that under capitalism, defenders of the system (e.g. industrialists, capitalists, and politicians) were able to extend their influences – or exert their power – over areas of life beyond business or capital in ways that reinforced the ideology of business and capitalism. Thus, viewed in this light, sport, art, science, media, and education may appear as independent elements of society but, in reality, they uphold and reinforce the values of the capitalist system. This may be illustrated in the way sport is practiced and encouraged (along capitalist and business-like lines) or as noted in Harry Cleaver's (in Carrington and McDonald, 2009) aforementioned observation, the way schools (and sport and exercise) embrace the structures and values of capitalism such as competition, league tables, hierarchies, specialised roles, and so on.

However, not denying their classical roots, neo-Marxists began theorising the world with subtler and less determined ways, and central to this endeavour was the Marxist-inspired Frankfurt School. There was, according to the Frankfurt School's critical theory, a need to incorporate the possibility of a non-totalising concept of power that rejected ideological determinism.

Neo-Marxists, often influenced by the Frankfurt School, began recognising that, although being inextricably linked to economics, wealth, and modes of production (and consumption), societies were much more complex, with ideology and power being necessary components of any worthwhile theory. Rather than cultural institutions (such as sport and exercise) reflecting capitalist society, sport and other cultural institutions were seen to be paradigms of it – reinforcing and reproducing the social forms and institutions that shaped and manipulated the activity in the first place. As you have seen, power inequalities (or imbalances) involve more than economic power and,

The Frankfurt School – founded in Germany in 1923 but its members later fled to the United States to escape the Nazis – 'sought to broaden the terms of … Neo-Marxist debate decisively' (Jarvie and Maguire, 1994: 100). They were committed to human emancipation and stressed 'the repressive effects of bourgeois thought and culture' (Hargreaves, 1982: 6). Rigauer (2000: 41) claims that they 'rejected any form of economic determinism and assumed dynamic relations and interdependencies between the economy and the culture of a society'. They were critical of orthodox Marxism, abandoning the traditional economic base-superstructure explanations in favour of analyses of ideology and politics. Gruneau (1993: 94) explains that the Frankfurt School 'was a hybrid of diverse philosophical and theoretical influences. But despite this mélange of influences, The Frankfurt School theorists always saw themselves as extending Marx's critical legacy'. They attempted to analyse and interpret social relations and meanings in a less determined (Rigauer, 2000), but still critical way and, simultaneously, respond to previous critiques. The over-determined theories have been criticised for being excessively pessimistic and overlooking possible liberating tendencies in cultural forms (Hargreaves, 1982).

resultantly, ascribing one single source to be the determinate factor in society was deemed over-simplified (i.e. mono-causalistic). Frederick Engels[5] foresaw the allegation of economic determinism, writing in an 1890 letter:

> According to the materialist conception of history, the *ultimately* determining factor in history is the product and reproduction of real life. Neither Marx nor I have ever asserted more than this. Hence if somebody twists this into saying that the economic factor is the *only* determining one, he transforms the proposition into a meaningless, abstract, absurd phrase.
>
> (Marx and Engels, 1890/1975: 394, original emphasis)

Despite Engels's assertion, Marxist accounts of sport have been accused of focusing too heavily on critiquing its economics, overlooking its liberating and positive elements (see Carrington and McDonald, 2009; Coakley and Pike, 2009; Craig and Beedie, 2008; Morgan, 1994). Similar to other social institutions and practices, sport and exercise are not exclusively oppressive and can also offer (perhaps in equal measure) various forms of resistance and opposition to ideological discourses (Carrington and McDonald, 2009; Hargreaves, 1982; Gruneau, 1983, 1988). Indeed, this represents one of the major paradoxes in neo-Marxist thought. The political *left* supports (sometimes radical) social change and reform to create (what they deem to be) a more balanced and egalitarian society: government involvement (nationalising) in key sectors such as education, health, transport, and energy resources. Historically, however, the political left has been acknowledged as having a deep-seated antipathy for sport (and some other popular cultural practices), viewing it, as they view religion, as an opiate of the masses and suppressor of 'true' human emancipation and one of the contributors to false consciousness. In other words, if the labourers, cleaners, waitresses, health workers, teachers, and so on are busy debating the latest drug scandal in the NFL or a golfer's extramarital affair (or the latest X-Factor contestant's nervous breakdown), they are being diverted from more important issues such as conflicts in the Middle East, global recession, environmental issues, and unemployment. Yet, conversely, sport has been (and arguably still is) a primary site for (largely male) working class expression and mass group cohesion – potential sites for the very mass-community action so desired (and predicted) by many Marxists.

It is sport's apolitical façade that helps equip it with such capitalist, nationalist, and sexist ideology, providing many an ideological battleground for competing causes. Yet the fact that sport is such fertile ground for the social, political, and economic manipulation of the masses by the powerful, as Marxists highlight, is largely due to the powerful potential sport has for expressing and representing a collective will and can equally be used effectively for liberating humans as constraining them. This is a major irony in Marxist analyses of sport. Sporting attachments can be so strong and historically and culturally embedded that they offer one of the few genuine arenas for group expression in a world rapidly characterised by rampant individualism. We see this in India, Pakistan, Australia, and England with cricket, in South Africa, Wales, and New Zealand

74

Consider our major group attachments – such as national, regional, and gender identities. It is no coincidence that sport is a major arena for group cohesion *and division* based on these aspects of identity. We see national (American) and continent-wide (European) identities expressed in golf's Ryder Cup. We see national identity (nation-state and/or nation) expressed around the Olympics and in the World Cups (football, rugby union, cricket). More locally, we see national identity rivalries between American and Canadian ice hockey clubs and English and Welsh rugby clubs. Even internally with ice hockey, we see alternative versions of Canadian identity expressed by fans of the Toronto Maple Leafs and the Montreal Canadiens. Regional/local identities are expressed around college/university/high school sports and some professional team sports in Europe, with regional rivalries between Barcelona and Real Madrid (which involve competing versions of national identities too), Liverpool FC and Manchester United FC or in cricket between Yorkshire and Lancashire's 'Roses match' rivalry due to its historic links to the War of the Roses in the fifteenth century.

with rugby union, and in South America and Europe with football, and to varying degrees in American baseball and Canadian ice hockey, each fostering genuine collective solidarity among many sports fans. Yet historically, some Marxists have overlooked this sports-centred collective solidarity, dismissing it as a bourgeois diversion. One possible reason for such fatalistic accounts of sport by Marxists is that when sport is 'allowed' to be used for ideological purposes, it tends to be supporting powerful or dominant bourgeois causes such as major corporate sponsors, government initiatives, or nationalistic and militaristic campaigns, few of which are likely to be supported by many political Marxists. This is not to deny that sometimes sport can be openly used for ideological messages that Marxists may support and do so knowingly. For example, environmental campaigns such as China's shark fin soup campaign to protect sharks and publicly endorsed by Chinese basketball player Yao Ming and the United Kingdom's Kick it Out anti-racism campaign in football are both likely to be supported by many Marxists.

BOURDIEU'S LINKS TO MARX

One of the most influential Marxist-inspired social theorists of recent times is Pierre Bourdieu, who managed to overcome some of the problems of economic determinism whilst still placing economic class at the centre of his work. Bourdieu was critical of the crude economic structuralism of previous Marxists and argued for more subtle analyses of class, extending beyond the basic economy-based analyses. So, for example, he considered class to be connected in less obvious yet important ways to eating habits, attitudes toward the body, theatre visiting (or not), clothing, housing, car choices, and many other forms of everyday lifestyle including sport and exercise (see Wilkes, 1990 for full discussion of these issues). Simply put, he showed that people belonging to one class seek to show their distinction from their closest neighbouring class (and sometimes their own class) group by accumulating social, cultural, and educational capital (power) over one's nearest class rival (from the same or lower class), thus maintaining their differential status. He called this process *maintaining distance*. Accumulating such power (capital) is compounded by having, and being seen to have, good taste – and this taste itself is viewed as being defined by those occupying higher positions in the class hierarchy. (For an excellent account of working class groups seeking such distinction, see Jones, 2011). This allows one to separate oneself from class rivals (or as Bourdieu also called it, to make 'gains in distinction').

The debt owed to Marx is explicit. Marx asserted that once a class begins the struggle against the class above it, it is involved in the struggle against the class below it (Marx and Engels, 1890/1975, vol. 3). Bourdieu (1984: 6) explained that class tensions and individuals are

> bound up with the system of dispositions (habitus) characteristic of the different classes and class fractions. Taste classifies, and it classifies the classifier. Social subjects, classified by their classifications, distinguish themselves by the distinctions they make, between the beautiful and the ugly, the distinguished and the vulgar, in which their position in the objective classifications is expressed or betrayed.

In other words, the lifestyle 'choices' we make, the sports we play and watch, the types of exercise we do, and the way we look after our

76

body are not class-neutral but are in fact class-signifying activities that reinforce our class and the class of the activity simultaneously. Our very involvement in activities that are perceived to be lower-/upper-class reaffirms the class status of these practices due to the upper-/lower-class of participant in the activity. They mutually reinforce one another's position. Additionally, according to this framework, the better one's taste, the higher up they are likely to perceive their own class.

Bourdieu's analysis of social life (or what he terms 'practice') can be described as emphasising the connections between individual preferences and behaviours (habitus), their financial, educational, and social resources (capital), and the specific environment, place, and situation (field) one exists in. In a passage from his major work *Distinction* (1984: 101) Bourdieu uses the following formula to express these relationships, allowing us to consider further the tensions between material conditions (structure) and one's independence (agency): '[(Habitus) (Captial)] + Field = Practice.' Here we see the connection between one's ability to act but to do so within circumscribed social conditions. Habitus disposes actors to perform

---

REFLECTION

Pause for a moment and think about your tastes. You can clearly see how sport and exercise and other cultural practices can become signifiers of one's good or bad taste and sometimes your class position. The training shoes or gym clothes you once wore are no longer trendy. The skirt or shoes you once thought were 'cool' are no longer 'in', perhaps because too many people have similar ones now, reducing your distinction. Consider what it may reveal about one's class if he or she has membership of an exclusive health and fitness club or if they attend an exercise class designed for young mothers at the local council-run leisure centre. What kind of cars do these groups drive? What types of sports clothing are these groups likely to own? These practices and tastes add to our accumulation of good capital and distinguish us from our nearest class rivals, whom we may even begin to label pejoratively as 'chavs' for encroaching into the class above by beginning to wear designer clothes, take foreign holidays, or attend 'high-class' cultural events they were previously distanced from.

certain practices, but these practices are themselves dependent on the situation (field), which, in turn, is influenced by the existence or absence of opportunities (capital). The debt owed to Marx is made more explicit when Bourdieu expands on habitus: 'We can always say that individuals make choices, as long as we do not forget that they do not choose the principals of these choices' (Wacquant, 1989: 45). In other words, like Marx before him, Bourdieu is arguing – albeit with less emphasis on pure economic capital and more emphasis on wider social and cultural capital – that despite appearances, people are seldom truly and completely free to make their own decisions. And even when they do appear to do so, a number of class factors weigh on these decisions. Bourdieu highlights that different people appreciate things differently according to class position. He called this 'schemes of perception and appreciation' and explains it in relation to sport in the following well-known passage that is worth repeating at length:

> … to understand the class distribution of the various sports, one would have to take account of the representation which, in terms of their specific *schemes of perception and appreciation*, the different classes have of the costs (economic, cultural and 'physical') and benefits attached to the different sports – immediate or deferred 'physical' benefits (health, beauty, strength, whether visible, through 'body-building' or invisible through 'keep fit' exercises), economic and social benefits (upward mobility etc.), immediate or deferred symbolic benefits linked to the distributional or positional value of each of the sports considered (i.e. all that each of them receives from its greater or lesser rarity, and its more or less clear association with a class, with boxing, football, rugby or bodybuilding evoking the working classes, tennis and skiing the bourgeoisie and golf the upper bourgeoisie), gains in distinction accruing from the effects on the body itself (e.g. slimness, sun-tan, muscles obviously or discreetly visible etc.) or from access to highly selective groups which some of these sports give (golf, polo etc.).
>
> (Bourdieu, 1984: 20, our emphasis)

It is these *schemes of perception and appreciation* that imbue sport and exercise (practice) with self-gratifying properties, making them attractive (or not) to different class groups. Bourdieu argued that this led to different class groups occupying different 'spaces of sport'.

One of us (Kelly, 2008) used a Marxist framework, utilising Bourdieu's 'schemes of perception and appreciation' to argue that different 'spaces' of rugby union existed in Scotland according to geographical and class-based factors. For example, whilst working-class and middle-class groups within Scottish rugby union both regretted the introduction of professionalism in 1995 – they did so for different class-based reasons. Fans from the cities of Scotland tend to occupy middle-class 'spaces' and differ from their southern Scotland (Borders region) working-class counterparts. The middle-class fans preferred their sport to remain tied to amateur ideals and not to be based on economic necessity. They viewed professionalism as tainting the pure amateur game. The working-class Borders fans regretted the loss of local identities in light of what they viewed as mercenary and nomadic players replacing loyal locals in 'their' teams.

Bourdieu showed that different class groups did not always agree on the values (or 'profits' as Bourdieu called them) of sport. Lower-working-class men may have different ideas about what a desirable male body should look like than an upper-middle-class male, for example. This may lead to different sport and exercise regimes. As well as some obvious male and female differences in perceived values attached to a number of sport and exercise activities, class groups often differ in their perceived values accorded to being toned or muscular, elegant or brash, slim or fat, being healthy and relaxed, and so on. As Bourdieu (1984: 211) summarised, 'one is practically never entitled to assume that the different classes expect the same thing from the same practice'.

Traditionally, Marxist concerns with sport have, unsurprisingly perhaps, focused on economic aspects of sporting worlds, with much attention paid to powerful elites exploiting fans/consumers – charging inflated ticket and merchandise prices (Gruneau, 1999; Sugden and Tomlinson, 1998). Others have charted the alienating conditions of athletes as being highly regimented and instrumental, allowing little room for self-actualizing expression (Adorno, 1981; Ingham, 2004, Beamish, 2009). However, perhaps one of the most significant sporting focal points for Marxist-inspired work in recent years has been on major sporting events, specifically the claims of positive legacy, most notably, the ubiquitous belief that such sports events serve as catalysts for local communities and national identities, renew urban development, and improve economic wealth and employment numbers. The Marxist-inspired *Urban Regime Theory* questions and sometimes refutes the extent to which such civic investment genuinely benefits a city, a community, or a country. As one of the major contributors in this field, Schimmel (2010: 57), summarises:

> This leftist-oriented urban framework emerged in the United States in the 1970s as a challenge to mainstream urban social science, which assumed that participation by city governments, urban planners, and businesses in local development policy was inherently apolitical ... Scholars debated the relative significance of the economy, the social production of space, competition for capital investment, significance of political processes, and the role of the state in urban development.

Thus, in true Marxist tradition, the 'benefits' to 'the community' are claimed to really be benefits to *some* of the community at the expense of others within the same community. As Schimmel reminds us,

> city boosters and urban elites often frame development agendas as 'the city's goals' and in ways that indicate a sense of territorial ambition through the use of slogans such as' Our city has big dreams!' But cities do not dream. Cities do not have aspirations. *People* do. *People* plan cities, and people share the benefits and bear the burdens of those plans unequally.
>
> (Schimmel, 2010: 64, original emphasis)

Stone's (1989) groundbreaking study of Atlanta questioned the extent to which the 'public interest' could be determined objectively. Schimmel (2010: 63) notes, 'public need gets defined through political arrangements made by urban elites who have similar interests and concerns. People whose needs differ from those within elite coalitions are often excluded from the planning process'. Thus, urban regime theory is useful when attempting to theorise the Olympic Games, the FIFA World Cup, and the Commonwealth Games, to question who the real beneficiaries are, at what cost and to whom.

The value in a Marxist sociology of sport is enormous in the sense that it allows greater understanding of sporting issues whilst also enlightening non-sporting relations, enabling us to make more sense of these society-wide issues. For example, the ongoing financial problems in some major professional sports – inflated salaries, fans struggling to afford tickets, clubs facing administration – has its equivalent in the 'real' world as revealed in the housing and banking examples outlined below. Yet, like the banking and housing industries, sporting industries often present their realities upside down (in Marxist terms). This *turning reality upside down* is illustrated when we consider some of the outcomes of the previously mentioned 2008 'credit crunch'.[6] As mentioned at the beginning of the chapter, despite overseeing the largest company losses in UK corporate history, the Royal Bank of Scotland's CEO Fred Goodwin still retired from the company with a £16 million pension package.[7] Marxists would argue that the legislative and ideological power that enabled this outcome flows from the almost universal concern with the money economy, a concern that leads to:

a.   The money economy replacing the true economy (according to Marxists) of humanity and human interaction in common language and lived expression whereby the money economy is (wrongly) assumed to be *the* economy. This occurs even to the extent that world leaders continue to evade meeting environmental targets with the often unchallenged defence that *jobs will be lost* and *the 'economy' will suffer*. This, quite simply, places jobs and money before the survival of the planet and the long-term survival of humanity itself. In sports, teams and major events get discussed in economic and cultural terms; how much they are worth to 'the economy', how many jobs they will create, how many tourists they will generate, how much the nation will 'pull together'. Marxists claim this leads to a false consciousness (obsession with money and financial systems over humanity and environmental systems).

b.   The powerful capitalist nation-states are willing to do whatever it takes – even 'nationalising' significant parts of the UK and US[8] financial sectors – to protect that money economy and economic system. The irony of neo-liberal United States adopting socialist principles to protect the very system that has led to their having to take this action, (and the fact this irony is seldom highlighted) reveals the true success of the ruling class ideology turning reality on its head. In sport, the American sports leagues adopt 'anti-free market' practices such as the draft system and salary cap to protect the overall system by ensuring competitions remain competitive.

Marxists see these outcomes as unremarkable and unjust in societies where the ruling elites are the chief benefactors of the capitalist system. Thus, the power (class) relationships and values derived from capitalism are reproduced in wider society.[9] As previously noted, the elite are often the major benefactors of these practices and ideas; thus, the aforementioned determination – by bankers, sports agents, and governing bodies alike – to defend these practices and ideas (ideologies) by citing the mantra that *top quality staff require top pay* and *if we don't pay, our rivals will*. Marxists, of course, would remind such demagogues that when the publicly paid workers – nurses, teachers, refuse collectors – demand higher salaries, these claims are often opposed by ignoring any concern to retain top-quality staff alongside warnings about *wage inflation* and *budget constraints* – two factors seldom applied to the billions of bonus pounds paid to top executives or star athletes and their agents.

The most powerful people and groups in society (who in Marx's time would have been the owners of the means of production) retain an interest in the intellectual culture as well and, therefore, also in sport and exercise practices and the ideas and values these foster in society. For example, Lord Coe, the Conservative party peer and former Conservative politician, who owns a sporting public relations firm, has been on the Olympic, FIFA, and UK government boards and committees. Lord Mawhinney, ex–Conservative party government minister of state for Northern Ireland, is also the chairman of the Football League in England and was instrumental in promoting the ideological narratives of their charity sponsor Help for Heroes (discussed in detail in Chapter 5).

CRITIQUES OF MARXIST THEORY

The major criticism of Marxism is that it is based chiefly on economic conditions and, when applied, the analysis sometimes reduces the importance of political, cultural, and other factors. In other words, economics and class conflict remain central to Marxist analyses and have resulted in orthodox Marxist accounts being criticised for downplaying or completely overlooking other intersecting factors such as gender, ethnicity, age, disability, and religion. Thus, one must keep in mind that Marxism in its classical form offers an economically determinist perspective, and thus, in the final analysis, it provides a mono-causal explanation. This is not to deny, however, that financial benefits and factors are significant components in modern sports, but it is necessary to note that there are other forces at play. These forces, such as culture, were later embraced and acknowledged by neo-Marxist theorists who, whilst retaining certain classical Marxist elements, reoriented the focus of their social analysis, thereby adding new dimensions to Marxism in general and to the Marxist analysis of sports in particular (specific branches of these are discussed in Chapter 5). This theoretical evolution, which is inherent in sociology and in most sociological theories, indeed reinforces that there is no *one Marx*. In fact, every student of his work must earn his or her own perception of it (Mills, 1962).

Marx's writings have raised some other important questions as well. First, in reference to his dialectical model, Marx so far inaccurately predicted that within the capitalist system, the workers/masses (proletariat) would become more unified and powerful and eventually engage in a revolutionary uprising, transforming the entire capitalist mode of industrial societies (see Marx, 1859/1977: 20–21). Consequently, Western Marxism became concerned to explain the failure of the proletariat revolution in industrial societies.[10] Rather than throwing the baby out with the bathwater, however, – instead of rejecting Marxism completely due to its apparent misjudgement of the capacity of the masses to revolt – some argued that to understand this failure, we must interpret it in Marxist terms. Rather than blaming Marx for not predicting that the masses would be unable or unwilling to revolt, we should consider the unforeseen success capitalism had (and still has) in concealing its 'true' (dehumanising and exploitative) nature and creating and perpetuating false consciousness.

This leads to the second major question, and this relates to Marx's conception of ideology. Questions have been raised about how society, manipulated by the elite, can distort our perception of reality and how are individuals deceived into accepting these perceptions as substitutes for reality? (see Smith, 1974; Larrain, 1983). This is part of the circular debate about structure and agency that in social science is in continual flux. In the current context, it is about how much we are culturally duped or in fact willing participants, and it forms one of Marxism's ever-enduring and perhaps unresolvable problems.

Although Marx and his intellectual legacy have been extensively critiqued, his views and sociological interpretations embedded in them still constitute an important framework for understanding and interpreting global and national sports (see Brohm, 1978). Mills (1962: 12) correctly observed that within the social sciences, 'those who reject (or more accurately, ignore) Marxist ways of thinking about human affairs are actually rejecting the classic traditions of their own discipline'. That is, 'there is a genuine powerful legacy to Marx's work upon which we can all still draw' (Beamish, 2002: 38). As we move onto Chapter 5 and discuss connections between Marxism and cultural studies, we should remember Carrington and McDonald's (2009: 1) reminder that 'these perspectives are defined in large part by their emphasis on the dialectic of *interpretation* and *transformation* of sporting cultures, institutions and practices' (original emphasis). Or as Rigauer (2000: 42) put it: 'The main purpose of a Marxist sociological theory of sport [and exercise] should be to explain the real societal functions of sport [and exercise] with the help of critical analyses focused on culture and ideology'.

FURTHER READING

For an historical overview of Marxist work within sport, Jarvie and Maguire (1994), Morgan (1994) and Riagauer (2000) are excellent sources. Brohm (1978) provides an orthodox Marxist analysis of sport, viewing it as an extension of state ideological repression. Gruneau's (1983/1999) seminal Marxist-inspired work rejects orthodox Marxism and turns attention to the culturalist Marxism that began to emerge in the 1980s and later developed into the cultural studies of sport and exercise. Ingham (1982) is another neo-Marxist who provided a sophisticated account of the power relationships within sport. John Hargreaves's book (1986) provides a Marxist-inspired analysis of the development of British sport and uses Gramsci's hegemony (discussed in detail in Chapter 5) to bridge the theoretical gap between orthodox and neo-Marxism. Carrington and McDonald (2009) provide a timely reminder of the importance and close connections between Marxism and cultural studies in the study of sport.

84

CHAPTER 5

CULTURAL STUDIES PERSPECTIVES

In recent years, sport has been one of the most prominent cultural spheres incorporated into promoting and supporting Western military forces in the post 9/11 'war on terror' context. The United Kingdom's most popular sport, football (soccer), has recently seen England's Football League competitions sponsored for a season by a newly formed military charity 'Help for Heroes'. As part of this sponsorship and public relations campaign, a series of photo shoots occurred that showed Football League mascots (cuddly cartoon-like animals) sitting on a military tank juxtaposed alongside the banner 'Help for Heroes'. The banner depicts two soldiers carrying a wounded comrade on a stretcher, and on the banner's left hand corner is a gold medal. An obvious reading of this image is: British soldiers are heroes doing humanitarian work (as shown by the wounded soldier being carried by two comrades) and they deserve medals and our support and help through the 'football for heroes week'. In a similar vein, Canada's most popular sport, (ice) hockey, has embraced the newly formed 'tickets for troops' initiative, which sees regular season ticket holders giving up their seats for a one-off match so that serving military personnel can watch the game for free. As part of the public relations work here, the military personnel are given special treatment such as being welcomed onto the ice at the end of the game to receive the applause of the non-military fans in the crowd. These and other similar events offer excellent photo opportunities and have received widespread media attention in these countries. Cultural studies theorists would argue that, far from being non-political acts, the use of sport in the context of the post-9/11 war on terror and its juxtaposition alongside positive images of national symbols of militarism serves to ideologically promote the political

Pause and think about the ideological messages being conveyed here. What other messages could be inferred (or read) through these acts or the mediated images they produce? Also, why do some sports events in the United States begin with the singing of the American national anthem, and why is this sometimes performed by a serving military person and/or accompanied by sanctioned militaristic references in the stadium and sports studio? (See Silk and Falcous, 2005 for a critique of the Salt Lake City Winter Olympics and the Superbowl in 2002, five months after 9/11, which involved military jet flyovers and numerous references to soldiers, heroes and homeland). Has this always been the case? Why are uniformed military personnel conspicuous figures at some major sporting events? For example, in the United Kingdom, they help supervise the fans in the arena at the Wimbledon tennis tournament, and they carry out ceremonial duties such as carrying the Cup into the sports stadium at nationally significant football and rugby union matches. What other ideological themes exist in sport and exercise that you can think of?

stance of their respective governments specifically and the ideology of militarism more generally.

CULTURAL STUDIES THEORY

In helping you to understand and apply a cultural studies perspective to sport and exercise, we begin this chapter by showing how culture is viewed as contested terrain to be understood according to particular social and political contexts, mainly by presenting them in specific ways that articulate for us their relationships to each other and us. The task of defining cultural studies is arguably a challenging one. It is not dominated by one theoretical or methodological position but rather is influenced by multiple approaches. Consequently, work within the cultural studies tradition is 'never a pure or distinct theoretical or methodological approach' (McDonald and Birrell, 1999: 287), nor is it related to an ancestral founder (as functionalism and Marxism are to Durkheim and Marx). Indeed, some analysts have described it as less of *a discipline* and more of a bricolage of disciplines (Hall, 1980; Hargreaves, 1982; Hargreaves and McDonald, 2000; Barker, 2008). McDonald and Birrell (1999: 286) suggest that cultural studies sports scholars are 'seeking to move beyond the confines of particular disciplinary boundaries'. They cite Nelson et al. (1992: 1–2) who claim 'cultural studies is not merely interdisciplinary; it is often… actively and aggressively anti-disciplinary – a characterisation that more or less ensures a permanently uncomfortable relation to academic discipline'. Hargreaves and McDonald (2000: 48) describe cultural studies as 'concerned with the social significance and systematic analysis of cultural practices, experiences and institutions'. Cultural practices and experiences are contested encounters, or a 'sort of constant battlefield' (Hall, 1981: 233) pitting the powerful against the less powerful in a competition to define the dominant (and, therefore, the valued) meanings associated with culture and cultural activities such as sport and exercise (as part of the wide array of culture industry activities). However, these 'battlefields' demand historical and theoretical excavation to unearth power relations, social and economic structures, and their effects. McDonald and Birrell (1999: 292) explain:

> A cultural studies perspective suggests that subjectivity and social life are always already embedded in particular relations of power that produce particular knowledges. The world has been made to mean according to which particular groups have access to the important cultural signifying systems (like the media) to proclaim a particular world view. People shape knowledge, and this knowledge is linked to relations of domination and subordination.

In other words, cultural studies emphasises that all social behaviour is to some extent enabled and constrained by economic, political, cultural, and gendered power relations and that the popular and dominant views formed in society are often those belonging to dominant and powerful groups. This means that cultural studies theorists often seek to understand how and why particular norms and values become established, and this often involves looking at the specific contexts of social relations. Grossberg (1997: 7–8) argues that 'context is everything and everything is context for cultural studies'. A key element of this context-specific understanding involves *articulation*: The true meanings of cultural practices (such as sport and exercise) can be understood only according to the ways in which they are articulated into a particular set of economic, political, and historical relationships (Howell at al., 2002). Articulation, then, refers to the juxtaposition or the 'putting together' of different elements to form one temporary symbol/meaning. So, it involves positioning different symbols or practices into specific contexts, often outside of their everyday context, to create particular meanings. For example, the cuddly football mascots sitting on top of military tanks gives the football mascots meaning beyond and different from that on the football pitch, whereas military tanks that blow people and buildings up assume a different meaning when cuddly football mascots sit on top of them. In other words, identities are part of socio-cultural contexts and (re)produced by discourse such as language and representation. Identities are neither fixed nor do they exist with essential qualities but rather are articulated and rearticulated according to established ideological viewpoints. McDonald and Birrell (1999: 294) note: 'an event (re)creates diverse meanings across time periods, while certain preferred readings become institutionalised or formalised as "history"'. For instance, Olympic sport produces and reinforces a sporting world that continually frames sport in terms of nations, perceived as 'naturally occurring' to be pitted against other nations in a battle of the fastest, strongest, and highest. Thus, Andrews (2002: 115) argues that cultural practices

> can only be understood by the way that they are articulated into a particular set of complex social, economic, political, and technological relationships that compose the social context... Moreover, whereas cultural practices, such as sport, are produced from specific social and historic contexts, they are also actively engaged in the ongoing constitution of the conditions out of which they emerge.

In other words, there is a cultural battle to define legitimate (and illegitimate) sporting practices continually emerging from everyday life, but these practices also reinforce and rebuild the relations of power around their original formation. Seen in this light, cultural studies rejects the view that sport is merely a reflection or constitutive part of society. Rather, sport simultaneously affects and is affected by wider society, namely its contextual relationships. To understand the perspective more fully, we now turn to its origins and chart its development from Marxism.

LINKS TO NEO-MARXISM

Though cultural studies had earlier antecedents grounded in the inter-war adult education classes, it was the 1964 opening of the Centre for Contemporary Cultural Studies (CCCS) at Birmingham University that paved the way for cultural studies as we recognise it today.

Although it seems self-evident that cultural studies is concerned with understanding the cultural aspects of society, this is too narrow a definition, not least because other perspectives study culture too. Theorists within cultural studies view sport and exercise (and wider cultural spheres) as sites of contestation over the meanings associated with cultural life. Therefore, it seeks to critically analyse how dominant norms and values within culture become normalised, experienced, and challenged but, crucially, it also seeks to provide an interventionist intellectual approach opening up the potential for active engagement rather than mere intellectual reflection. Unlike other perspectives that may analyse culture, cultural studies is concerned with academic and political struggles over competing definitions and the power to decide upon which definition (or value) becomes accepted as the 'norm'. Barker (2008: 5, our italics) reiterates the political aspects of cultural studies as

> a body of theory generated by thinkers who regard the production of theoretical knowledge as a political practice. Here, *knowledge is never a neutral or objective* phenomenon but a matter of positionality, that is, of the place from which one speaks, to whom, and for what purposes.

Jarvie and Maguire (1994: 124) summarise some of the general aims of a cultural studies approach to sport. These include a consideration of the relationship between power and culture and demonstrating the extent to which sport and leisure (and exercise) have been consolidated, contested, maintained, or reproduced within society. If we think about sport specifically, cultural studies views sport as a contested site of struggle, with some sporting cultural forms becoming marginalised at the expense of others that become monopolised as natural, dominant and valuable (Gruneau, 1988). For example, think about the marginalised 'sports' of fox hunting and hare coursing.[1] As sporting pursuits, both have longer histories than the modern

The CCCS at Birmingham University was instrumental in establishing cultural studies as a distinct field within and beyond the United Kingdom. Its longstanding director, Stuart Hall (1932), is perhaps the most significant figure in British cultural studies and was highly influential in the centre's development. He led the centre from 1968 to 1979 and, in doing so, helped cultural studies become established as a recognised approach to studying society. The CCCS traces its main origins, however, to the work of Richard Hoggart (1957), its original founder, and to the collective works of Raymond Williams (1958) and E. P. Thompson (1963) who wrote about the culture and experiences of the working classes in the United Kingdom. To understand the cultural studies project, we need to think of it as a product of post-war Britain's shifting class relations, in particular, the effects of consumer capitalism on Britain's working classes. The leftist theorising of class, which had traditionally relied on mono-causal economic explanations imprisoned by binary oppositions such as *exploitation* versus *emancipation*, were increasingly proving inadequate for explaining the multifaceted lived realities of post-war working class life in Britain. For instance, during this period, for the first time, large sections of the working classes enjoyed the benefits of mass consumerism and, rather than being viewed as exploited victims, they appeared to be willing participants embracing and benefiting from this new age of mass consumption. Many also continued voting for the Conservatives who historically were not aligned to working-class causes.[2] These were among the factors that posed problems for the left-wing intellectuals of the time who, with the help of *the culturalists* of Hoggart, Williams, and Thompson, were realising the importance of culture on society. Moreover, they stressed the ordinary, everyday nature of culture, reminding people that opera, theatre, and classical art were not the only cultural mores worth knowing or practising. Thus, working-class culture became visible, real, and legitimate. Culture was increasingly conceived as less a 'thing' to see or view and more a set of relational experiences, beliefs, practices, and outcomes that were the lived realities of people's lives. This approach to culture recognised that people's lived experiences in the present were part of the complex tapestry of culture. Such a position entailed being aware of the selection (and omission) of certain traditions that 'we' embrace, celebrate or reject today. Williams (1977) referred to these shared values and outlooks of culture as 'structures of feeling'. The structures of feeling of any given culture reveals their values but also that these values are in part formed by the subjectively selected and interpreted traditions of the past. Ultimately, therefore, these processes are products of power relations.

Olympics, major league baseball, or the FIFA World Cup. Both are embedded deeply in the social and cultural histories of their respective geographies, with class, status, and countryside issues intersecting. In recent years, these sports, which both involve hunting and killing animals, have been marginalised and made illegal in the United Kingdom (see also Chapter 7). Contrast these 'cruel' practices with Britain's annual Grand National horse race, which is also viewed by many as being cruel and dangerous and often results in horse deaths.[3] Despite its inherent animal cruelty, this event remains a celebrated national sporting occasion in the UK sporting calendar and retains its legitimate and legal status.

REFLECTION

Think about your sport and exercise experiences and the values and norms that have traditionally been encouraged as *the* values and *the* norms of 'our' sport and society. Is exercise always healthy? Is being heavier or bigger than some other people really such a bad thing that one should be pejoratively labelled 'overweight' or 'fat' and prescribed exercise routines? Are the increasing health and fitness concerns in many Western countries constitutive of our failure as individuals to self-discipline or are they linked to the broader social and political milieu? What is 'appropriate' use of time for teenagers and young adults? Compare the likely reaction from most people to the contrasting activities of one teenager who sails around the world in a catamaran to the teenager who spends two hours per day skateboarding in the local city centre pedestrian square. What value judgments might we make and why?

cultural studies perspectives

CULTURAL STUDIES AND HEGEMONY

The cultural studies project, then, involves questions around power and ideology generally and the power to define and reinforce values and norms more specifically. Yet the perennial problems the neo-Marxists grappled with were inherited by their cultural studies descendants: What about sport's and exercise's positive contributions to the lives of individuals, groups, and society, including the working classes? To address this question required moving beyond overly determined and one-sided accounts of sport and exercise and not overlooking their potential role as oppositional movements or forms of resistance. However, whilst sport and exercise offered opportunities for cultural resistance – illustrated clearly by Tommie Smith's and John Carlos's clenched fist salute at the Mexico '68 Olympics – it was still the case that some people's views and social and cultural preferences became dominant at the expense of others, and the ways in which this occurred also remained a major question for cultural studies theorists. Ideas are not fixed, nor are people irrevocably programmed in how they ought to behave and think.

Marxist-inspired work more broadly began acknowledging the latent and complex reality of power, realising that Marx's failed prediction of a workers' revolution (and eventual overthrow of an unfair capitalist system) required focused attention. These issues can be partly explained by turning attention to what became known as the differences between the culturalists and the structuralists. McDonald and Birrell (1999) contrast the Marxist inspired works of structuralist Louis Althusser (also introduced in Chapter 4) with culturalist E. P. Thompson. Althusser rejects any notion of ideologically free education, religion, or civic authority, implying that human behaviour (agency) is fatally inscribed with a false consciousness. In contrast, E. P. Thomspson's culturalist outlook rejects this fatalistic view of agency, maintaining a more positive agency-centred outlook. Though both extremes pose problems – structuralists potentially being over-determined and lacking human agency and culturalists potentially romanticising working class agency – cultural studies work began bridging this theoretical divide.

So, whilst many Marxists still viewed sport and exercise as overly oppressive, nationalistic, sexist, and sympathetic to the excesses of capitalism, with greed, hyper-competitiveness, drug-taking, human alienation, and prize accumulation, cultural studies began to develop explanations that also acknowledged the freedom and enjoyment (agency) for many engaged in them. Put simply, cultural studies theorists, like their Marxist predecessors, acknowledged that sport and exercise could distort human relationships but, unlike many traditional Marxists, they also accepted and encouraged viewing sport and exercise as potentially liberating cultural spheres with (perhaps equal measure of) various forms of resistance and opposition to ideological discourses. Thus, structurally determined explanations made way for more culturally sensitive theories that recognised under certain conditions sport could be semi-autonomous from its overarching structures and could in fact offer a rich environment for alternative and oppositional force. In other words, sport and exercise activities and the values associated with them must be viewed according to their varied and changing contexts, and these contexts can be *both* limiting (constraining) and freeing (emancipatory). One of us (Kanemasu and Molnar, in press) illustrates this with Fijian rugby migration. It is argued that rugby assumes both constraining and liberating features for both the athletes and the people of Fiji. For example, it is shown that despite representing a rival nation, Fijian migrant rugby players continue to symbolically represent their native country and act as a collective source of pride (for both player and Fijians). However, this is contrasted with others who accuse them of representing a foreign nation, being unavailable for their own country, and of ultimately exhibiting mercenary behaviours. This study reveals the subtle social, economic, and political factors that can give sport very different cultural meanings at the same time for different people depending on their sense of self and national identity and in relation to their personal and national aspirations.

In relation to the emancipatory potential of sport, Carrington (2009: 22) explains: 'This, perhaps, is where those Cultural Studies scholars who would describe themselves as being on the left and most probably socialist would part company with those who would self-identify as Marxist'. Despite the recognition of sport's positive qualities and its potential for resistance (cf. Bale, 2000), including for the working classes, questions continued to be asked of how some of the existing unfair relations of production and false consciousness that still occurred were maintained – as many continually experience poverty, unemployment, poor working and living conditions, and other hardship. Antonio Gramsci's concept of hegemony was influential in much of the culturalist work seeking to avoid both deterministic structuralist explanations and overly romanticised notions of working-class emancipation. In other words, how can a system that is not always or fully in the majority's interests be accepted and maintained by this majority who, far from being culturally duped, enjoy large degrees of agency, power, and decision making? The cultural studies answer is that subordination involves coercion and consent, and the concept of hegemony reveals how cultural products of power become camouflaged as apparently universal truth. Morgan (1994: 66), for example, describes social order as guided by 'patterns of action' that induce us to act in certain ways and impress upon us that social actions have to be done in accordance with what is regarded to be the 'normal', 'expected', and 'official' way to do and value them. Taylor (1989) refers to these as 'strongly valued goods' – the way one ought to behave, act, value, and so on. A hegemony-oriented framework allowed for Marxist-inspired analyses to go beyond Marx 'to analyse the ways that political, cultural, and ideological institutions and practices are integrated with the economy to form the whole' (Sage, 1998: 21). Hegemony rejected simple class-based concerns, encouraging theorists to recognise the incomplete, unfixed, and diverse nature of power relations (Hargreaves, 1982; Hargreaves and McDonald, 2000; Sugden and Tomlinson, 2002).

The old-fashioned leftist conception of naked exploitation of the working classes was being superseded. 'On the contrary, there are dominant social groups whose intellectual members – both in the ruling and subject classes – develop, define and negotiate values, norms and class fractions' (Rigauer, 2000: 43). McDonald and Birrell (1999: 288) stress hegemony, therefore,

> involves a struggle for cultural leadership. Leadership is secured only to the extent that particular ruling ideas or ideologies are made to appear natural, that is, as commonsense. Power relations are never merely imposed from above but involve the active consent of subordinate groups and the taming of resistance through accommodation.

As Hargreaves and McDonald (2000: 51) state, 'hegemony theory provided the potential for understanding both the liberative and

94

controlling features of culture'. Hall states that Marxism was 'imprisoned' by its orthodoxy, its doctrinal character, its determinism, and its reductionism and suggests that Gramsci allowed certain (cultural) questions to be asked. Hall (1992: 280–281, original emphasis) notes

> While Gramsci belonged and belongs to the problematic of Marxism, his importance for this moment of British cultural studies is precisely the degree to which he radically *displaced* some of the inheritances of Marxism in cultural studies.

These new questions revolve around culture, especially pop culture, and cultural domination through hegemonic power. In a passage that Crehan (2002: 138) describes as 'one of the most frequently quoted glosses of hegemony', Gramsci (1971: 12) explains the concept as a relation of

> 'spontaneous' consent given by the great masses of the population to the general direction imposed on social life by the dominant fundamental group; this consent is 'historically' caused by the prestige (and consequent confidence) which the dominant group enjoys because of its position and function in the world of production.

Hegemony, therefore, 'resists the idea that people are passive recipients of culture and keeps intact what is arguably the inherent humanism of Marxism … it allows for cultural experiences such as sports to be understood as both exploitative and worth while' (Hargreaves and McDonald, 2000: 50). Hegemony consists of the ongoing struggles involved in legitimising and normalising ruling ideologies to appear natural and sensible rather than forced and oppressive. Hegemony became such an important conceptual tool in the cultural studies armoury that Jarvie and Maguire (1994: 108) describe it as the 'most significant concept' while Hargreaves and McDonald (2000: 54) believe it to be the 'specific character and meaning of the cultural studies project'.

Hegemony was the central conceptual tool used by John Hargreaves (1986) in his classic text *Sport, Power and Culture*. The book deals primarily with the notion of hegemonic struggle in British society from

BIOGRAPHIC NOTE

Antonio Gramsci (1891–1937) is now one of the most widely used cultural theorists of modern time. He was born in Ales, a small town in the Italian island of Sardinia. He lived in poverty for much of his childhood, exacerbated by his father being jailed for alleged corruption in his role as a registrar when Gramsci was seven years old. The translators of Gramsci's notebooks, Hoare and Nowell-Smith (Gramsci, 1971: xviii), state that the charges were 'undoubtedly motivated by his opposition to the political party in power locally'. Gramsci's mother was a seamstress and, with his father in jail between 1898 and 1904, the young Gramsci was forced to interrupt his school education to work to help feed the family. He eventually completed his schooling and, in 1911, won a scholarship to study at the University of Turin but left before completing his studies. This was partly due to his growing political commitments and his health problems that plagued him all his life. He had a debilitating spinal condition. During Gramsci's life, Italy was politically divided by north and south factions of workers, with the industrial north and agricultural south being divided on government protectionist policies that appeared to favour the factory workers in the north and penalise the peasant famers in the south. Gramsci's older brother was a committed socialist and helped influence Gramsci's political development that shifted from an early sympathy for Sardinian nationalism to class-based issues and peasant problems. This is where hegemony comes in. Gramsci was troubled by the fact that what he viewed as an unfair system (capitalism), which kept many poorer working-class workers in their desperate conditions, was only possible if these workers complied and conducted much of the work required for the system's success. If it was so unfair, why would the workers keep it going? The concept of hegemony helped Gramsci explain this state of affairs, but this theoretical insight coupled with his increasing political activism made Gramsci an enemy of Mussolini's state. At a time when Mussolini's fascist dictatorship was gaining momentum by crushing democratic opposition, Gramsci, who was now general secretary of the Communist party, was arrested and eventually jailed for twenty years. The prosecutor famously demanded, 'We must stop this brain working for twenty years' (Gramsci, 1971: xviii). Unfortunately for the fascists, Gramsci's brain was not prevented from functioning, and it was from his prison cell that Gramsci produced his influential writings that became known collectively as the *Prison Notebooks*.

the eighteenth century to the mid-1980s, detailing the emergence of modern sports forms. As Stuart Hall, notes in the book's foreword, 'Hargreaves' study has the considerable merit of treating sport as a social phenomenon and setting it in the context of power and culture where it properly belongs' (p. xi). Hargreaves explains that Gramsci's concept of hegemony involves power relations functioning largely in terms of voluntary compliance. Hargreaves argues that increased state intervention occurred in British sport since the 1960s to provide a cathartic effect and to foster a stronger sense of national identity. Hargreaves draws attention to state and national ceremonies such as the opening of Parliament, Remembrance Sunday, and the Football Association (FA) cup final day and demonstrates how, through hegemonic processes, they became national symbols designed to invoke mass loyalty. For Hargreaves, whereas the national identity being invoked was voluntarily adopted, it represented a 'national unity in a manner more consistent with the dominant class's preferred view' (1986: 155).

At this juncture, you may ask why this is not highlighted as another form of cultural duping? The answer lies in part in the success of hegemonic processes in that when they are successful they are difficult to see. Stephen Lukes's (1974/2005) advanced model of power[4] enables us to consider this further. Lukes (1974/2005: 27-28, our italics) states,

> the most effective and insidious use of power is to prevent such conflict arising in the first place... Is it not the supreme and most insidious exercise of power to prevent people, to whatever degree, from having grievances by *shaping their perceptions, cognitions and preferences in such a way that they accept their role in the existing order of things, either because they can see or imagine no alternative to it, or because they see it as natural and unchangeable, or because they value it as divinely ordained and beneficial*?

So, there may be times when we are unaware of uneven or unfair social, cultural, and economic relationships due to their hegemonic success. Yet, when hegemonic processes do become apparent, even to the extent of being challenged, they sometimes remain difficult to criticise. Cultural studies theorists would suggest that hegemonic processes succeed precisely because unless one is extremely self-aware and able to see the ideological wood amongst the trees, human agency is likely to reinforce the dominant ideology itself, as you will see now. One of the most influential contributions to cultural studies and sport came from Paul Willis's (1982) *Women in Sport in Ideology*. Willis outlined an approach he called 'analytic cultural criticism', which attempted to reveal some of the subtle ways that preferred readings of culture became fused as common sense. In his illustrative example, he discussed the ways female involvement in sport is conceptualised. Willis (1982: 125) argued 'ideology can only exist precisely if it can embody itself in the concrete common sense of actors' in specific contexts. Common sense is a powerful shield against recognising ideology. In other words, if we think of something as natural and inevitable (common sense), we are unlikely to see its ideological connections to social, cultural, political, and economic power relationships. Furthermore, the real power of hegemony lies in the fact that even when there is the veneer of challenge to ideology, this is often framed in such a way that it accepts the underlying definitions in the first place. Before turning to some sport and exercise examples, it is worth quoting Willis at length as he explains the full power of hegemony even when faced with on the surface challenges:

> Frequently the immediate response of the actors involved will be one of opposition, but the opposition, unless it is extremely self-aware, can only take up the issue in the terms within which it has been offered, the terms which render the phenomenon apparently concrete and real. The reaction of the local actors, then, though hostile to the surface forms of the penetration, in fact gives completely new life to the underlying definitional power of the ideology. To take certain questions up is already to have given up the right to challenge the epistemological foundations of those questions. The 'battle', so to speak, is conceded as soon as it is started, *by* starting it. If the local cultural participants do not attempt to challenge the immediate apparent issue, and have no

other account of reality, then they have no choice but to collude in the ideological definition of what confronts them...They have conceded the battle without even realising that there was a 'battle'.

(Willis, 1982: 128, original emphasis)

So, on the one hand, human agency is possible, but the ideological work of the power elite can be so effective a force it requires sophisticated levels of self-awareness of one's situation (cf. Sociological Imagination in Chapter 2). An example used by Willis is trade union members fighting for more wages. By framing their demands in monetary terms, they accept the legitimacy of waged labour. The most militant demands for more money, therefore, appear to challenge the dominant hegemonic power but, simultaneously, serves to reinforce the power of a market economy, surplus value, and waged labour. Another example can be seen in the tax debate that monarchists and republicans sometimes engage in. On the surface, republicans appear to challenge monarchy by demanding the queen pays the same rate of income tax as everyone else. However, by engaging in this battle (over how much tax the queen should pay), republicans have inadvertently accepted the underlying definition of the situation that the queen holds a legitimate position. So, rather than challenging the basic premise of royalty per se, royalty becomes accepted in a debate about the taxation rules being applied to royalty.

SPORT, EXERCISE, AND CULTURAL STUDIES

In turning to sport and exercise specifically, we present two of the main types of cultural studies examples (representation and articulation) by looking at media and sport relations. We begin with a sporting example Willis provides in his influential chapter, involving women being measured against men's performances. We then discuss in detail an example of articulation by looking at sport, popular culture, and militarism (that we introduced at the beginning of the chapter).

Willis notes the *fact* of female and male difference becomes ideologically normalised into presenting females as being physically inferior or being sexually caricatured. He argues that sexual caricaturing is reinforced by women who collude by presenting themselves as overly feminine/ sexy in interviews and media articles. Female physical inferiority, meanwhile, is reinforced by women who appear to challenge sexist assumptions but end up reinforcing maleness or masculinity as desirable (by measuring themselves against men and/or highlighting their masculine traits in sport such as aggressiveness or strength). A clear example of these representations occurred in a BBC interview with UK Olympic cyclist Vikki Pendleton (see Inside Sport, BBC 1, 7/4/08). The male interviewer framed large sections of the interview on how she maintained her femininity whilst 'balancing' out the aggressiveness and assertiveness required to be a top-class athlete. She willingly responded to a number of comments with 'I can't help liking girly things. I like putting dresses on, I like wearing make up. I like having my hair done and I like wearing high heels. I just can't help that. I like painting my nails and doing acrylics and things like that.' She then justified the aggressiveness that enables her to push on in the last lap but not without informing the viewer that this 'did not come naturally' to her and that this 'is not the way I am in everyday life'. Thus, she emphasised her feminine qualities as 'natural' and her athletic qualities as unnatural. She then highlighted her (and other women's) inferiority to men by informing the viewers of how much she relies on her male coach to guide her through because 'he has all the things that I need in his repertoire; that I need to be the best in the world. They're the things that I lack'. Viewed in cultural studies terms, these combine to reinforce and normalise sexist stereotypes even when on the surface, high-profile female athletes getting prime air time on national television might appear to some – including the athlete, interviewer, and audience – as challenging dominant ideological assumptions.

Sometime, such trivialisation of females can be achieved without the female's direct involvement, as the next example illustrates. On the surface, it appears to be challenging the sexist attitudes of male sports presenters, yet it serves to reinforce such sexist ideologies. In 2011, two prominent male Sky television presenters were reprimanded for sexist comments about a female assistant referee. Yet, in an apparent defence of the female official, the Daily Mail served to reinforce the stereotypes it appeared to criticise (see Daily Mail, 25/1/11). Accompanying a full-page-length photo of the female official, Sian Massey, wearing a mini skirt and revealing blouse, dancing in what looks like a bar, the paper reduced the on-the-surface criticism of the two male commentators to another sexist piece on women in sport.

100

It is the articulation of sport, popular culture, and militarism that we wish to focus our next illustrative example on, exposing the ideological, latent power dynamics of sport as conceptualised in cultural studies. Although it relates to a small number of specific events, its focus can be more broadly applied to the theme of a powerful (yet widely challenged) value being associated with sport (or in cultural studies terms, inherently promoted as a strongly valued good). In 2007, the UK Chief of the General Staff, the acting head of the British Army, General Dannatt, lamented what he described as a lack of public support for the UK military amongst the general UK population.[5] With increasing questions of legitimacy surrounding the original invasion and occupation of Iraq (and the occupation of Afghanistan) by US-led forces (including a third official UK inquiry into the Iraq invasion), a number of initiatives[6] have emerged within sections of the American, Canadian, and British political and cultural spheres that appear to promote universal acceptance and support for the armed forces and their actions (ideology) in highly questionable conflicts (see Kelly, in press for detailed analysis of these issues) .

For example, in the United Kingdom since season 2008–2009, in the lead-up to Remembrance Day weekend, all Premiership football clubs in England and Scotland have been asked to wear specially embroidered club kits with Earl Haig poppies displayed prominently on them. In the United Kingdom, this poppy has historically been associated with remembering the sacrifices (rather than celebrating the outcomes) of UK and Commonwealth soldiers in the two world wars. A number of similar US and Canadian examples have also occurred (see Silk and Falcous, 2005; Butterworth and Moskal, 2009; Scherer and Koch, 2010). Additionally, in June 2010, days before the opening ceremony of the South Africa Football World Cup, UK Prime Minister David Cameron addressed serving soldiers in Afghanistan, reading out a letter of support from the England football team manager, Fabio Capello.[7] The letter outlined the team's 'support' for the 'work' being done on 'our behalf' and volunteered that the armed forces were the real 'heroes'. Viewed through a cultural studies lens, these practices are merely part of a range of newly created cultural initiatives that are becoming institutionally accepted events normalising 'remembering heroes'. By manufacturing a set of new 'traditions' such as military homecoming parades, annual Armed Forces Day, and newly hatched memorial services for soldiers killed after WWII and articulating these as popular culture under the ideological umbrella of 'helping heroes', these politically imbued practices combine in seeking to simultaneously create a culture of uncritical acceptance and pride in military actions whilst buffering opposition to United States–led militarism. Cultural studies theorists view these processes as part of a wider ideological aim that seeks to legitimise highly unpopular militaristic acts. That is, linking the invasion of Iraq (and Afghanistan) with the Earl Haig poppy and its potent symbolic currency of fighting 'just' wars in World Wars I and II and embedding this into the nation's favourite sporting pastimes serves the political purpose of simplistically framing United States–dominated Western military actions as positive, right, necessary, and morally just. Not only does this link controversial and unpopular wars (and their devastating effects) with defeating Hitler, but it insulates the powerful militarist ideologues from criticism. Grieving family members and injured personnel are co-opted into pleading for 'the nation's' support and understanding. Who can argue with a grieving mother? Who can deny an eighteen-year-old soldier casualty wasn't brave? Cultural studies theorists might turn here to Gruneau (1983) who reminded us that resistance always needs to be understood in the ways it both opposes dominant ideology and is contained by it. Cultural studies theorists would, therefore, argue here that resistance to unpopular wars is being contained amid a continual herofication of militarism process.

Refusal to 'support the troops' is quite separate from feeling deep sorrow for those killed, though it is seldom presented as such. However, cultural studies theorists would argue the powerful elites are determined to weave both issues inextricably together in attempting to manufacture consent and contain dissent, and sport is one site among many for doing so. Sports officials, players, fans, and the media are co-opted into promoting and justifying the narrow agenda of political and militaristic elites helping cement nationwide support whilst socialising young army recruits into feeling 'the nation's gratitude'. As cultural studies theorists would assert, if the 'nation' is proudly remembering 'heroes' and imagining them as interchangeable with those who defeated Nazism, there is less risk that sections of that nation will question the morality and legality of their nation's involvement in unpopular wars in the first place. Many will be put off from criticising 'war heroes' whereas others will be routinely ostracised for any such displays of criticism and be positioned within the dominant paradigm

102

as 'traitors' and deviants and, at worst, extremists or supporters of 'terror'. For example, see Falcous and Silk (2006) for an analysis of the negative treatment of Australian boxer Anthony Mundine after he refused to support Australia's involvement in the 'war on terror' and see Kelly (in press) for an analysis of the critical comments directed toward the Archbishop of Canterbury and a section of Celtic FC supporters who deviated from these normative 'support-the-troops' articulations.

As these examples illustrate, according to cultural studies, dominant ideology can be powerful even when there is opposition to it. Unless one is extremely self-aware, expressing opposition is very difficult. As these examples demonstrate, even when the support-the-troops message is questioned, those questioning it get stigmatised. Additionally (and crucially), if one does not publicly reject the dominant position, she or he faces being co-opted into the dominant framing of everyone supporting it. The end result is that even self-aware objectors to the dominant ideology end up falling silent or actively playing the expected role, and the result is the inevitable reinforcement of this dominant ideology over and over (for more on role playing, see Chapter 6). Lord Mawhinney's 2010 pronouncement on behalf of England's football fans illustrates this perfectly. In his role as chairman of the Football League, whilst announcing the governing body's new sponsorship partner as 'Help for Heroes', he proclaimed via the governing body's website:

> The contribution being made by our armed forces around the world is truly humbling. The football for heroes week will provide an excellent opportunity *for supporters to show their appreciation for the outstanding work being done.*
>
> (Lord Mawhinney, 2010, our emphasis)

Whether one likes it or not, one is incorporated into showing appreciation by virtue of the fact they are football fans attending a match that is officially being used to endorse the UK military. Viewed in this way, both with one's support being incorporated by proxy and with objections being difficult to express, the hegemonic process becomes clearer for cultural studies theorists. In other words, if there is any public rejection to the strongly valued good, this objection often inversely reinforces the position being rejected in the first place –

as a result of the objection being stigmatised and simultaneously reinforcing the righteousness of the cause being objected to. Put simply, this results in either the appearance of everyone supporting X or any objection to X being stigmatised (for examples, see Kelly, in press).

Other sporting issues of representation and articulation might include the power held by some to define and (il)legitimise certain practices in sport and society. These may include the ideological construction of drug taking or engaging in dangerous sports. For example, consider the discourse surrounding athletes ingesting 'drugs'[8] and the arguments constructed around the themes of 'danger', 'cheating', 'unnaturalness', and so on. When non-sporting 'performers' consume some of the banned substances – such as alcohol and other such suppressants – these same arguments disappear. For example, the teacher who takes an artificial pain killer and/or stimulant to perform her classroom duties would seldom be accused of cheating or endangering herself – if we accept it is not a regular or addiction-induced behaviour. Likewise, some iconic bands' most celebrated albums have allegedly been produced amid high levels of drug taking, yet few accuse rock bands of 'cheating' or of relying on performance-enhancing drugs rather than their own 'pure' ability. Arguably, few label the creation of such albums as invalid or band members as deviant. Or consider some of the undoubtedly dangerous sporting activities that result in deaths or serious injuries and the ideological construction of these. For example, when the eighteen-year-old sets sail alone around the world, she is seldom criticised (never mind prevented) from doing so or reported by commentators as being irresponsible on the grounds of engaging in dangerous activities likely to endanger herself and others who may have to rescue her at great expense and risk. Neither is she held up as someone who is setting a bad example for fear that she is influencing the nation's impressionable youth to do the same. On the contrary, she is likely to be ideologically framed as a positive role model who is courageous and driven. Of course, she may or may not be these things. What is significant for cultural studies is, however, understanding the ways sports, exercise, and other cultural forms get articulated into particular socio-political, historical, and economic relationships. It is precisely this type of representation that was evident in the aftermath of the 2009 climbing tragedy in the Alps, which saw the death of two twenty-one-year-old British men. Their

Consider the numerous debates that occur in the media around sports people and their alleged personal indiscretions such as extramarital affairs or drunkenness. The ways in which these events become represented in media discourse accept the ideological assumption that people who are successful at sport should be role models for wider society. There are no inevitable or natural reasons for such a position that, rather, relies on being re-contextualised in such ways as to recreate these relationships.

premature and tragic deaths were widely reported in discursive terms that framed them and their actions as 'heroic', 'inspirational', and 'adventurous' (see the *Metro* newspaper, 12/1/09: 13) as opposed to an alternative discourse of gratuitous, self-indulgent, and dangerous.

McDonald and Birrell (1999: 288) adopt a cultural studies approach whilst asserting that 'power relations are never merely imposed from above but involve the active consent of subordinate groups and the taming of resistance through accommodation'. Viewed through this cultural studies lens, we could suggest that this *taming of resistance* occurs at Scottish rugby union matches when Princess Anne is captured on television and front page newspaper headlines singing the Scottish national anthem – Flower of Scotland.[9] Placing this in the political context of rising nationalist sentiments in Scotland, Scotland's 'special princess' adopting a nationalistic battle tune that reminisces of fighting the English can be re-articulated as a harmless folk tune embraced by perhaps the most visible manifestation of the Union of the United Kingdom, its royal family. Thus, potential resistance is tamed by accommodating the song in this way.

A further example worth thinking about is the issue of sports stadium naming rights. Debates about this often become dominated by questions of how much it will be worth to the sports club. However, this accepts the underlying definition that replacing a stadium name with a corporate sponsor name is in itself acceptable (as long as the price is right). Of course, the cultural and emotional value invested in stadium names differs from context to context, but in the United Kingdom in particular, football stadium names have remained central parts of some football club identities. Newcastle United FC recently experienced high levels of opposition to their newly instigated name changing of the iconic St James's Park, with some supporters spray-painting the original 'St James's Park' on the stadium wall in protest to the renaming.

As we have seen, cultural studies work is varied and can be applied to sport and exercise in a variety of ways, with gender and sexism, militarism, national identity, fair play, ethics, and the economics of sport being some of the issues a cultural studies perspective could analyse. Additionally, it could be applied to analyses of alternative sports and exercise forms such as midnight cricket and parkour, which both challenge dominant sport/exercise forms in terms of the values attached to each activity and their use of space offering counter-hegemonic challenges to existing dominant values. Cultural studies can also offer ways to critique the increasing politics of the body – lifestyle, healthy living, keeping fit, and so on – in particular, the ways in which social, historical and political conjunctions disappear and become replaced by moral demands on the individual to 'take control' or, as the corporate giant Nike would say: 'Just Do It!'

CRITIQUING CULTURAL STUDIES

Though cultural studies in sport extends back thirty years, advocates of the perspective sometimes lack genuine comprehension of what distinguishes it from other (mainly Marxist inspired) perspectives. Andrews (2002: 110) notes, 'cultural studies is also oftentimes used as an empty metaphor, a bland descriptor of any study focused on sport as part of the cultural realm'. Given the fact that cultural studies writers examine culture, power, and politics, viewing all three to be interconnected, their belief in producing theoretical accounts as a political practice can sometimes be viewed as producing biased or over-politicised work. In other words, the fact that they wish to change the world and understand it leads to criticism of being too involved and having an agenda. This sometimes results in critics viewing it as politicised and subjective, lacking objectivity and rigour. An obvious cultural studies response to this is that those claiming or seeking true objectivity and value-free research are merely producing analyses that implicitly support dominant positions/groups often by overlooking power struggles that are rendered invisible to them in their misguided belief in the nirvana of objective social science. Nevertheless, producing trustworthy and authentic social accounts as opposed to being a political cheerleader is difficult to achieve and something that most cultural studies theorists continue to grapple with.

Another major challenge facing cultural studies is that it is difficult proving or illustrating hegemonic processes by virtue of the fact they are often unobvious, hidden, open to interpretation, and ultimately involve active consent by subordinates who misrecognise the true nature of human relations. This merely becomes another false consciousness position and risks accusations of determinism and of being rather patronising – to assume that the enlightened cultural studies theorists can see the real truth that others do not. Given that much of the methodological work carried out in cultural studies is ethnographic, seeking to understand the lived realities of the everyday world, particularly struggles between subordinate and dominant groups, these realities are often intangible. For instance, sexism, racism, or sectarianism can be experienced in subtle ways that might be unobvious to many.

FURTHER READING

For an introduction to cultural studies theory, Barker (2008, 3rd ed.) is an excellent text. Some useful sources focusing on sport and cultural studies include Hargreaves and McDonald (2000), Andrews and Loy (1993) and Howell at al. (2002). Carrington and McDonald's (2009) edited collection on Marxism, cultural studies, and sport is an excellent source, too, for students wishing to develop deeper knowledge of the perspective, its journey from Marxism, and its application to sport. One of us has used a cultural studies approach to explain the relationship between the Scottish press, football and sectarianism in Scottish football (Kelly, 2011) and has integrated a cultural studies and symbolic interaction approach to analyse the sport, militarism, and popular culture relationship during the post-9/11 'war on terror' (Kelly, in press). Scherer and Jackson (2008) use a cultural studies approach to examine the production, representation and consumption of an Adidas television advert in relation to New Zealand's All Blacks rugby union teams and national identity. Hargreaves' (1986) aforementioned book is essential reading for any sports student wishing to research this perspective, and we would also recommend reading the classic cultural studies account of post-colonialism, cricket, and identity politics by C. L. R. James in his rightfully celebrated *Beyond a Boundary* (1963). For those wishing to read more on the deeper hegemonic processes of sport, the 1982 chapter by Willis in Jennifer Hargreaves's edited collection is recommended.

CHAPTER 6

SYMBOLIC INTERACTION PERSPECTIVES

Many of us are familiar with the various roles we tend to adopt when involved in different social settings. Our behaviour, manner, and even appearance often differ according to where we are, with whom, and in what context. For example, contrast being in your living room with your parents, being with your teammates in the locker room before an important game, being with your friends at a bar on a Saturday night, or enjoying (or not) a first date with a potential new boyfriend or girlfriend. How might your speech, body language, clothing, expressions, and overall demeanour differ from situation to situation as you manage to portray yourself as best you can for each occasion? In terms of sport and exercise, let us consider a unisex coaching session for teenagers in volleyball or baseball and the roles that different participants adopt. Both girls and boys are treated equally and encouraged to compete on equal terms. On the surface, this appears to be a positive practice in breaking down barriers between the sexes. For example, it may foster reciprocal respect and understanding between both groups. Boys might realise that 'girls can play', and girls might gain additional confidence when they confirm to themselves and others that they are as talented as the boys. Yet, using symbolic interaction, we can read this differently by beginning to understand situations such as this from the perspective of the participants (youngsters and coach). Perhaps some of the children have had recent growth spurts and/or become more interested in their appearance. Looking their best will almost certainly be important to some of these teenagers. They might not feel overly comfortable wearing the ill-fitting and unflattering sports shorts and revealing sleeveless vests. Perhaps this is compounded by the fact that during a unisex session, the girls have to wear this uniform in front of the boys and vice versa. Some of the children might feel anxious about showering in the communal shower areas and may, therefore, be reluctant to get dirty or sweat too much during exercise in the hope that they can avoid showering among their peers. This affects their commitment and enthusiasm for the rigorous athletic activities being encouraged by the coach.

Understanding the ways young teenagers define a situation may help us gain a deeper insight into this scenario. Showing off and acting out may be the way in which some of the boys think they can prove their macho image to the girls whom they wish to impress. Maybe the girls remember the last time the boys made fun of them when they tried to serve the volleyball or pitch the baseball. The last time they tried to discuss tactics with the boys they were mocked and ridiculed with cries of 'What do girls know about curve balls?' It is unsurprising, then, that some of the girls have no desire to be subjected to such mocking again. Understanding the ways the coach perceives the situation reveals another social dimension. Perhaps the female coach feels the best way to approach her teenage participants is to be strict and forceful, showing she is boss. Some of the children might feel put off by such an aggressive and dominating coaching approach. The stern and regimented impression of sport and exercise may have been confirmed and reinforced to many of the children by such autocratic coaching behaviour. Yet, the coach feels this is necessary to prove herself to some of the larger boys who previously questioned her authority. Moreover, her more experienced male colleague witnessed this dissent last week as he was instructing nearby, and he is here again casting curious and concerned glances over to see how things are going this week. On the surface, unisex sports coaching sessions might be beneficial but, in certain situations, viewed through a symbolic interaction lens, they might equally lead to a breakdown in the coaching setting, making the experience unpleasant or unproductive for both athlete and coach.

Symbolic interaction is a term given to a sociological perspective that belongs to interpretive approaches to studying society. Interpretive approaches are those sociologies that base their interpretations on human meaning and understanding with particular sensitivity to the point of view of the actors themselves. Symbolic interaction is linked to what is sometimes called *the sociology of everyday life* due to its focus on the ordinary that most of us witness and act out on a daily basis. It is sometimes closely associated with social-psychology, which is unsurprising, given that both approaches involve studying the individual and the ways in which the individual interacts with larger groups and organisations in society. This perspective views social life as a series of interactive events (interactions) that become 'read' or understood according to the symbolic meanings accorded to these events and the behaviours that actors engage in within these contextual situations. Though social interaction is inevitably affected by the norms, values, and rules of any given society (making symbolic interaction sociological rather than merely psychological), these are not fixed or determined but instead are continuously (re) made by involving human subjectivity and mutual negotiation of interpretations of each situation.

Human action is complex, involving multiple relationships in ever-increasing webs of interaction and interdependence: In Chapter 3, we learned that Durkheim explained this increased interaction as the shift from *mechanical solidarity* to *organic solidarity* (see also Chapter 7 for social figurations). Symbolic interaction acknowledges this complexity and views human interaction as consisting of people defining situations and their meanings in interaction with others. Therefore, symbolic interaction theorists suggest that people act on the basis of the meanings of symbols that acquire their meaning from everyday interaction within the confines of society or what we may call social structures. These interactions and meanings are fluid and subject to change in time and according to each situation. However, interaction is affected by societal norms and values we internalise, which help us define situations by giving meaning to them, thus imbuing us to act in particular ways that are socially judged by wider groups in society. Therefore, our behaviour in one social setting may be deemed friendly, polite, welcoming, professional, motivated while, in other social settings, the same behaviour might be viewed as unfriendly, rude, unwelcoming, unprofessional, lazy, and so on. Depending on our knowledge and sensitivity of the setting and the expectations that accompany it, the perceptions of our behaviour may not match the social situation. When this happens, we are sometimes described as lacking tact or, in extreme cases, manners. To begin understanding the perspective more fully, we begin by turning attention to its origins.

CLASSICAL THEORY

Symbolic interaction developed in the post–WW II years in the United States partly as a response to the perceived limitations of the popular functionalist approach, specifically its preoccupation with the large-scale/macro-world at the expense of the small-scale/micro-worlds. In other words, face-to-face interaction was increasingly recognized as an important feature of society that helps explain our social and cultural life in ways that functionalists tended to overlook by focusing on structural elements such as the law and political and economic systems. Additionally, symbolic interactionists opposed the view that social life is governed by objective systems, rules, or patterns that are independent from human actors or can be reduced to scientific laws (in the ways that the natural sciences could). Symbolic interactionists (among others) became increasingly dissatisfied with what they viewed as functionalists concocting abstract theories to explain human interaction without due consideration of the circumstances and contexts of this interaction or the subjective meanings that might collectively arise for different individuals and groups in society. For example, to relate back to our initial example, conducting a coaching session involving teenage boys and girls might be more successful when understanding their face-to-face interaction from their perspective rather than trying to apply some general model of learning from a sport and exercise motor control book.[1] Symbolic interactionists accused functionalists of trying to fit social life into a preconceived theory rather than trying to observe it under authentic circumstances. This grand theorizing, the symbolic interactionists claimed, resulted in unsatisfactory sociological explanations. Indeed, celebrated symbolic interactionist Erving Goffman (whom we later discuss in detail) rejected such grand theorizing: 'Better, perhaps different coats to clothe the children well than a single splendid tent in which they all shiver' (Goffman, 1961: xiv). In other words, one grand theory may not be as effective and realistic as numerous smaller theories.

Symbolic interaction has its roots in the inter–world war years when Chicago School social theorists and some of their colleagues (e.g. George Herbert Mead and Charles Cooley) stressed the importance of sociologists taking (as much as it is possible to do so) the position and attitudes of *the other* (human actors) to try to empathize and ultimately understand the nature of human interaction more authentically. Cooley labelled this 'sympathetic introspection'. This attempt to put oneself in the other's shoes forms half of what we now call *reflexivity*. The other half involves seeing oneself from the other's perspective. Mead described this as 'the self', the ability to objectify oneself, to see oneself from outside of one's own mind'. Mead was influenced by Cooley's concept of 'the looking-glass self' that suggested individuals formed their notion of self according to how they perceived others to view them, sometimes even adapting their behaviour and/or appearance as a result of these perceptions. Therefore, to better understand our own self, we need to look at other people with whom we interact. Subsequent anthropologists Marcus and Fischer (1986) refer to these processes as 'making the foreign familiar and the familiar foreign'. Taking such reflexive positions requires understanding and sensitivity of the values and meanings others give to symbols (behaviour, appearance, objects, mannerisms, and so on) that must have some level of mutually understood meaning if they are to be meaningful in any way in a society. Therefore, on one level, individuals interpret symbols for themselves, but these interpretations are influenced by the established meanings society has given them. Moreover, individuals must also try to interpret the meanings that others give to these symbols. However, social settings involve more than simply interpreting the expressions, actions, and symbolic acts occurring between individuals. That is, to more fully understand social life, sensitivity is required around how others (and the self) act and modify behaviour when in the company of others, and these concerns formed the basis of the symbolic interaction project.

As these concerns around modified behaviour grew during the post-1950s, questions increasingly emerged around the extent to which it was possible to create an objective philosophy of social science, one that could be quantified along similar rigid methodological lines as was so for the natural sciences. Academics began challenging traditional explanations of social life based on the methods of the natural sciences, claiming these were not appropriate for understanding the nuances and realities of social life. They argued that understanding societies required reconciling the objective facts with the subjective experiences of human beings in particular situations. One way of doing this was to try to see the world from the view of the group being studied. Symbolic interaction became a major perspective dedicated to this approach. Methodologically, this approach shared many of the practices of anthropology and the newly emerging methods of its urban ethnographers who increasingly researched subcultures in American cities from the position of the actors within the subcultures. Another Chicago School[2] theorist, Everett Hughes, was a key figure in the emerging field of urban anthropology that focused on subcultural groups such as the mentally ill, prostitutes, and drug addicts. Urban anthropology, which is also referred to as *urban ethnography*, was later systematised into the symbolic interaction perspective by Chicago School pioneers Herbert Blumer, Howard Becker, and Erving Goffman. Like the newly emerging anthropologists, symbolic interactionists shared a desire to understand how society and subcultures were experienced and understood by those who inhabited them.

While symbolic interaction focused on the micro-aspects of society as opposed to the macro-aspects that occupied much of functionalist analyses, a particular branch of functionalism – interpersonal functionalism – helped symbolic interaction develop some of its central ideas and connect these to macro-structural factors. A. R. Radcliffe-Brown, a key figure of interpersonal functionalism, outlined a series of social behaviour mechanisms that reduced social tensions and facilitated social integration (see Loy and Booth, 2000). These 'strain accommodating mechanisms' (sometimes called 'functional equivalents') included everyday practices such as joking, avoidance, and gift giving. In functionalist terms, these mechanisms were viewed as helping maintain the overall system – in this case, the mundane human interaction of daily life – by reducing social friction that accumulates through everyday interaction. Symbolic interaction took this further and developed ways to understand the face-to-face interaction of individuals and groups to explain them as grounded in wider societal norms and values. In other words, what appear to be idiosyncratic and individual acts are, on closer inspection, part of broader patterns that develop over time to help regulate and maintain social order at the local face-to-face level and ultimately civil society at the structural macro-level.

MODERN THEORY

George Herbert Mead's former student Herbert Blumer is recognized as formalizing symbolic interaction in the modern era. He summarized the approach as being based on three central premises. First, people act on the basis of the *meanings* that things have for them. These can include both the physical (flags, uniforms, sports/gym equipment) and social (sports events, fitness classes, parties, surgical operations). Second, meanings arise out of the *social situation*. For example, the steroid-using bodybuilder may view his or her banned drug as a mere ergogenic aid in the way that you may view vitamin pills for your everyday health. His or her environment is full of fellow users seeking similar effects, each viewing their own and others' behaviour as valid, necessary, and beneficial to their particular objectives in their particular world (i.e. subculture of bodybuilding). Third, meanings are *fluid* and *interpretative* in that they change according to time and situation, and this often involves the individuals negotiating and defining these meanings in joint partnership. So the steroid-using bodybuilder might reach a stage at which his or her values change and he or she alters his or her definition of what the drugs are doing to his or her body and what they represent. This may be due to his or her gaining a better education, having been to college for a few years now or perhaps it was due to his or her getting fined or banned for drug use, or to experiencing medical side effects.

Although Blumer outlined these three premises of the perspective, arguably the most influential symbolic interactionists were Blumer's ex-student Erving Goffman and his Chicago School contemporary, Howard Becker. Becker's work on deviance has been hugely influential, whereas Goffman is perhaps symbolic interaction's most famous exponent, and his work has been widely applied and read beyond the world of academia. Thus, we now turn our attention to Becker's work on *deviance* and Goffman's work on *the interaction order*.

Given that social scientists were increasingly rejecting the scientific rationality associated with the natural sciences, sociologists placed increasing importance on the context of the situation when interpreting society. In other words, symbolic interactionists and other interpretivists increasingly asserted that one can judge an act only by reference to its contexts rather than some general 'scientific' yardstick. For example, Goffman showed that the seemingly irrational behaviour of mental patients hoarding and safeguarding pieces of string or foil (materials of little value for most of us) needed to be fully contextualized and understood to grasp its significance and

BIOGRAPHIC NOTE

Erving Goffman (1922–1981) was born in 1922 in Alberta, Canada to Jewish Ukrainian parents. He grew up in Winnipeg and, in 1939, enrolled at the University of Manitoba (Winnipeg), majoring in chemistry. Before completing his degree, Goffman began working at the National Film Board of Canada alongside Dennis Wrong, who later became an eminent sociologist himself. It was during this period that Goffman's attention shifted toward social sciences, and he eventually enrolled at the University of Toronto, where he graduated with a BA in sociology. At Toronto, Goffman was introduced to the works of Durkheim and Talcott Parsons. In 1949 he obtained his MA at the University of Chicago. The 'Chicago School', as it became known, enabled Goffman to interact with some of sociology's major figures, including Herbert Blumer, Everett C. Hughes, and fellow postgraduate student Howard Becker. After receiving his MA, he remained at the University of Chicago and, in conjunction with the University of Edinburgh, he completed his PhD in 1953, which was based on fieldwork he had carried out on the Shetland Islands. Having been supervised by Herbert Blumer, Goffman became associated with the emerging approach of symbolic interaction. Goffman's *The Presentation of Self in Everyday Life* (1959) 'not only announced his arrival as an important, if unorthodox social commentator, [it] also ushered in a new approach to sociology: a sociology of everyday life' (Birrell and Donnelly, 2004: 49). He contributed to linguistics, psychiatry, social psychology, anthropology, and sociology, publishing eleven books, many of which still figure prominently in undergraduate courses. His appeal was popular, and this was in part linked to his diverse topics but also the accessible nature of his writings. Birrell and Donnelly (2004: 58) claim that he 'anticipated the major shift' in the sociology of sport in the 1990s towards media, textual, and discourse analyses in his later work with *Frame Analysis* (1974), *Gender Advertisements* (1979), and *Forms of Talk* (1981). Goffman was constantly 'at work' observing and taking notes, even stopping at accident scenes to observe people's behaviour (Birrell and Donnelly, 2004). His most famous model is probably his *dramaturgical model* (1959). Birrell and Donnelly suggest 'most researchers see Goffman as a generator of sensitising concepts and insightful interactional principles rather than a social theorist' (2004: 50). He was reluctant to become engaged in academic dialogue with his critics, believing it counterproductive to furthering our knowledge about society. As a person, Goffman was often described as enigmatic. Despite becoming an intellectual whose work and fame transcended the world of academia, he eschewed the trappings of celebrity, never appearing on television or radio. He was fond of second-hand clothing, perhaps maintaining a link with his parents' clothing store past. One of his most insightful comments occurred in conversation with fellow sociologist Stanford Lyman, when he proclaimed, 'Sociology is something that you do, not something that you read' (cited in Smith, 2006: 4). In 1982, just before he died of cancer, he was elected president of the American Sociological Association and was perhaps the most famous sociologist of his generation.

meaning. He convincingly argued that contextualisation must involve seeing such behaviour from the patients' perspective. Within the confines of (1950s) mental hospitals, patients were deprived of their own clothes, personal belongings, and secure lockers to house their own possessions. In this context, a generally insignificant possession becomes a personal vestige to be protected and kept safe from potential thieves. Rather than being irrational behaviour, then, under such conditions patients' behaviour appears completely rational.

In extreme cases, however, some perceived irrational behaviour was branded deviant by sections of society. Symbolic interaction accounts of deviance began to contrast the established accounts that had traditionally framed deviants as differing from 'normal' people. Symbolic interactionists (such as Howard Becker) instead showed how deviance was socially constructed. In other words, rather than looking for measurable differences (what natural scientists might call variables) between deviants and non-deviants, symbolic interactionists explained these differences as the result of the structures and guidelines put in place to deal with so-called deviants and explained how these structures guided their treatment by those in authority such as the psychiatric doctor and prison warden. In an

symbolic interaction perspectives

illuminating passage from his well-known book on deviance, Becker (1963: 35) explains this in detail while making symbolic interaction connections to wider societal structures and power dynamics:

> Since he [drug addict] cannot get drugs legally, he must get them illegally. This forces the market underground and pushes the price of drugs up far beyond the current legitimate market price into a bracket that few can afford on an ordinary salary. Hence the treatment of the addict's deviance places him in a position where it will probably be necessary to resort to deceit and crime in order to support his habit. The behaviour is a consequence of the public reaction to the deviance rather than a consequence of the inherent qualities of the deviant act.

So rather than so-called deviants having biological or psychological failings that set them apart from 'normal' people, their behaviour was viewed as the result of human action produced in social, political, and cultural contexts.[3] In sport, we might consider the symbolic aspects of labelling top-class athletes' deviant for engaging in unsporting conduct such as the professional foul in football or sledging in cricket or using illegal performance-enhancing substances and, therefore, being judged as poor role models or cheats according to such socially constructed measures.

Symbolic interactionists reject abstract general theories that claimed to know how people *would* act for accounts of actual social conduct observed in real circumstances that reveal how people *do* act. Although symbolic interactionists and functionalists share the view that actors seek to function in ways that lead to a shared successful

---

REFLECTION

Are verbal abuse (sledging) or purposely and illegally fouling an opponent who is about to score acceptable forms of deviant behaviour? Is taking a legal drug that a sports governing body has deemed to be a source of cheating better or worse behaviour than the professional foul or sledging? Is the practice of bench clearing[4] in baseball and ice hockey more or less deviant than engaging in a bar brawl?

symbolic interaction perspectives

outcome, symbolic interaction places more emphasis on these contextual contingencies than functionalism does. As mentioned before, symbolic interaction is also more concerned with the small-scale/micro-worlds in which interactions take place. Unsurprisingly, then, unlike many of their functionalist peers, symbolic interactionists were/are less interested in the overarching (macro-) questions about society's structures and systems and more interested in the face-to-face behaviour of humans in particular settings; Goffman called this the *interaction order*. Following the Chicago School's urban ethnographic approach to studying society, which viewed the city as a natural laboratory, Goffman harnessed his ability to collect ethnographic data from the minutia of everyday interaction and, despite its micro-focus, to scientifically explain it in relation to wider societal factors. Preferring the term 'student of society' to sociologist, Goffman applied his principles of the interaction order to show, as Durkheim had previously done with suicide (see Chapter 3), that even the most apparently individual acts of behaviour were in fact meaningfully connected to wider societal norms, expectations and values. As Smith (2006: 32) neatly summarises:

> Goffman showed how many of our seemingly insignificant and idiosyncratic concerns (our expletives when we drop a glass, our discomfort when a stranger holds a glance at us too long) are consequences of the normative ordering of interactional conduct. Goffman the Durkheim revisionist is never more clearly present than when he is drawing our attention to the social sources of a feeling or item of conduct we had thought uniquely ours.

In seeking to explain the workings of human interaction in everyday life, much of Goffman's work focused on what others considered abnormal forms of society; hence his work on stigmatised groups such as mental patients and gamblers. It was in these settings where behaviour that was often different from the expected occurred that Goffman illuminated (and interpreted) the everyday patterns of 'normal' behaviour and interaction. From his earliest writings, he became known for focusing on the discrepancy between the public show and the actual reality.

One of Goffman's most powerful and widely used frameworks was his dramaturgy model as expressed in his (1959) book *The Presentation of*

Self in Everyday Life. In it, he presented society as a metaphoric stage where people perform specific roles in a series of social situations. These roles enable individuals to maintain high degrees of *impression management* to avoid embarrassment or faux pas and to present themselves in the best possible light. However, to a large extent, these roles are inscribed with particular society-wide expectations in terms of behaviour, dress, and demeanour and to successfully carry them out three interconnected elements are necessary: the physical environment (what Goffman called the 'setting'); the appearance and manner of the actor ('personal front'); and the institutionalized collective expectation ('front'). Collective representations arise with regard to what should happen in certain fronts, and these fronts are socially constructed and reinforced. Goffman (1959: 36) referred to these as 'the vocabulary of fronts'[5]:

> Instead of having to maintain a different pattern of expectation and responsive treatment for each slightly different performer and performance, he (observer) can place the situation in a broad category around which it is easy for him to mobilise his past experience and stereotypical thinking. Observers then need only be familiar with a small and hence manageable vocabulary of fronts, and know how to respond to them, in order to orient themselves in a wide variety of situations.

For instance, think about the brain surgeon, lawyer, teacher, or personal trainer and their settings and fronts. We each know the expected role that they and we play in joint interaction, for if we did not, social life would be near impossible, requiring us to work out each situation anew every time it occurred. There is an existing vocabulary of front for these relationships and settings. These roles and our behaviour within them are the products of the shared and expected behaviour associated with the interaction between surgeon-patient, lawyer-client, teacher-pupil, and personal trainer-exerciser.[6] Randall Collins (1981) referred to this as 'situationalism'.

According to Goffman, we usually expect to see consistency between setting, appearance, and manner and front. When there is a discrepancy, the subtleties of human interaction emerge. For instance, if we witnessed an apparently drunk and dishevelled brain surgeon about to operate, we would be concerned. Or if a defence lawyer turned

120

up in court wearing jeans and a T-shirt and littering his questions with profanities, we would think it odd. This is because the institutionalised front (brain surgeons being sober or lawyers being professionally dressed and properly spoken) for a particular setting (operating theatre, court room) is not being matched by the personal front (appearance and behaviour of the surgeon and lawyer). In sports, we might think about the high school sports coach. She or he will probably have a personal front of whistle, tracksuit, clipboard (appearance) and be confident, controlled and, perhaps, brusque (manner). In the context of the high school sports arena (setting), we would expect a certain type of institutionalised, collective representation to arise (front). If the coach were not dressed appropriately, did not act in the ways we expect of coaches, there would be a discrepancy between the actual reality and what we have come to expect in such situations due to the collectively understood vocabulary of front. In this example, the joint performance between coach and children could break down.

For Goffman, some of the most interesting and revealing insights occurred where 'virtual social identity' (idealized front) and the 'actual social identity' (actual reality) differed to some degree. The difference between them would be called the discrepancy, disruption, or stigma (depending on which Goffman book you are referencing; he was well known for starting each new book with new terms). Goffman viewed interaction as consisting of a team performance. In other words, most actors work to secure the success of the performance. He writes, 'We commonly find that the definition of the situation projected by a particular participant is an integral part of a projection

---

REFLECTION

Think about your sport and exercise worlds. Think about the university gym, its single-sex locker rooms, its unisex cardio room and free weights areas. Or consider your parents' golf club or your yoga class where you are a participant/performer. What institutional settings and fronts exist? What appearance and behaviour do you witness and engage in? Do your behaviour and appearance (front) change according to the setting you find yourself in? Are there different expectations placed on you in these different settings?

that is fostered and sustained by the intimate cooperation of more than one participant' (1959: 83).

Goffman elaborated further on this in a famous article called *The Nature of Deference and Demeanour* (1956/1967). Here, he outlined that, 'individuals must hold hands in a chain of ceremony, each giving deferentially with proper demeanour to the one on the right what will be received deferentially from one on the left' (1956/1967: 85). In other words, people act as a team to carry out social acts successfully by presenting themselves appropriately and in convention with the expected norms of the situation. This may involve calling the coach 'boss' rather than by his name or the ex-player, on becoming the coach, expecting his old teammates to call him 'boss' and show him due respect. Either way, social interaction such as this requires teamwork for it to be successful. For example, the student and lecturer will usually team up to prevent 'performance disruption' by students' willingly taking their place in the rows of seats facing the whiteboard and lecturer and having their pens and notebooks ready in anticipation of the lecture. The lecturer will stand at the front and instruct the students accordingly, and both parties will engage according to convention to ensure a successful performance (lecture). Or think about the previously discussed sports lesson. The children also have to perform their part successfully or the performance would break down. If they were not dressed appropriately, did not listen or act in accordance with the teacher's instructions – play to the whistle, for example – the lesson could fail.

Goffman stressed that performances were staged 'backstage' (or back region) and 'frontstage' (or front region). In the student café (back region), the student may question the authority or ability of the lecturer whereas the lecturer in turn may harbour negative feelings toward a lazy or disruptive student and talk in unprofessional terms about her or him in the comfort of his or her office (back region) to a colleague. Or the lecturer may (as students sometimes do) hastily prepare his or her notes for a lecture at the last minute unprepared for the talk, but when in the lecture presenting to the class (front stage), he or she is concealing this information from the audience. This all amounts to front- and backstage management. In sports, you may think about the sports coach media interview. The coach may conceal disruptive information from the interviewer (such as his or her backstage instructions to his or her players to try to injure their opponent's best player). He or she attempts to ensure that he or she is shown in good light. His or her media persona (face) most likely differs from his or her locker room persona, and he or she must manage both faces carefully to foster his or her preferred identity in each stage of the television studio (frontstage) or locker room (backstage).

APPLYING SYMBOLIC INTERACTION TO SPORTS AND EXERCISE

Much of the symbolic interaction work on sport and exercise has been influenced by Goffman (hence our focus on him). Birrell and Donnelly (2004: 53) observe that Goffman has had limited *direct* influence on the sociology of sport, but 'his *indirect* influence is widespread' (original emphasis). They add that he 'deserves renewed attention from sport studies scholars because his work connects in exciting ways with the new climate of critical cultural analysis that increasingly characterises our field' (2004: 55). It is clear that symbolic interaction has much to offer students of sport and exercise. It has been used to explain pattern maintenance, subcultures, and deviance (revealing its historical connections to Durkheim and functionalism). It is unsurprising that some studies combine all three elements to show how individuals within subcultures engage in deviant behaviour (see Curry, 1991 for a symbolic interaction account of sexist male behaviour in the locker room). We should remember that though symbolic interaction may have historical connections to functionalism, this does not mean explanations of pattern maintenance are functionalist in nature. Pattern maintenance does not in itself require a functionalist explanation. What determines whether it is or is not functionalist is the type of explanation given for the pattern maintenance. For example, in describing the use of sport for endorsing the British military in the post-9/11 'war on terror', one of us (Kelly, in press) uses deference and demeanour to explain pattern maintenance – in this case, the rhetoric of 'support the troops' and British military being 'heroes', doing 'good work'. However, this is explained from a critical perspective combining both cultural studies and symbolic interaction.

Goffman's dramaturgical model can be insightfully applied to the study of sport and exercise groups who engage in 'standard maintaining routines' (Goffman, 1959: 81). One example is Beames and Pike (2008) who utilise Goffman's dramaturgy framework to discuss students and instructors in the world of rock climbing. They showed that both student and instructor engage in impression management routines of over-communicating and under-communicating certain facts to show good face. For example, the rookie instructor spent extended periods in the back region (her own cabin) to practice knot tying and other practical rope exercises to ensure confident and successful front region performances the following day in front of the group. Meanwhile, when asked about their rock climbing abilities, some students staged a performance designed to maintain the appropriate front of sufficient levels of confidence and ability. For one of the student climbers in the study, this included the wearing and owning of role-appropriate clothing and equipment (appearance) and exuding over-confidence when asked about his abilities (manner). Each of these combined to confirm for the audience the actor's desired face (of a competent climber who knows what to do and has the 'correct' attire for performing such a role successfully). Such staged performances were noted by Goffman, who suggested 'if the performer is to be successful he must offer the kind of scene that realises the observers' extreme stereotypes' (1959: 49). Goffman explains this type of behaviour as *dramatic realisation*, noting that, 'while in the presence of others, the individual typically infuses his activity with signs which dramatically highlight and portray confirmatory facts that might otherwise remain unapparent or obscure' (1959: 40).

Symbolic interaction can also be applied to subcultural groups such as sports supporters, bodybuilders, boxers, and surfers. Wacquant (1992) conducted a well-known ethnographic study of a boxing club in Chicago to reveal the subtle and intricate layers of social order existing among its members yet unobvious to outside observers. Smith (2008) explored and explained the social construction of pain for a group of professional wrestlers to conclude that pain became an attractive source of authenticity and solidarity among wrestlers. Armstrong (2007) examined minor league ice hockey fans to conclude the sport offered a form of consumption that allowed fans to express themselves in identity-affirming ways leading to increased chances of fans repeat attending.

Goffman's concepts inform our understanding of sports supporter behaviour and interaction if we consider the interactive nature of supporter culture and its performative conventions such as singing, chanting, cheering, flag waving, and so on. For example, consider the ways in which sports supporters behave when playing certain teams, the contrasting behaviour exhibited against other teams, and the 'suppressed' behaviour adopted when fostering the preferred impression in order to avoid providing 'destructive information'. One of us (Kelly, 2007) analysed the supporter (sub-)culture of Scottish soccer club Hibernian[7] by combining a symbolic interaction and cultural studies approach, showing how Hibernian supporters engaged in subtle forms of impression management. The supporters practised what Goffman called 'audience segregation' by expressing different elements of their identity according to the audience present to maintain their preferred fostered impression when in the company of different audiences (teams). In this case, Hibernian fans became more or less Irish in expression according to their impression of what the opposition's identity was. This is another type of 'dramatic realisation'. So, for example, when playing major opponent Celtic football club – perceived by many in Scotland to have a dual Irish-Scottish identity – Hibernian supporters became less Irish, concealing important information (such as Irish flags and supporter emblems) in attempting to be a rival to Celtic. When playing other Scottish teams with no Irish connections, however, Hibernian supporters became more Irish, thus maintaining their role as authentic rival to these other clubs. Additionally, destructive information such as sectarian or antisocial behaviour was consciously downplayed to the extent that some supporters tried to manage the front given off by their fellow supporters (e.g. by informing the researcher at opportune times of their fellow supporters' 'unrepresentativeness' in attempting to discredit any damaging information these other fans may have given the researcher). Goffman's concept 'discrepant roles' is particularly useful when applied here, illuminating the corporate character of many supporters groups. Goffman (1959: 88) stresses, 'each team-mate is forced to rely on the good conduct and behaviour of his fellows, and they in turn, are forced to rely on him. There is then, perforce, a bond of reciprocal dependence linking team-mates to one another'. Goffman stresses:

> One overall objective of any team is to sustain the definition of the situation that its performance fosters. This will involve the over-communication of some facts and the under-communication

of others ... There are usually facts which, if attention is drawn to them during the performance, would discredit, disrupt, or make useless the impression that the performance fosters. These facts may be said to provide 'destructive information'.

(Goffman, 1959: 141)

As Goffman recognises, there are some teams that have a corporate character and

whose members are so closely identified in the eyes of other people that the good reputation of one practitioner depends on the good conduct of the others. If one member is exposed and causes a scandal, then all lose some public repute.

(Goffman, 1959: 164)

The corporate character among supporter groups helps explain why their individual members might illuminate certain aspects of their group behaviour while suppressing the 'dirty work' a minority of the supporters engage in such as swearing, drunkenness, or even violence.

Giulianotti (1991) also utilised Goffman's work to analyse football supporters in Scotland. He showed that fans of the Scotland national team rejected 'violent machismo' in favour of 'instrumentally ambassadorial' behaviour, attempting to foster their preferred definition of being Scottish, not English (in part response to the common mistake made by many non-British of labelling the Scots as 'English'). Giulianotti argued that Scotland supporters promoted a definition of the situation 'which could generate an enduring conscience collectif' (1991: 509). He adds, 'this was achieved through the unanimous depiction of stereotypically English cultural properties, against which they could define themselves' (1991: 509). Giulianotti presented supporter behaviour as situationally dynamic, with Scotland supporters fostering a particular definition of their own situation aided by the Scottish press juxtaposing the 'ambassadorial bonhomie' of Scotland supporters with the 'problems' 'of English soccer' (1991: 504). [8]

Symbolic interaction emphasises the team cooperation among actors trying to successfully carry out performances. It can also help explain how new team members are welcomed almost immediately into groups as a result of what Goffman terms 'familiarity'.

symbolic interaction perspectives

Among team-mates, the privilege of familiarity – which may constitute a kind of intimacy without warmth – need not be something of an organic kind, slowly developing with the passage of time spent together, but rather a formal relationship that is automatically extended and received as soon as the individual takes a place on the team.

(Goffman, 1959: 88)

In addition to 'familiarity', Goffman adds

It is to be noted that a given front tends to become institutionalised in terms of the abstract stereotyped expectations to which it gives rise, and tends to take on a meaning and stability apart from the specific tasks which happen at the time to be performed in its name. The front becomes a 'collective representation' and a fact in its own right. When an actor takes on an established social role, usually he finds that a particular front has already been established for it.

(Goffman, 1959: 37)

Thus, it is common for strangers when among sports supporters of the same team to feel an immediate connection to others that is mutually returned by these fellow strangers. Second, it is also a common occurrence to witness apparently spontaneous bursts of behaviour in which many fans (team members) know how to 'perform' (dress, dance, sing, and chant) in successfully carrying out the performative conventions despite having never previously met and, in some cases, having never attended a game. Alternatively, in newly acquiring a position within the 'team', inexperienced supporters (or other subcultural members) may try to camouflage their inexperience and quickly learn how best to become established as one of the group. Goffman (1959: 93) adds, 'It may be necessary for the members of the team to learn what the line is to be, and take it, without admitting to themselves and to one another the extent to which their position is not independently arrived at'. This may help explain those new group members who behave in ways they feel they are supposed to and expected to in order to fulfil the role of authentic member. As Armstrong (2007) and Smith (2008) found with ice hockey fans and professional wrestlers, symbolic interaction can help us explain the processes of individuals being socialised successfully. Playing up the stereotype, showing one's authenticity as a 'true' fan or group member is common among subcultures, and this type of *anticipatory socialization* is valuable for students of sport and exercise. This form of impression management can enable us to understand the behaviour of new and established members of such groups. Goffman (1956/1967: 33) stated,

> The human tendency to use signs and symbols means that evidence of social worth and of mutual evaluations will be conveyed by very minor things and these things will be witnessed, as will the fact that they have been witnessed.

Thus, we may see individuals within surfing or skateboarding groups adopting (subculture-appropriate) established group behaviours in deliberate and conscious attempts to fit in. This may involve wearing the 'correct' clothes, having the latest kit, or speaking in the slang that is common among the group, for they know that by displaying such behaviour and dress, they will be more easily accepted.

It seems clear that the extent to which supporters engage in confirmatory acts, dramatically highlighting certain facts to confirm the moral values of that community – perhaps by reproducing the expected stereotype – can be understood by utilising Goffman's dramaturgical model. Alternatively, the extent to which subculture members under-play particularly negative aspects of behaviour and identity by eschewing the disdainfully viewed discrepant role, engaging in standard maintaining routines and, thus, avoiding destructive information, may also be understood more fully.

In broader practical terms, symbolic interaction accounts of sport and exercise can help us form richer understandings from the perspective of the participants that may enable us to facilitate education, funding, and coaching decisions in a wide range of situations. Beames and Pike's (2008) rock climbing example may, for instance, help outdoor instructors be on guard against student learners exaggerating their abilities and possibly endangering themselves and others. Additionally, consider the original sporting example of a unisex coaching session. On one level, this might be seen to break down barriers and offer equity to both sexes. Yet, as we learned, the reality for these youngsters may be different due to their interaction with their own peers, leading to 'on-paper' theories about inclusion

128

being useless unless due consideration is given to the children's own definition of the situation (of playing sport with the opposite sex). Similarly, the example of athletes using steroids is likely to be better informed if we connect these practices to the subcultural values and norms within the worlds of bodybuilders, football players, and other potential steroid using athletes. We can understand their use – and legislate/govern it – only by understanding the individuals and cultures of the users. As we have seen earlier, deviance may be better conceptualized as the product of social relationships between individuals and groups within society. The users of steroids, therefore, may view their behaviour as normal and, in some cases, desirable. Rather than trying to solve this situation by 'punishing' the athletes, symbolic interaction allows us to see the situation from their perspective, allowing us to see that it may be more beneficial to influence the groups' values from within rather than seek to punish them for something they internally conceive of as normal, helpful, and socially acceptable within their subcultural group.

CRITIQUES OF SYMBOLIC INTERACTION THEORY

Symbolic interaction has a problematic relationship with sociology. This is due to two main reasons. First, many of its practitioners make no attempt to claim symbolic interaction is a complete theoretical perspective, preferring to view it as an approach to the study of society. Furthermore, its urban ethnographic approach is often accused of lacking methodological robustness and rigour. Symbolic interactionists along with other interpretive sociologists became known for writing in rich descriptive detail, contrasting sharply with the rigidity of traditional scientific report writing, leading to criticisms of symbolic interaction as being unscientific, emotional, and overly descriptive in nature. Anthropologist Clifford Geertz (1973) would make this writing style more fashionable with his 'thick description' approach to writing most famously immortalised in his study of Balinese cock fighting. Second, symbolic interaction is often associated with social psychology, and part of its central ethos – understanding local face-to-face interaction – is sometimes accused of lacking sociological significance, offering us ephemeral snapshots of interaction rather than explicitly connecting them to structural factors. For example, with regard to its application to sport and exercise, Coakley and Pike (2009) and Delaney and Madigan (2009) outline in their respective critiques of symbolic interaction[9] that it overlooks social processes and power inequalities. We feel that symbolic interaction has been unfairly judged regarding the attention it does afford social structures and power dynamics. We would argue that some of the classic symbolic interaction texts (Goffman, 1959; Becker, 1963) imply to varying degrees that face-to-face social meaning arises in situations and conditions that have pre-established institutionalized meanings that are largely the outcome of various power holders such as the opinion formers in the mass media or 'public opinion'. Goffman is pretty explicit about this. For example, in discussing the historic behaviour of black men in the southern states of the United States, he highlights that when in the company of white people, they would often perform the role of the 'ignorant, shiftless, happy-go-lucky "negro"' conforming to the white people's stereotypical preferences. The wider societal power relationships and codes shaping this face-to-face interaction are obvious. Reducing any doubt about this, Goffman adds (1959: 45):

> Thus, when the individual presents himself before others, his performance will tend to incorporate and exemplify the officially accredited values of the society, more so, in fact, than does his behaviour as a whole. To the degree that a performance highlights the common official values of the society in which it occurs, we may look upon it ... as a ceremony – as an expressive rejuvenation and reaffirmation of the moral values of the community.

The symbolic meanings forming, emerging, and classifying particular human interaction is shown in much of the symbolic interaction work to assume its symbolism precisely due to the larger societal processes and values that become normalized. Therefore, it may be more accurate to say that symbolic interaction is focused on interpersonal conflict – on the interpersonal rather than the societal – and it relatedly deals with societal issues inadequately rather than not at all. Nevertheless, it is correct to stress that some still view symbolic interaction as lacking a macro- or conflict view of society. As previously stated, it has, however, been synthesized with more critical accounts during the last thirty years, allowing insight into the meanings of interaction for excluded or subordinate groups such as females and non-whites.

FURTHER READING

For some brief textbook introductions to symbolic interaction and the sociology of sport and exercise, you can read Coakley and Pike (2009), Delaney and Madigan (2009), and Berry (2010). For an introduction to the more general interpretive approaches to the sociology of sport, Donnelly (2000; 2002) are excellent chapters with the latter one elaborating on George Herbert Mead's influence on symbolic interaction. Birrell and Donnelly (2004) provide an excellent overview of Goffman's influences on the sociology of sport and call for sport and exercise theorists to reclaim the valuable theoretical insights Goffman left us with for understanding sport and exercise more clearly at this micro level of analysis. Beal (2004) offers us theoretical and methodological insights into the connections between symbolic interaction, cultural studies, and critical ethnography. Some of the more detailed studies influenced by symbolic interaction include Ingham (1975), Carroll (1980), Birrell (1981), Hughes and Coakley (1991), Wacquant (1992), and Schmitt (1993). Weiss (2001) provides a general overview of symbolic interaction's usefulness in explaining identity reinforcement in sport, particularly showing the ways that self-identity often seeks external affirmation from others to confirm to both parties their value. We would strongly encourage students to read some of the original texts such as Goffman (1959/1967) and Becker (1963) and to begin to develop their own interpretation of symbolic interaction and its application to sport and exercise.

CHAPTER 7

PROCESS SOCIOLOGY
THE CIVILISING PROCESS

To carry out good quality sociological analysis and to better understand contemporary social practices we must develop our historical sensibilities ([see Mills, 1959] i.e. our understanding of history and of links between past and present). It is, however, common to take our current culture for granted and develop present-centred views of our society. Polley (2007) observes that it is easy to overlook the fact that sports began sometime in the past. 'No sports with which you are engaged started this morning' (2007: 14). By ignoring our past, we fall prey to being ahistorical, which can lead to only partially realistic, fragmented explanations. It is not a difficult exercise to see in what ways our present society is different from what it was 100, 50, or 30 years ago and to develop an appreciation for historical analyses. Let's look at an example that will highlight some of the changes our society has undergone.

Imagine that you are in 1900 and partaking in the Paris Olympics as an athlete. You are a sprinter, and your main event is the 100 m race. You have been performing well and have reached the final. The moment of truth has come. It is time to run that final race, and you are standing on the cinder track, donning the colours of your country, along with your fellow competitors. You feel anxious, but ready and are thinking about all the hard training you have done. You are focused on your goal and trying to block out the noise of the cheering crowd. What happened before the sound of the starting gun is a blur, but you vividly remember your run: You are gasping for air, your muscles are burning, and you are first to blast over the finish line. After being declared the winner of the 100 m Olympic race, your minute of glory comes, and the celebration begins. You have done yourself and your country proud.

132

Now, let's stop and think about this example and how we can use processual/historical thinking to see whether this illustration is realistic and in what ways the Olympics and our society's perception of it have changed over time. Relying on your experience of watching and, perhaps, participating (as spectator, volunteer, or athlete) in one of the more recent Olympic Games, you might be expecting that such a commercially, financially, and politically important mega event must have assumed similar social roles and status throughout its history. To see whether there is stark contrast between the early (e.g. 1900 Paris Games) and the most recent (post-1984) Games, you may want to imagine yourself in the early 1900s. Consider the following questions:

What do you think the atmosphere might have been? How many athletes might you have had to compete against? Do you think that there was extensive media hype and a large number of countries represented? How many sporting events do you think the organisers arranged to have? What do you think the sporting facilities might have been? Based on the preceding example, can you identify the gender of the runner? Would your fellow country people have heard of you winning the Olympics? Would you have had a crowd to block out? What would have been your finishing time?

REFLECTION

Relying on your historical knowledge, try to answer these questions and/or discuss them during seminars with your tutor. If you wish to improve your historical understanding of the modern Olympics, you will find plenty of sources available (e.g. see Guttmann, 2002).

Perhaps not surprisingly, when you look at historical evidence, the dissimilarities between the early and later stages of modern Olympics become conspicuous. For instance, early Olympics were not as well and widely received in society as they are nowadays. The number of participating countries and athletes was also much smaller. Early Olympics certainly did not have the same quality and quantity of media coverage and, thus, social significance. The number of sporting events was fewer, and women were not allowed to compete in most of them. For instance, the 100 m race was an exclusively male event in 1900 (changed only in 1928), and the winner finished with a time of 11 seconds. (Consider that the current Olympic record is 9.69 seconds.) To sum up, the 1900 Paris Olympics were

> part of a world fair or exposition, Exposition Universelle Internationale. The exposition *organizers spread the events over five months* and, thus, underplayed the significance of the Games. The Olympic aspect of the sporting events was presented as being so insignificant that some of the *competing athletes did not know that they had actually competed at the Olympics...* The conditions athletes had to face were appalling. For instance, *scheduling problems were so common* that many contestants never made it to their events. When they did arrive on time, they often found conditions unfit for an international sporting event. For example, the area for the running events was covered with grass rather than cinder and was dangerously uneven. The competitors in the throwing events did not even have enough room to throw. Furthermore, the *hurdles were made out of broken telephone poles* and the *swimming events were conducted in the River Seine* with its extremely strong current.
>
> (Bairner and Molnar, 2010: 222, italics added)

This description of the Paris Games clearly indicates that from its inception, the modern Olympics has undergone major transformations in almost all areas. From a disorganised and ordinary sporting event, the Games have changed to become one of the most prestigious and extraordinary mega events in later modernity (see Roche, 2000). However, this transformation is not unique to the Olympics. All sports, to some extent, have been and are being transformed as part of wider socio-cultural processes. For instance, modern football has also (processually) changed over time and moved away from ad hoc mob football to become association football. Elias (1986: 127) explains: 'The transformation of a polymorphous English folk game into Association Football or "soccer" had the character of a fairly long development in the greater regulation and uniformity.' Hence, what is to note is that we cannot formulate an adequately critical and realistic sociological account without exploring the history of whatever is being investigated. By doing so, we avoid process-reduction models that 'isolate individuals from "society" and involve reducing processes to monocausal, static and non-relational variables' (Jarvie and Maguire, 1994: 132). To view social phenomena as long-

134

term processes is a fundamental strength of process sociology as sociological explanations must be relational and historical involving references to sequences over time (Dunning, 2002). To emphasise the importance of history in sociological thinking, Elias (1983) strongly argued against the 'retreat of sociologists into the present.' In this chapter, we will frequently reference the work of Norbert Elias to help explain and illustrate processual thinking and process sociology, as he was the originator of this theoretical perspective. One of his colleagues, Eric Dunning, observes that 'Elias spent his adult life striving to construct a reality-oriented, equally theory-centred and research-centred synthesis between a modified psycho-analysis and the best features of the classical and modern sociological traditions' (2002: 211–212). Krieken notes that Elias essentially provided 'a set of sensitising concepts, an orientation to how one thinks about and practices sociology with the potential to draw many of the various threads of sociological thoughts together' (1998: 8).

Moreover, Elias had another important role to play in sociology, especially in the sociology of sport. This role was the legitimisation of the sociological study of sport and leisure. Before Elias, mainstream sociologists had only given sporadic (if any) attention to sports, leisure, and exercise and, thus, they were on the periphery of sociological inquiry. Kelly (2007) observes that there is still a paucity of sport-related comment in much of the mainstream academic literature and that people still have the tendency to make claims such as 'It's only sport'. Elias (1986: 19) himself wrote, 'I well remember Eric Dunning discussing with me the question of whether sport, and particularly football, would be considered by the authorities to be a respectable subject of research in the social sciences'.

For those of you who have been involved in sport and/or regular exercise, this may come as a surprise, as you are probably very well aware of the importance of specific sporting events or activities in your life. You can recall your feelings when your local or national team wins or loses, the fluctuation of emotions from the lowest to the highest, and the driving force behind the willpower to get up one hour earlier/stay up for one extra hour to be able to swim, run, and kick the ball about. In other words, sports are much more than institutionally or self-regulated forms of physical activities. Dine and Crosson (2010: 2) write, 'sporting practices and representations contribute significantly

BIOGRAPHIC NOTE

Norbert Elias (1897–1990) was born in Breslau (now Wrocłow in Poland) into a Jewish family. At the age of twenty-one, he began his university studies, with medicine and philosophy being his subjects at the University of Breslau. Later he dropped medicine to focus on philosophy, in which he completed his doctoral studies in 1924. A few years after the completion of his studies, he moved to the University of Frankfurt to study with Karl Mannheim (a Jewish Hungarian sociologist). His academic career in Germany, however, was prematurely terminated with the Nazis coming to power in 1933. He moved to Paris and then, two years later, to England, where he spent three years writing his magnus opus *The Civilising Process* (Elias had begun working on this project prior to moving to England). Generally speaking, Elias had a hard life. He lost his parents in German concentration camps during World War II and, being a German migrant in post-war England, constantly struggled economically. Finally, in 1954, he was offered and accepted a full-time academic post at Leicester University where, after initial frustrations, he made a significant impact on sociology, in general and the sociology of sport, in particular. His real breakthrough came in the 1970s, when both inside and outside academia he began to earn recognition. There are a range of views on his genuine contribution to sociology, resulting in his life and his academic heritage being viewed by some as controversial. His followers argue that he has 'seen the light' whereas his opponents say that the 'light' was viewed through a narrow tunnel. Regardless of these contradictory opinions, what Elias managed to achieve during his long life was the legitimisation of the sociological study of sport, as he was the first mainstream sociologist to pay appropriate heed to sport and leisure. (For more information on his life, see Krieken, 1998).

to the social construction of identities, through the elaboration of discourses and networks of power relations'. To put the social relevance of sports into perspective, here are some statistical data. In 2007, the BBC reported that approximately 60,000 English fans travelled to Paris for the Rugby World Cup final. In November 2010, the Guardian reported that around 50,000 students protested against the raising of tuition fees in London. Even if you argue that protests took place all over the United Kingdom (which they did) and, in turn, the total number of protesters must have been higher than 50,000, we would still argue that sports have a significant role in and effect on our society and is an important social mobiliser. Elias and his colleagues recognised the social relevance of sports and put them under rigorous sociological scrutiny, specifically with the help of the concept called *the civilising process*.

THE CIVILISING PROCESS

Elias's most prominent work, *The Civilising Process* (1939/2000), challenged monocausal thinking and supported the idea of equally theory- and evidence-based research. The basic idea of this work is 'that there is a link between the long-term structural development of societies and changes in people's social behaviour and habitus' (Mennell and Goudsblom, 1998: 15). That is, the way(s) we behave has(have) an effect on how societies develop, and then the development of societies affects our behaviour. To map long-term changes in social behaviour, Elias looked into people's interpersonal conduct in European societies.

In *The Civilising Process*, Elias arbitrarily (Ritzer, 2003; cf. Krieken, 1998) decided to look into Europe in the Middle Ages. What Elias managed to discover is a process of changing manners and habits (i.e. 'gradual changes in expectations of people's interpersonal conduct... as well as the way they approached their own bodily functions and emotions'; Krieken, 1998: 95). Public social behaviours that had been once acceptable and normal were later considered uncivilised and repugnant. This is referred to as the threshold of repugnance (or 'delicacy of feelings', Elias, 1939/2000: 98). 'As time went by, he [Elias] found that the standards applied to violence, sexual behaviour, bodily functions, eating habits, table manner and forms of speech became gradually more sophisticated' (Krieken, 2009: 359), with an increasing sensitivity to shame, embarrassment, and repugnance. In other words, Elias's analysis revealed long-term changes in table and social manners. For instance, in relation to blowing one's nose, Mennell (1992: 39–40) writes,

After reading the quotation about the social practice of blowing one's nose in the seventeenth century, think about your feelings whilst reading the passage. What were your thoughts? Did you feel disgusted? Would you consider blowing your nose with your fingers? There might be slight cultural and regional variations when responding to these questions but, we think, it is safe to say that most of us in Western societies would be appalled by witnessing such practices in public, which is due to a processual change in our threshold of repugnance. Elias (1939/2000: 51) observes that 'the different standard of repugnance which is still to be found today in many societies which we term "uncivilised", [indicate] the standard of repugnance which preceded our own'.

Medieval people blew their noises with their fingers... Handkerchiefs were known as a luxury item, not in general use. To blow one's nose on one's clothing was already 'rustic', but seemingly common enough. By the late seventieth century, upper-class people had ample stock of handkerchiefs and their use was obligatory. Eighteenth-century books laid down polite ways of using them, and for a person to gaze at the product or poke his or her nose was disgusting.

So, we can see that the threshold of repugnance was decreasing as time went on. That is, people became repulsed more easily than in previous times, and this affected people's attitudes and behaviour.

Elias later applied the theory of gradually increasing levels of civilisation to analyse sport and leisure.[1] He named the development of modern sports the 'sportisation process', which depicts the increasing civilisation and codification of contemporary sport and leisure (and, we could include, exercise) activities. In addition to improvements in manners and increasing levels of repugnance (due to a lowering of the *threshold of repugnance*), 'Elias noted a consistent decline in the level of violence permitted and enjoyed in contest and games' (Krieken, 1998: 144). Over time, the degree and form of violence associated with sports and games began to decline, and physical injuries and deaths associated with sports became less

138

acceptable. This argument can be and has been demonstrated via the development of a range of sports (see for example, Maguire, 1991) but Elias paid particular attention to fox hunting. Unintentionally, the fairly recent ban on fox hunting has made this leisure activity an apt example to demonstrate the sociological relevance of the sportisation process and how certain social practices, once socially acceptable, go out of fashion – so to speak (regarding fox hunting see, Elias, 1986; Dunning, 1999).

Initially, fox hunting was a bloody activity, involving the hunters not only killing but eating the fox. These practices, in line with the civilising tendencies of society, gradually disappeared and were replaced by less-violent behaviours. Ritzer (2003: 130) writes that: 'over the years, fox hunting has become increasingly civilised... instead of people doing the killing, the hounds do it...[and] it is no longer the norm for people to eat the fox'. In other words, fox hunting underwent a civilising process, the result of which was the decreasing violence and the delegation of the killing of the fox to the hounds. Regardless of this activity becoming more civilised in comparison to early modern blood sports, it is often perceived as a cruel, uncivilised from of leisure by many in contemporary society. Dunning (1999: 60) makes the following observation: 'Fox hunting... is widely considered to be "uncivilised" today... Looked at in solely present-terms, it seems absurd to suggest that an activity which is judged "barbaric" by so many people can be said to have undergone a "civilising process"'. Although fox hunting has indeed undergone a civilising process, as Dunning suggests, it is now considered socially undesirable as our society's threshold of violence-related repugnance has changed since the late 1800s and early 1900s. This increasing intolerance for violence is evident by the fact that 'fox hunting with dogs was banned by the Scottish Parliament in 2001, and in England and Wales in 2005 (Coakley and Pike, 2009: 206). (For a literary account on fox hunting, see Sassoon, 1979.)[2]

REFLECTION

Think of other examples in sport and exercise, the development of which could also be explained through the civilising process.

We have now established that our behaviour and social norms change over time, and good historical analyses would help us identify these transformations. It is essential to recognise that social practices and society are not set in stone and change over time, but it is just as important to question why such changes manifest. Let's now turn our attention to how Elias interpreted gradual cultural changes over time.

Elias argued that the cultural elite had a specific function in terms of establishing and reinforcing what it means to be civilised in a given historical era. Elites set the norms and people are, to varying degrees, pressured into obeying them; otherwise they have the tendency to become socially stigmatised. 'Those who breached the dominant rules and codes were viewed as "uncivilised"' (Maguire, 1999: 42). Nonetheless, Elias also recognised a counteraction, what he called the 'double-bind tendency' (or double dependency). As 'functional differentiation increased and interdependencies widened, the upper classes were 'forced' to refine their behaviour and seek to retain exclusivity over the codes that maintain their distinction' (Maguire, 1999: 42). Differently put, the elites ensure their privileged social positions and their value systems, and they influence (directly or indirectly) people in other social strata to internalise and follow them (cf. hegemony theory and Raymond Williams' (1977) dominant-emergent-residual cycle. For similar themes around maintaining distinction in this way, also see Bourdieu (1984: 212), who describes these shifting value systems as 'schemes of perception and appreciation'). Thus, we are reminded of the lower middle classes trying to distinguish themselves from their working-class neighbours by labelling them *chavs*, *neds*, or *Essex girls/boys* to demarcate themselves from their social 'inferiors'. However, on occasions, upper strata can be and are forced to change their old values and adopt new ones due to their links and dependence on other, lower classes. The growing interdependence between various social strata 'was inexorably leading to a diminution of their exclusivity, and thereby, a loss of power '(Maguire, 1999: 42). One form of this process is called 'reclaiming monopoly' (Elias, 1939/2000: 270). Moving back for a moment to violence, one of us used the concept of 'reclaiming monopoly of violence' to explain the initial spread of football. It is worth briefly reviewing this argument as an example of using Elias's civilising process to explain the formation of sport-related social processes.

Molnar (2007) observed that football experienced a steadily growing popularity in Hungary in its initial years. However, due to its inherently violent nature and the sporadically occurring injuries, especially when compared to other already dominant sporting practices, the development of the game was inhibited at the turn of the nineteenth century. A violence-prone image of football was distributed to the public, fuelled by the traditionalist ruling class with the view to turn football into a 'folk devil'. The idea to outlaw football was debated in various forums but, despite strong opposition by conservatives, a football ban never materialised.

Molnar (2007) argued that this aversion to football in Hungary derived chiefly from the tension between the nature of football and the level of tolerance for violence in the Hungarian upper stratum. This game challenged the increasing monopolisation of violence and attempts to internal pacification in social relations by the ruling class (Elias 1939/2000). Mennell (1992: 69) observes that one aspect of the monopoly mechanism is the gradual concentration of means of violence, which is essentially 'the gathering of the control of means of violence into fewer and fewer hands'. By the monopolisation of

---

REFLECTION

This is only one example of the great many clashes between acceptable and unacceptable behaviour. Think about any sport activity (or any activity); they all have rules and regulations, which you have to adhere to if you want to take part. If/when you break those rules (e.g. you are more violent than acceptable or employing a prohibited technique), there usually are consequences (e.g. removing the violent player from the playing field).[3] Gradual (full or partial) elimination of some violent sport/leisure activities from mainstream culture has also been observed (see fox hunting example above and Dunning, 1999). The civilising process and the sportisation process make us aware that rules and social practices and standards do not establish themselves but are set by people (predominantly members of the ruling class) and change over time. Elias paid particular attention to the ways in which traditional behaviour patterns (habitus) gradually gave way to new, more civilised forms in the *The Court Society* (1969/1983).

violence and internal pacification, the ruling class endeavoured to increase the level of civilisation and set standards for what is considered to be acceptable or unacceptable violence. Hence, members of the Hungarian upper stratum, based on their elitist value-system and their assumed control over the monopoly of violence, declared football repugnant because of its uncivilised characteristics, which were not in line with the acceptable level of violence. By virtue of this, football was portrayed as a physical activity that should not be practised, and the ruling class made a forceful attempt to eliminate it from Hungary (Molnar at al., 2011).

The conclusion of this debate around football was possibly the result of the level of popularity football had already achieved among a wide range of social groups in Hungary, and thus the upper class's monopoly of violence became fragmented and was overruled by the large number of people from various social circles who believed that football was no threat. We argue that this process of 'reclaiming monopoly' (Elias 1939/2000: 270) played a significant part in the initial diffusion and development of football in Hungary and is helpful in understanding the early developments of many similiar sports.

SOCIAL FIGURATIONS

Elias conceived of the structure of societies as a dense and flexible network of human figurations (or relationships). Thereby, he criticised Western philosophy to the degree it filtered into and contaminated contemporary sociology. As a way of overcoming Western approaches to explaining the nature of society based on dichotomies (e.g. viewing individual and society as separate entities), Elias developed his own concept of *social figurations* (hence the name: figurational sociology) and argued that 'given the present state of sociological discussion, there is a specific reason for introducing the concept of 'figuration'' (1978: 129). Through the concept of figuration, Elias asserted, the complexity of social reality could be better illustrated: 'It [figurations] makes it possible to resist the socially conditioned pressure to split and polarize our conception of mankind, which has repeatedly prevented us from thinking of people as individuals at the same time as thinking of them as societies' (Elias, 1978: 129; cf. agency-structure dialogue).

142

Figurations 'refer to groupings of interdependent human beings, to specific situations which people form with each other' (Elias, 1978: 13). Figurations are the nexus of interdependencies between people, the chains of functions, and the axes of tensions that can be identified in any social context. Figurations are not stable or unchangeable social structures; they are socially produced and reproduced, and constantly change during the course of history. Thus, Elias viewed the change of societies as the result of the interconnectedness of various social processes. Human societies, from this perspective, 'can only be understood as consisting of long-term processes of development and change, rather than as timeless states or conditions' (Krieken, 1998: 6).

Figurations are real and describe societies as human beings living together as parts of complex, interdependent networks (Burkitt, 1991). The concept of figurations reveals that 'human beings are interdependent, and can only be understood as such…these figurations are continually in flux, undergoing changes of different orders… [and] that the processes in such figurations have dynamics of their own' (Mennell and Goudsblom 1998: 131). Figurations also involve power balances and are influenced by long-term, largely unplanned processes (e.g. the civilising process). Human beings constitute these figurations, creating a flexible lattice-work of tensions and interdependencies between them (Elias, 1978). Figurations can be imagined as people with a given number of valencies (bonding capacities), some of which are shared, some of which are unique to particular individuals. Individuals connect to others, making friendships or developing work partnerships, and this constitutes a framework of figurations (Elias, 1978). Bonds can be strong, firm, and long lasting or weak, short, and superficial. In other words, some bonds will last longer whereas

---

REFLECTION

Elias (1978) further explained the nature of figurations via the 'personal pronouns model' and 'game models'. These representations are meant to help in the interpretation of the network of social figurations and to provide a simplification of social reality (for further details on figurations, see Elias' personal pronouns and game models, 1978: 71–103; 121–128).

others are temporary, and the constant search by human beings for new linkages and the atrophy of old bonds fuel the perpetual change of human figurations.

Let us engage your sociological imagination at this point to help you establish your understanding of what social figurations are and in what ways you, and everyone else, are connected to them and interconnected through them. You are not an island separate from everything and everyone. You interact with others around you on a daily basis. You are in contact with and, to varying degrees, dependent on others, meaning, for instance, that you expect your local coffee shop to be open as usual and serve you your choice of beverage. This means that the baristas have to turn up for work, know how to make coffee, make coffee, and be willing to serve you (you depend on baristas for your coffee, and baristas depend on you and other customers to purchase coffee, as their jobs are created on that basis). After your coffee, you wander into your university and get yourself ready for a lecture. For that lecture to take place, you expect the lecturer and your classmates to show up at the right place and at the right time. After your lecture, you have sports training or you pop to the university gym for a workout. Again, you are dependent on a range of people in these situations. You depend on your lecturer for the lecture, on your coach for the training session, and on the gym staff for your workout. However, they are also dependent on you as student, athlete, and/ or exerciser. Without you and others like you subscribing to their services, their social roles could not exist as they currently do. These are examples of the interconnectedness and power balances that exist between humans in society.

To further your understanding of the ever-changing nature of social figurations, consider the fairly recent changes in Western exercise culture. For instance, like Elias, look at evidence regarding the number of gyms in your local or regional area and how this number changed over time. In fact, consider whether they are called gyms. Perhaps you now visit a fitness centre, a fitness clinic, or a health and well-being centre? See whether you can link what you find to larger social discourses such as health and sport.

144

According to Elias, 'in order to understand what sociology is all about, one has to look at oneself from a distance, to see oneself as one human being among others' (1978: 13).[4] This means that if you want to understand the operation of your society you have to distance yourself from that society and must be viewed as an individual in the network of human interactions. Therefore, Elias refuses the concept of 'Homo Clausus' (closed human – a view advocated by Western philosophy at that time) or 'closed box' as a way of understanding social relations and interdependencies. These types of human beings are prone to believe that their actual selves somehow exist inside of them and that an invisible barrier separates their inside from everything existing outside (Elias, 1978). The reason for this, as Elias writes, is that 'they cannot imagine that there are people who do not perceive themselves and the world in which they live in this way. They never ask themselves which part of them actually forms the dividing wall and which part is shut away inside it' (1978: 119).

By rejecting the idea of 'closed humans', the concept of 'Homines Aperti' (open people) is advocated (i.e. people who recognise the interdependency chains of human societies [social figurations] and can imagine themselves as a part of them). As open people, you already know that you are part of various social figurations via your connections to others as explained in the examples above. However, these connections are not set in stone and may not stay with you for the rest of your life. That is, you will (we hope) eventually finish your degree, may become a regular exerciser instead of being an athlete, or may decide that tea is an option healthier than coffee. You, like others, constantly create, reform, and lose connections with various actors in society. For instance, as part of your transition from school (or work) to attending university, you decide to move out of your parents' house and rent a house with five other university students. You had not known these students before and, thus, you had had no social valencies. After moving in together, your social relations to them changed. You, and they too, created new social connections, enriching the complexity of social figurations. Some of your new housemates are enrolled on the same degree programme and you go to lectures and seminars together. You may also share similar sport and exercise related interests. You may end up working out with one of them in the gym on a weekly basis. You may go to the cinema with another and go out clubbing with all of them. So, as you can see, you have created new connections and are now, to some extent, dependent on these newly formed relations and they are dependent on you (e.g. to pay your share of the rent, to keep certain parts of the house clean, to do the shopping, but you may or may not equally be dependent on each other). Whilst you were creating these new social links and you were busy with your studies, you neglected some of the older friendships you had in your home town. You do not go back home frequently, and the old friends you used to meet daily you do not see for weeks. Because of the lack of maintenance of your old relations, they began to change or, perhaps, even wither away. You may still keep in touch with friends from your home town via social networking sites (cyber social figurations – could be perceived as a novel feature of the civilising process) or over the phone, but you do not see them as often as you used to. Consequently, you transformed (or even terminated) some of your old relations (social valencies) and developed new ones. This is essentially how social figurations, and you as social actor in/through them, change over time. Social figurations are not exclusive to interconnecting individuals. They are also a useful concept for explaining the commingling of larger social structures such as sports and local, regional, and global sporting structures.

GLOBAL SPORTS: DIMINISHING CONTRASTS AND INCREASING VARIETIES

Specific aspects of process sociology have been employed to interpret the global diffusion and spread of modern sports as part of the sportisation process. Though Elias paid only partial attention to the global spread of modern sport in terms of looking for correlations between the process of globalisation and civilisation, Joseph Maguire (1993, 1994, 1999, 2005) has done significant work in this area.[5] Various elements of sports globalisation have been investigated on account of process sociology, including the global role of media/sport complex (Maguire, 1993), national identity/policy (Maguire and Tuck, 1998, 2005), athlete migration (Maguire, 1994; Maguire and Stead, 1996, 1998), Americanisation of European sports (Maguire, 1990, 1991), and the global diffusion of sports (Maguire, 1999, 2005). Through the following lines, some of the contributions of process sociology to the discussion on global sports will be introduced.

146

Process sociology as regards global sports is suggestive of the emergence of hybrid (combination of) or trans-cultural formations, a fine line between cultural homogeneity (sameness) and heterogeneity (difference). That is, one culture does not simply exist in isolation or overtake another culture; rather, they fuse together by retaining some and discarding other elements of two (or more) cultures. Maguire (1999), building on Elias (1939/2000: 382–387), utilised the 'diminishing contrasts and increasing varieties' concept to interpret global cross-cultural relations and differential popularisation of sports. He notes that 'concepts such as diminishing contrasts and increasing varieties arguably steer the analysis between the excess of homogenisation and heterogenisation' (1999: 41). Therefore, the commingling of Western and non-Western cultures and the subsequent emergence of new cultural amalgams is supported. In other words, power struggles that facilitated the civilising process now encircle the entire planet, and global interdependencies are driven toward diminishing contrasts and increasing varieties across the globe (cf. double bind tendency). In corollary, the impact of Western powers on the non-Western part of the globe is perceived to be a cultural interchange rather than a one-way process (i.e. cultural domination; regarding an overview on various perspectives of globalisation, see Beynon and Dunkerley, 2000). Maguire (1999) provides the example of the diffusion of polo from India to England and the spread of English sports in India to illustrate such processes of cultural interchange.

Modern sport is an optimal example of globalisation and cultural interchange (i.e. 'sport is a significant touchstone of prevailing global, national and local patterns of interchange'; Maguire, 1999: 76). The worldwide spread of modern sport has been recognised by scholars as a long-term historical process that began to emerge around the mid-nineteenth century (Elias and Dunning, 1986; Maguire et al., 2002). Modern sports originated in England, and many types of them are practised globally today. Sports predominantly spread from England to other countries mainly between the second half of the nineteenth and first half of the twentieth centuries (Elias, 1986). This type of organised physical activity was mostly unknown in the receiving countries. Therefore, those countries adopted not only the activities and their rule systems but the word 'sport' as well (see Elias, 1986). Elias writes: 'The English term "sport", too, was widely adopted by other countries as a generic term for this specific type of pastime' (1986: 126).

To confirm (or reject) the validity of Elias's observation regarding the global spread of sports, check in what ways (if any) other languages have adopted and been using English sport-related terms. As we are not talking about a one-way traffic but a cultural interchange, you could also investigate what sport terms you use or are familiar with that originated from another country.

The global dispersion of modern sports, an aspect of the sportisation process, is bound up in globalisation processes (Maguire, 1999) and has been described via different historical phases.[6] Initially, Elias (1986) differentiated between two phases of the sportisation process. Later on, Maguire (1999) further developed this framework and added three more stages to it in line with Robertson's (1992) *Minimal Phase Model* of globalisation. The latest contribution to the interpretation of the sportisation process is also done by Maguire (2004) incorporating the work of Therborn (2000) and his concept of historical waves of globalisation. In the following part of this section, some of the historical stages of the sportisation process shall be unfolded based on the works of Maguire (1999, 2004) and tied to the framework of globalisation developed by Robertson (1992; see Table 7.1).

The significance of the sportisation phase-model (see Table 7.1) is that it not only expresses the social significance of sports but ties it to the framework of globalisation.[7] The roots of modern sports do not go as far back in history as do those of globalisation. There can, however, be seen essential similarities between these two processes as indicated by Table 7.1 (see italicised sections). The last four phases of the *Minimal Phase Model* of Robertson (1992) highlight certain social issues that interacted and are still intertwined with the development of sport and refer to the interconnectedness of globalisation and sportisation processes, which cannot be unequivocally separated from one another in terms of their starting and ending points. They are intertwined. In other words, from a process sociology perspective, globalisation, in line with sportisation, is perceived as a complex, long-term, unevenly distributed process.

For instance, the 'incipient phase' stresses the emergence of formalised international relations and standardised citizenly individuals that are indicators of the increased level of civilisation that perhaps led to parliamentarisation and to less-violent ways of settling debates. This probably gave an opportunity for sport to gradually replace 'uncivilised' leisure activities (e.g. blood sports such as cock fighting) and become the 'civilised' way of enjoying leisure time. Furthermore, the third phase is described as the 'take-off' phase in both models. During this period, both sportisation and globalisation were beginning their extensive and speedy world-wide travel. Western cultures in general and sport culture in particular spread over the globe. The fourth stage, struggle for hegemony, describes the realignment of Western and non-Western nation-states on the global scale and the establishment of a new world order. Nonetheless, this period also suggests the increase of the resistance of non-Western countries and the re-colonisation of Western ones. The last stage, the uncertainty stretch, indicates that, despite the fact that global issues are becoming more clarified, the outcome of the process of globalisation cannot be clearly seen. The mélange of intended and unintended human actions has brought to light new (hybrid) social circumstances, some of which can be considered unexpected and have begun to force Western powers from their economic and cultural core position toward the periphery. 'For process-sociologists globalisation [and sportisation] processes have a blind, unplanned dimension... [and] these processes, then, are also bound up in a multiple set of "disjunctures", which... have a high degree of unpredictability' (Maguire, 1999: 40). This social analysis of sport and globalisation gives a broad understanding of not exclusively the social phenomena but their interconnectedness as well.

REFLECTION

Demonstrate your understanding of how the sportisation/globalisation processes, specifically the de-civilising phases of them, work by explaining the switch from amateurism to achievement ethos as the dominant value system in mainstream sports. To provide a good analysis of this shift in value systems in sports, you would need to combine what we have discussed in the processual/historical thinking, the civilising process, and diminishing contrasts and increasing varieties sub-sections (for an aid, see Gruneau, 2006).

149

Table 7.1 Sportisation and globalisation interconnectedness

Sportisation Process Maguire (1999)	Globalisation Process Robertson (1992)
First phase (1750-1800) Sportisation started in the 18th century in which the principal past times began to emerge as modern sports such as cricket, fox hunting, horse racing and boxing.	**The Germinal phase** (1400-1750) Expanding the scope of the Roman Catholic Church, the beginning of Heliocentric view and modern geography, and the spread of the Gregorian calendar.
Second phase (1800-1870) The second wave consists of the spread of modern sports among the lower social strata in Britain. Also, football, rugby, tennis and athletics began to take on modern forms and traditional folk games commenced their decline. In the first two phases, sportisation was linked to parliamentarisation. These two processes indicated a higher level of civilisation that led to the *development of less violent leisure time activities*.	**The Incipient phase** (1750-1875) Emergence of the idea of the homogenous and unitary state; the formalised international relations, *standardised citizenly individuals and a more solid conception of humankind*.
Third phase (1870-1920) The global 'take-off' of sportisation: *International spread of sports, the establishment of international sport organisations*, the occurrence of first international championships and competitions, and the evolution of standardised rule systems. In this phase, the English were the dominant players. They tended to win international competitions and reform other nations' movement cultures.	**The Take-off phase** (1875-1925) The manifestation of globalising tendencies increases. *Exponential development in number and speed of global forms of communication*, emergence of increasing economic and political connections, along with global competition - for instance, the *Olympics* and Nobel prizes, and global conflicts such as the First World War.
Fourth phase (1920 - 1960) The beginning of Americanisation in sportisation, which began to replace the English gentlemen fair-play values by the achievement sport ethos. The inchoation of *struggle for (sport) hegemony* between the West and the rest but, also, within the Western nation-states. Decline of modern sports' founding nations and indigenous *resistance against Western (sport) culture*.	**The Struggle-for-Hegemony phase** (1925-1969) Constant fights, disputes and wars over *establishing a new world* order and domination such as the break out of the Second World War and the occurrence of the *Cold War*. This phase also includes the *crystallisation of the Third World*.

Fifth phase (1960 - Present)	**The Uncertainty phase** (1969 - to
This involves a degree of creolisation/ hybridisation of sport cultures, the increase of cultural interchange, increasing standardisation of modern sport and the challenge of hegemony of modern achievement sport. Also, sport as *a male preserve began to be challenged*. Western control of global sport began to wane off the playing field. Western nations are possibly experiencing *self-doubts and uncertainty (e.g. English national football team's international performance)*.	date) The clarification of global consciousness, the number of global institutions increases, exponential acceleration in global mass communication and mass media. Also, civil rights become a global issue and *world-wide debates emerge around race, sex and gender.*

At this juncture, we must point out that the preceding models represent both sportisation and globalisation in phases, which may not directly seem to be in line with process sociology. However, these phases are only an estimated indication of the ends and beginnings of stages in both the sportisation and globalisation processes. That is, both globalisation and sportisation are and should be considered as ongoing, long-term historical processes but, as Therborn (2000) observes regarding globalisation, they should not be perceived as a linear process of continuous development. Societies do not develop following a straight line. Their development usually fluctuates, creating what is called 'de-civilising' and/or 'de-globalising' phases. Examples of de-civilising phases could be the breaking out of wars such as the World Wars and, as a more recent example, the conflicts in Iraq, Afghanistan, and Libya. These events represent setbacks in the civilising process as well as in globalisation for the reason that wars usually lead to loss of human life and the breaking down of political and economic partnerships between the warring parties and their allies (e.g. consider the history of the Cold War and see Wagg and Andrews, 2007). Also, think of the economic crisis of 2008, the effect of which still can be clearly felt at the time of writing, which could be claimed to be a de-globalising spurt in the globalisation process, having an impact on, amongst many social spheres, sports and sports development.

CRITIQUES OF PROCESS SOCIOLOGY

Process sociology, similar to all other theoretical perspectives, has been critically evaluated on a number of accounts. Here we introduce a few of these criticisms to provide a more rounded account of process sociology and to help you hone your critical thinking skills. We will outline some of the major critiques of the nature of the civilising process and of social figurations.

The concept of the civilising process has been criticised for being evolutionist in its logic and ethnocentric in its attitude to interpreting relations between Western and non-Western peoples. Elias claimed that during the course of history Western societies, despite occasional de-civilising spurts, had gradually been reaching higher levels of civilisations, meaning that the level of violence has dropped and our control over our emotions and bodily functions has increased in the course of time. This observation has been critically evaluated, arguing that the degree of violence has not changed much as we still have ongoing wars, we continue to develop more efficient military machineries for killing, our means and forms of symbolic violence have become more sophisticated, and even sports, regardless of growing codification, remain a preserve of (mostly necessary) violence. Gulianotti (2004a: 157) argues, 'We may congratulate ourselves on the felicitous control of bodily emissions, while exercising our more incisive, "civilised" skills in sarcasm, insult and calumny'. In other words, in spite of the continuously growing number of rules and regulations in society, which should safeguard our level of civilisation and pacify us, we still celebrate both pre-modern and late-modern forms of violence as long as violence is carried out in line with the grand narrative of society. For instance, with regard to boxing, Murphy and Sheard (2006) observe that the introduction of regulations and protective gear in boxing has not significantly changed the violent or damaging nature of the sport. The establishment of weight categories has obviously created a more level playing field and long-term damaging effects by forcing athletes to lose or gain a significant amount of weight in a matter of weeks. Also, protective gear may have reduced the chances of specific types of injuries occurring but has not eliminated them (see Murphy and Sheard's [2006: 548–549] discussion on the use of gloves). Also, military action, as a form of instrumental violence, is welcomed and celebrated as long as it serves the perpetuation of Western cultures – or to be precise, powerfully dominant groups within Western nation-states. Not to mention the fact that the mass media are laden with violent stories, movies, images, and video games. Giulianotti

(2004a: 157) adds that 'civilian rape, murder, starvation or forced migration' are still part of the 'civilised' tapestry of contemporary societies.

As the civilising process is embedded in the history of Western cultures, it has been questioned whether it provides a too-narrow, Western-centred outlook on societies. The main critique here is that sociological observations regarding other, non-Western cultures are fundamentally influenced and measured by Western standards. If we consider Western cultures as societies spearheading the civilising process, all other cultures being less concerned with health and safety, controlling emotions and bodily emissions (or whatever we hold socially important and dear) should logically be considered less civilised or representing de-civilising spurts in the civilising process. Following this logic, folk games or leisure activities of non-Western peoples that do not resemble the structures and aims of modern Western sports such as strict adherence to rules and winning at all costs can be perceived as activities of lesser value or even barbaric. Or, peoples who do not exercise and do not watch their diet because they have not been overly scientised and, perhaps, never heard of the negative physical consequences of high cholesterol, are deemed primitive because of their (lack of) knowledge when compared to Western standards. These are examples of evaluating other cultures according to preconceptions originating in one's own culture (i.e. ethnocentrism). Cultural relativism seems to offer a remedy to ethnocentrism by stating that cultures and social practices embedded in them should not be judged based on the values of another culture. Hence, each culture must be understood and interpreted on its own terms, not judged in relation to others.

We think that the most inveterate critique or objection toward Elias's sociology, especially his introduction and use of social figuration, is questioning its necessity and genuine contribution to the field of socio-cultural studies. Essentially, this debate is focused on the argument that Elias had nothing new to say about society and sociology. He simply regurgitated what others had already unfolded before him. This claim seems to be underpinned by Elias's minimalism in terms of acknowledging works and concepts of other scholars. Elias's lack of referencing is persistently pointed out (see Giulianotti, 2004a; Smith, 2001), which leads to claiming that Elias 'tends to ram in open doors'

(Coser, 1980 , cited in Kireken, 1998: 74). Bairner (2006: 596) well captures this argument with regard to process sociology's contribution to understanding sport:

> Those who do not subscribe wholly to the figurational approach will be tempted to argue that everything that Dunning and his colleagues have impressively revealed...could have been said without an almost slavish adherence to figurational sociology.

Process sociology is not a 'stepchild' of sociology in terms of being overly criticised. All sociological theories have been, must be, and are under academic scrutiny (Smith, 2001). Critical thinking and debate are what propels sociological inquiry into sport and exercise forward. Being complacent with our own knowledge and formulaic approaches to understanding society will not greatly enhance our sociological imagination (see Chapter 10). Therefore, sociology is as much a quest for understanding as it is a quest for critique. With regard to process sociology, a good summary of critiques can be found in Krieken's (1998: 73–83) work and in one of the special issues of *Sport in Society* journal (2006), in which the exceptional contribution of Eric Dunning, and, to a large extent, figurational (process) sociology, to the sub-discipline of sociology of sport is discussed by selected scholars.

FURTHER READING

For a brief but thorough general overview of most of the sociological concepts developed by Elias, see Robert van Krieken (1998). A more detailed and in-depth account on Elias's work could be found in Stephen Mennell's (1992) overview. For a more detached and contrasting analysis of process sociology, we would recommend Dennis Smith's (2001) work on Elias. It is also a useful source to trace the ways Elias' sociology links with other social theorists. With regard to sport, research carried out by Eric Dunning (1999), Joseph Maguire (1999; 2005), Jason Tuck (2005 – with Maguire), Louise Mansfield (2009) and Dominic Malcolm (2007 – with Ian Waddington) would be recommended as further reading.

CHAPTER 8

FEMINIST PERSPECTIVES

SPORT AND EXERCISE – GENDERED BORDER CROSSINGS

Sociology and sport appear to have a specific common feature: Both areas began as male preserves. This observation is not exclusive to sport and sociology but cuts across most (if not all) academic disciplines and areas of society. For instance, Beddoe (1998: 1) writes the following about history's oversight of women: 'We [women] had been left out of the history books for so long that we have come to accept what was in reality a male view of history'. So feminism and women's movements emerged as a reaction to the structures (e.g. sports) implemented by a male-dominant society. As women have historically been marginalised, excluded from specific social spheres (e.g. business, media, technology, politics, education, and sports) and confined to others (e.g. child minding and household), clear gender roles began to emerge that have now been somewhat challenged, but their social footing is still firm in most modern Western societies. The degree to which traditional gender roles and expectations are embedded in our society can be clearly observed through the instances featured in feminist literature (see Gill and Grint, 1995; Adams, 2000; Birell, 2002; Caudwell, 2006) and is illustrated by an example below.

Imagine that you are an amateur, budding female bodybuilder who works out for two to three hours, six times a week. You are proud of the body you have crafted over the years and take great care of looking after it. The gym is your second home, your shrine where you show up religiously every evening after work or university. You like the calming, metallic coolness of free weights and the monotony of the exhausting exercise regime that you designed for yourself and carry out on a daily basis. You train on your own or with your brother most of the time, as there are only a few women who lift free weights in your gym, and all of them prefer weights lighter than those you do. Despite all the pleasure and satisfaction you gain from being a bodybuilder, you realise that the more you train, the more devoted and larger/muscular you become and the more disapproving looks you receive. Smaller men may try to avoid you and, perhaps, look at you with surprise, curiosity, pity, and/or disgust. Other women in the changing room may meekly note that you might have become a 'little' too big and masculine. Maybe even your friends and parents appear unsupportive of your obsession with bodybuilding, and they are concerned about you losing your femininity. (Interestingly, your parents and friends are perfectly fine with your brother displaying the same type of enthusiasm toward muscle and bodybuilding; see Choi, 2000.) This makes you feel uncomfortable, but you do not want to give up bodybuilding, so you try to combat disapproval by appearing more feminine. You decide to paint your nails, get your hair done, wear makeup to training sessions, and dress the way many other (perhaps most) women of your age tend to do in the gym (i.e. ensuring that their feminine beauty – as arguably envisaged by men – is appropriately maintained and displayed.[1] You are also very conscious about other aspects of your physical appearance. You have extensively trained and dieted to reduce your body fat to appear leaner and your muscles more defined. One of the visible by-products of this strict regime and self-discipline is the reduction of the breast tissue. The fact that your breasts have almost completely vanished worries you a great deal for two reasons: One of the distinctive markers of your femininity is withered, and you have not had a boyfriend for sometime.[2] Your solution to these worries is breast augmentation surgery (given that you can afford it). After surgery, you return to your training regime gleaming with hope and makeup carefully applied on your face. You feel more confident and more feminine with the dainty silicon cushions carefully tucked under your chest skin. You think that you have done everything to fit in, to look the (female) part, to appear (what is considered) feminine, and to be desirable for the male gaze. Yet, you feel that something is still not right. Despite all your efforts and transformation, the disapproving looks remain, your insecurity returns, and you pose the question: 'Should I not be here?'

156

Drawing upon her personal experience in marital arts (another male preserve), Choi (2000:1-2) introduces her gendered sporting battle:

> not being allowed to play football at school, the indifference of my fellow male martial artists in the dojo, the hostility of the men in the gym – all leading me to question myself. Should I not be here? Am I not good enough? Do I not train hard enough?

Though bodybuilding, similar to martial arts, can be considered as acting against the gender status quo (Wesely, 2001) and thus empowering and liberating for women, it can also disempower and alienate them from normative social practices and roles (see Roussel et al., 2003). The issue is that, by developing a large musculature, you have done something women are not supposed to. They are not supposed to have large muscles, lift weights heavier than those most men can, and have a great deal of confidence. When you decided to become a female bodybuilder, you, perhaps unknowingly, crossed a range of preestablished gendered borders and challenged gender logic (see McGrath and Chananie-Hill, 2009). As a result of your well-developed, 'ripped' physique and your masculine disposition (i.e. your transgression of corporeal gender norms, your femininity and sexual orientation) may be questioned. To stay within the established gender norms, you were – what Ussher (1997) called – 'doing girl', that is, employing a range of feminising practices (e.g. wearing makeup, feminising your hairstyle, and undergoing plastic surgery) not because you wanted to but because you were (directly or indirectly) socially pressured to. That is, despite the progress feminist movements have made over the years, a nonconformist muscular/athletic woman can still face a range of social stigma and have her sexuality challenged. Concepts, values, and practices of femininity and masculinity are deeply and historically rooted in our society, and gender roles socially manufactured hundreds of years ago still hark back to our (post) modern societies. Let's take a brief look at some of these gender norms/binaries i.e. male-female and the ways in which we socialise into them (for a more extensive discussion on gender, see Bandy, 2010a).

From birth, society (we) often distinctly differentiate between girls and boys, for instance by assigning gender-specific colours (i.e. pink to girls' wear and blue to boys' wear). As they grow up, children are introduced to gender-specific activities (gender logic) and given gender-appropriate

Consider the above-mentioned bodybuilding example and ponder upon the following: Why is it that your brother, who works out just as much as you do, does not have to face the same issues? He does not have to go the extra mile to fit into society (he does not need to accessorise and undergo plastic surgery to reinforce his gender identity) and few, if any, disapprove of his highly muscular, lean body. His drive for muscularity seems to be perfectly acceptable, whereas yours is questioned. Why?

As another exercise, use the Internet to look up pictures of two female bodybuilders: Cory Everson and Bev Francis. Analyse photos of these ex-bodybuilders you come across on the World Wide Web and explain why one of the women might have been more successful than the other.

toys and clothing (e.g. football, boxing gloves, toy guns, and cars for boys and dolls, tea sets, and cuddly stuffed animals for girls). Even at this early stage, we begin to see the ways gender logic shapes attitudes towards sport. Lever (1978: 482) observed that boys are more likely to be exposed to complex games than girls, which may give boys 'an advantage in occupational milieus that share structural features with those games'. In other words, games played by boys have the tendency to create an effective social environment akin to modern organisations, whereas girls' play is less structured and more spontaneous and imaginative. Even if we question as to whether boys playing structured games more often than girls gives an unfair advantage to boys when trying to fit into a sport team or into a new work environment, we must acknowledge that gender learning and socialisation have many aspects through which we internalise gender appropriate behaviour.

For instance, Greendorfer (1983) investigated the family's role in gender socialisation and identified a range of activities that are instrumental in teaching, learning, and reinforcing gender identity in children. Parents have the tendency to pass on traditional gender perceptions that they had internalised during their own socialisation, thereby perpetuating gender-specific status quo. In line with traditional gendered views, girls are perceived as fragile and requiring more attention/support and would

Feminism is certainly one of those social theories that captivate students' attention and sociological imagination. They can relate to it as links between arguments produced and observations made by proponents of this perspective regarding gender inequality, and their personal lives/troubles are clearly visible. It is not unusual that students develop heated discussions with regard to the relationship between sport, exercise, and gender. Naturally, it is mostly women who embrace and become advocates of feminism, although it is not exclusive to them. Some men (pro-feminists), too, learn to appreciate feminist theory, specifically its deconstruction and critical analysis of social gender roles. Yes, feminism is first and foremost about women and their role in society. However, it can be and has been argued that ossified gender-specific social roles are not only curbing women; men also suffer them. To illustrate this point, we refer to the movie *Billy Elliot*. Billy is brought up in a traditional working class family in the (post-) industrial north of England, and it is expected of him to take up a 'manly' sport activity, in this case, boxing, as his father and brother did. Billy has no desire to be trained in the 'sweet science'; instead, he wishes to practice ballet, which he does without his father's consent. When his father discovers that Billy does not attend boxing training but dances with girls wearing white tights and tutus, family quarrels begin. Fortunately for Billy, his talent for ballet is recognised, he is given an opportunity to further his skills in London, and his father learns to appreciate Billy's 'unusual' obsession. Although the movie's end is Hollywood-esque, it powerfully depicts Billy's desperate struggle against well-established gender stereotypes. The movie's story runs along multiple threads, but one moral is that society and social structures are not 'one-size-fits-all'. (Compare Billy's case with the bodybuilding example outlined at the beginning of this chapter and discuss the similarities.)

have to be 'rescued' from challenging situations. Conversely, boys are given more space, allowed to be more exploratory, and not necessarily disciplined when they express moderately aggressive behaviour toward their toys. Mothers also have the tendency not to allow female children to venture away from them too far, whereas boys, again, are given greater

To demonstrate one of the flows of patriarchal arrangements with regard to sports, we refer to the example of the sex test and Ewa Klobukowska. Gender verification (sex test) in sport was the direct result of the Cold War and involved confirming the eligibility of (only!) female athletes to compete in sporting events. As evidenced in debates around the so-called muscle gap (see De Oca, 2007), there was general concern in the United States that modern Western culture feminises its male citizens, which was compounded by the masculine appearance of successful female athletes of the Eastern bloc. The effeminising impact of modern culture and the physical dominance of communist female athletes fundamentally shook Western gender values. In an attempt to restore the 'natural' Western gender order and Western sporting dominance, a sex test for women taking part in international competitions was introduced and first carried out in 1966 at the European Athletic Championships. Ewa Klobukowska, a Polish short-distance runner, became the first victim of this gender ideology and male insecurity-driven practice. In 1967 at the Women's European Athletic Cup (Kiev, USSR), Klobukowska was submitted to the sex text and was examined by six physicians who unequivocally declared that she was *unfit* to be a woman as she had one chromosome too many. As a result, Klobukowska was banned from future competitions and, essentially, her womanhood was deprecated. Ironically, in 1968, Klobukowska proved the gender verification committee's decision wrong by providing the ultimate evidence of her womanhood, i.e. giving birth to a baby.

degrees of freedom and independence (see also Mitchell et al., 1992). By virtue of this, Greendorfer (1983) argues that what we often consider the 'natural order' regarding gender divide and, more specifically, women's underrepresentation in sports (and in other public domains) is *not natural at all*. Rather, women's lack of participation and/or interest in sport is socially engineered and often perpetuated by traditional values and socialising agencies such as the family. Consequently, to explain women's marginal involvement in sports (and in other social arenas perceived as male preserves) in comparison to men by claiming that it is 'natural' in our society blatantly misses the point of gender-specific socialising influences in society.

RATIONALES FOR MALE DOMINANCE

To assume that women are fundamentally different from men is a key aspect of Western civilisation (Weedon, 1999), and men have relied on three main rationales for maintaining 'natural' gender order and for women's exclusion from sport (Kay and Jeanes, 2009). These are *aesthetic, biological*, and *social* (which are aspects of theories of gender difference; [Lengermann and Brantley-Niebrugge, 1992]). Aesthetic rationale argues that it is not visually pleasing to view women taking part in sport and exercise activities that are not considered feminine and graceful and require them to assume masculine (dis)positions, build a muscular physique, and carry out overly strenuous activities. In the bodybuilding example previously, aesthetic rationale was used to object to the unfeminine appearance of the female bodybuilder's body, which was challenging/transgressing gender norms and thus considered unacceptable. Essentially, most men did and do not want their masculinity challenged and their male-specific spaces invaded by women, as those are part of their male identity. Women displaying socially unacceptable gendered behaviour (e.g. having manly physique and self-confidence) have the tendency to challenge and sometimes undermine male preserves. This rationale, driven by male insecurities and hegemonic values, reflects what allegedly most men would want women to look like and dress like (e.g. wearing makeup and high heels), which do not necessarily lend themselves to pursuing sport and exercise. There are many examples in the sport world that demonstrate men's control over women's looks, one of which is the Amateur International Boxing Association's decision to 'phase in' skirts instead of shorts for women fighters for international competitions for achieving a 'womanly appearance' (Creighton, 2011). Beach volleyball regulations regarding women's uniform have been another controversy that signifies men's control over women's appearance – dress code in this case. These cases are directly dictated by aesthetic rationale from a male's point of view.

The second rationale, biological, seems to be rather convincing as it is often supported by (pseudo-) scientific evidence to claim that women are not genetically and biologically fit or 'designed' to partake in strenuous physical activities and that women are both physically and intellectually inferior to men. Accordingly, women should assume specific, restricted social roles that revolve around childbearing, motherhood, domestic duties, and other activities that are often viewed as requiring lesser physical strengths and intellectual skills.[3] For example, in the early 1900s, it was noted that women have narrower shoulders and less muscle than men, as they did not need 'the brawn from lifting and labouring …in the harder coarser ways; she is broader through the hips to give ample room for cradling her children' (Drake, 1901, cited in Weedon, 1999: 7). Weedon (1999) mentions that craniometry (measurement and study of the human skull) was frequently used to justify women's lesser intellectual and reasoning powers, given that they had smaller skulls than men. That is, biological reasoning has been used to exclude women from politics, education, and sports. In using both aesthetic and biological rationales, De Coubertin, founder of the modern Olympics, went to great lengths to exclude women from the Games by arguing that it was unaesthetic and against the laws of nature for women to partake in sports (Bandy, 2010b). He viewed the Games as 'the solemn and periodic exaltation of male athleticism, with internationalism as a base, loyalty as a means, art for its setting, and female applause for reward' (De Frantz, 1997: 18). Even in recent years, women's sports are trivialised/under-represented as they are considered not as good as men's and 'real' sports always involved men. The British Boxing Board of Control, for example, used biological reasons such as 'risk to an unborn child, menstrual pain and that premenstrual women were more accident and injury prone and more emotionally unstable' (Choi, 2000: 24) to refuse Jane Couch, welterweight boxing champion, her licence to box professionally. Couch took her case to a tribunal that ruled in her favour; thus, she is now allowed to fight professionally. Cases such as Couch's and the fact that elite female athletes can run faster, jump higher, and are stronger than the vast majority of the male population (think back to the preceding bodybuilding example) fundamentally undermines biological rationales for women's sport-related exclusion and marginalisation.

Finally, women's participation in sport was opposed based on the clash between qualities and behaviours associated with sports and femininity. Sport is one of the ultimate male preserves, an arena in which masculine values and behaviours can be learnt, reinforced, and displayed (Dunning, 1994). Sports 'are historically grounded in the values and experiences of men' (Coakley and Pike, 2009: 276). Consequently, features of sports are appropriate for and associated exclusively with men and masculinity (see Carroll, 1986). As a

162

corollary of this logic, female athletes are either considered as usurpers of this male domain or breakers of the traditional values of femininity. Women athletes are still often accused of having masculine features and displaying macho behaviour, thereby transgressing gendered borders and challenging gender logic. As outlined in the bodybuilding example, female athletes frequently put great effort into preserving their (traditional) femininity by employing various feminising practices such as wearing makeup and undergoing plastic surgery (see McGrath and Chananie-Hill, 2009). Therefore, Griffin (1998: 26) is correct in saying that 'women taking sport seriously is a feminist activity' as that entails violating conventional gender roles and crossing traditional gender barriers and expectations. The previously discussed rationales have been responded to by different branches of feminisms and generations of feminists, to which we will now turn our attention.

REFLECTION

Generally speaking, seminars are forums to look forward to when discussing gender issues. It is fascinating and educational (for both students and lecturers) to witness how traditional rationales and more modern views collide forming numerous debates. Here we provide some tips to get the debate going.

Sport participation and access to facilities are good starting points, and they provide plenty to talk about. It is often claimed that the playing field with regard to gender is more balanced now and that men are not as dominant anymore. Try to debunk these claims by bringing a daily newspaper to the seminar and check the sports pages bearing gender equity in mind.

In terms of access, men often believe that women involved in the same sport are afforded the same opportunities. So check whether it is true. Select a sport and athletes (both men and women) involved in it and ask them to describe what they are required to do to be able to train, such as do they have to pay a fee? If so, how much? How many times a week do they practice? What time of the day does their practice take place? Do they have to pay for travel and equipment? Do they have sponsors? Or go along to your local golf or bowling club and ask about their playing times and competitions. Are males and females treated identically?

FEMINISMS

Different feminist perspectives emerged at various points during the course of history. Branches of feminism surfaced in response to women's gradually changing social circumstances and to both external and internal critiques toward existing approaches (see next section). Generally, the history of feminist movements can be divided into three separate but interconnected waves, during which feminisms were and have been shaped.

The first wave (approximately 1860s–1930s)[4] of feminism was predominantly concerned with combating women's exclusion from the public sphere, legal inferiority, forced emotional and financial dependence on men, and fighting for suffrage. This historical era is characterised by the steady increase of feminist writings and the foundation of key women's rights organisations (e.g. Women's Social and Political Union, 1903) that became instrumental in promulgating feminist perspectives and ensuring that women's rights became part of political discussions. Women fought for voting rights, education, and access to paid jobs other than domestic duties. In sociology, women were in the shadow of men and received little encouragement and mention for their contribution. 'The classical women sociologists were perceived only as a marginal presence in the male discourse groups constructing sociology' (Lengermann and Brantley-Niebrugge, 2009: 127). For example, Marianne Weber, wife of Max Weber, was discouraged by her husband to continue with her intellectual journey and was advised to focus on domestic life instead. Due to blatant inequalities across the social tapestry, women of this era fought for equal rights, independence, and emancipation, leading to the emergence of liberal and Marxist feminism.

Liberal feminism

This branch of feminism revolves around the concept of *sameness* (i.e. men and women are socially capable of carrying out the same tasks and achievements if the same opportunities are provided) and is founded on the idea of liberalism, which is a political doctrine centred on creating and defending liberty and equal rights. Liberals generally believe in human rights, free speech, free and fair elections, principles of free market, and freedom of belief and religion. Liberalism as a political movement began to emerge in Europe in the seventeenth century and became widespread during the Age of Enlightenment (eighteenth century). Liberalism initially was a reaction to authoritarian governments such as monarchies and god kings. Early liberals (e.g. John Locke and Jeremy Bentham) argued against absolutist social control and advocated the formation of governments that were driven by rational laws and subject to the consent of the governed.

Liberal feminists thus see particular features of patriarchal social systems as oppressive to women and advocate that men and women should have equal rights and opportunities in all spheres of society, including sport and exercise. It has been observed on this account that, in Western societies, women are relegated to the private sphere (household), in which they perform an 'endless round of demanding, mindless, unpaid and undervalued tasks associated with housework, child care, and emotional, practical, and sexual servicing of adult men' (Lengermann and Brantley-Niebrugge, 1992: 463). Hence, generally speaking, liberal feminists attack sexism, which is a range of prejudices and discriminative practices often, though not exclusively, against women purely based on their gender. The underpinning argument against male dominance is that 'when women are given equal opportunities, they will actualise their potential ... and be rewarded equally for their talents' (Boutilier and SanGiovanni, 1994: 98–99). Interestingly, liberal feminists do not attack the foundation of existing social systems; they, however, believe that appropriate reforms within current socio-political structures can lead to gender equity. Feminists adopting this approach would campaign for equal opportunities in and access to, for instance, politics, education, and sports. They also insist on women's political and social issues to be in the public domain, which was traditionally and exclusively occupied by men's agendas.

Despite the argument that liberal feminism is now a minority approach in contemporary feminist theory (Lengermann and Brantley-Niebrugge, 1992), it has been instrumental in re-developing policies regarding equal rights, especially in America. Ratified in 1972, Title IX provision was based on principles of liberal feminism and thus prohibited any form of gender discrimination in state funded educational institutions with specific focus on women's and girls' access to sports facilities. Although sometimes received ambiguously

BIOGRAPHIC NOTE

Dissimilar to other theoretical perspectives, it is a challenging task to find a main originator for feminism, as it was and is a concerted effort of predominantly women to fight against the constraints of male domination and oppression. 'Twentieth-century feminism has no *Das Kapital*, no *New Testament*, no *Little Red Book*, no originating or primary text from which it derives and to which it constantly defers for guidance' (Humm, 1992: 13). Despite Humm's observation, some feminists may identify the work of Simone De Beauvoir (*The Second Sex*, 1949 and 1953 in English) as fundamental to the development of second-wave feminism. Nevertheless, here we focus on one person who played a crucial part in the early development of feminist movements. For us Charlotte Perkins Gilman stood out.

Charlotte Perkins (1860–1935) was born in Hartford, Connecticut. Having had a trying childhood and an unfulfilling marriage, Gilman often suffered from bouts of serious depression, for which the treatment of the time was complete rest and domestic isolation. She wrote about this personal experience in the short story entitled *The Yellow Wallpaper* (1890), a semi-autobiographic piece depicting the psychological sufferings of an idle married woman. Unusual of that time, she left her husband and remarried to Houghton Gilman with whom she lived until her husband's sudden death in 1934.

Gilman believed that with modernity, humankind acquired the chance to develop into a much more balanced and equal society, in which novel, more cooperative gender roles would emerge. Therefore, she became an advocate for women's active involvement in public life and education. Gilman developed a solid and growing reputation as a writer toward the end of the nineteenth century, but her international recognition came only after the publication of *Women and Economics: The Economic Relation between Men and Women as a Factor in Social Evolution* (1898). In this work, she fundamentally critiques women's continuous economic dependency on men (sexuo-economic relations); a situation that greatly hinders women's liberation from the shackles of the household and prevents women from achieving their potential. Gilman believed that social, gendered structures and the uninterrupted perpetuation of those by both genders are responsible for women's enslavement (and, to some extent, men's enslavement, too; see her short story on *Mr. Peebles' Heart*, 1997). To break from this enslavement, she suggested the professionalization of housework, encouraging women to hire housekeepers and cooks to release them from housework (See also Gilman's short story entitled *Making a Change*, 1997).

Gilman was most productive in the first decade of the 1900s when she released *Concerning Children* (1900), *The Home: Its Work and Influence* (1903), *Human Work* (1904), and *The Man-Made World, or, Our Androcentric Culture* (1911). In these, she generally challenged social stereotypes about women and, to some extent, men by arguing against the 'natural' divide between the genders, which had led to a specific division of labour. Gilman claimed that women are not allowed to achieve their potential if they are tied to the kitchen, household, and raising children. When they are tasked with such duties, they cannot develop otherwise as their time and energy are consumed by those activities. Hence, she advocated the foundation of nurseries that were to benefit both women and children. Gilman argued that the common belief that after giving birth women automatically became knowledgeable (god-given wisdom) of how to raise children was nonsensical. 'So she preached that a majority of children under school age were being ruined in their homes' (Gale, 1990: xl). Despite her advanced views on the social construction of gender, Gilman harboured racist and xenophobic sentiments (see Gilman, 1990; McLennan, 2011). (For more information about the fascinating life of Gilman, see *The Living of Charlotte Perkins Gilman*, 1990.)

(see Boutilier and SanGiovanni, 1994), Title IX has been considered a milestone in the fight for gender equity in the field of organised sports. Progress toward a more egalitarian society can also be observed in the Olympic Games, where the number of events for women has significantly increased since the inception of the modern Olympics. Choi (2000) also notes that as women gained wider access to and more opportunities in sport, their performances in many events have begun to closely match men's achievements. Progress is undeniable. Nevertheless, we still do not live in a completely egalitarian society. (Regarding women's marginalisation in the media, see studies by Duncan and Messner, 2005, and Messner and Cooky, 2010.) Having equal opportunities in sport and other social spheres may not be sufficient for women to participate and achieve their potential in sports and find fulfilment in exercise.

MARXIST FEMINISM

Enjoying the full benefits of equal access (presuming its existence) can be curbed by the material and economic subordination that women were/are often subjected to in pre-modern, modern, and contemporary societies. One could argue, 'What is the point of granting wider access to women in sport and exercise if women do not have the financial means to take advantage of them or have to rely on their husband for the necessary financial support?' In other words, 'Marxist feminism rejects the possibility that any real equality of opportunity can exist in a society where wealth and power rest in the hands of an elite ruling class' (Boutilier and SanGiovanni, 1994: 99). Marxist feminists would go further than most liberal feminists and would point out that making amendments to the existing legal system to create a more egalitarian society is only paying lip service to women's social needs and opportunities because, in a capitalist, free market-driven society (supported by liberal principles), women are financially marginalized and in dependency and hold little economic power. Consequently, Marxist feminists argue that class division and related structural oppression are chiefly responsible for women's marginalisation in public spheres that are in some shape or form associated with economic power. In this sense, 'Marxian feminism brings together Marxian class analysis and feminist social protest' (Lengermann and Brantley-Niebrugge, 1992: 466).

This branch of feminism is associated with the work of Karl Marx, although it was Friedrich Engels (Marx's junior partner) who laid the foundations of this feminist perspective in *The Origins of the Family, Private Property and the State* (1884). Marx and Engels both focused on the economic oppression of the working classes by the upper class. In brief, according to Marx, the upper class owns the means of production and raw materials and, thus, workers find themselves in a socially and economically disadvantageous, subservient position (for a detailed account on Marxism, see Chapter 4). The feminist translation of Marx's economic dependency argument is that in addition to the upper–working-class exploitative relation, women form another sub-layer of exploitative relations as they, most of the time, perform labour that, although deemed essential, is unpaid. That is, sexism is perpetuated across society as it serves the needs and dominant position of the male power elite. This observation was also true to male-centred Marxist organisations such as trade unions, in which men restricted women to having only family support roles to play. In fact, Weedon (1999: 17) notes that 'first-wave feminism was identified by Marxists as a bourgeois deviation from class struggle for a socialist revolution'. Therefore, the chief focus of Marxist feminism has been 'to determine the ways in which the institution of the family and women's domestic labour are structured by, and 'reproduced', the sexual division of labour' (Humm, 1992: 87).

In sports, men still have more and wider opportunities to turn professional and make a living out of practicing and performing sports (for examples, see Coakley and Pike, 2009, and Kay and Jeanes, 2009). For instance, to relate back to the bodybuilding example at the beginning of this chapter, female bodybuilders generally have fewer opportunities than men to turn professional. We use the case of Joanna Thomas to illustrate women's financial marginalisation in sport. Joanna was born in England in 1976 and became interested in bodybuilding at the age of fourteen. When she first entered the gym and declared her intention to build muscle, the gym owner's wife said, 'You leave that to the men, dear' (http://joannathomas.com/about.html). Regardless of the advice, Joanna became serious about bodybuilding and, after the age of seventeen, began a successful campaign as an amateur athlete, winning the British championship in 1998. Later she moved to America to partake in further competitions and increase her muscle mass and definition. In 2005, she was the focus of a documentary (*Supersize She*), broadcast on Channel 5 in the United Kingdom, in which she confessed that her opportunities for making sufficient money out of bodybuilding were limited and, to supplement her income, she featured on web sites that exposed nude pictures of herself to paying customers (see http://joannathomas.com/home.html). She bemoaned that she was often treated as a sex object, not as an athlete; could not secure sponsorship; and had to fully rely on revenue generated from her web site. Marxist feminists would argue that Joanna's situation derives from inequality in social structures that operate within bodybuilding (and society at large). Those structures have preferential treatments for men and their activities and discriminate against female athletes. To indicate the still-significant differentials in earning power between men and women, in 2011 the prize money allocated for the Mr. Olympia competition was $600.000 and $60,000 for the Ms. Olympia. In a few sports, the gap between financial rewards for men and women have been redressed (e.g. tennis) but, in most instances, financial inequalities are still present.

Radical feminism

During the first wave of feminism, Marxism was the main alternative to liberalism (Weedon, 1999). However, in the 1960s with the advent of the second wave of feminism (1960s–1980s), new issues began to emerge, along with a new body of feminism. Consequently, the second wave of feminism, and radical feminism that grew out of it, concentrated on turning private troubles into public matters by acknowledging that 'the personal is political'. Radical feminism, a progressive movement promoting fundamental social change, rejected both liberal and Marxist approaches due to their inherent limitations. Liberal feminists have the tendency to speak of and represent an abstract group of women and thus neglect class, gender, and race issues. Marxist feminists, conversely, pay too much and almost exclusive attention to class and economic issues, which, although relevant, do not fully explain the sophisticated and deeply rooted system of male domination. Radical feminists argue that gender oppression is 'the historically earliest, the most universal, and the most difficult to eradicate' (Boutilier and SanGiovanni, 1994: 99) and, in turn, suggest alternative strategies to combat it. So, if patriarchal domination is deeply ingrained into societies, more complex than outlined by liberal and Marxist feminists and is a subtle gendered controlling force, what can women do to challenge and, perhaps, defeat it?

Sub-groups of radical feminism may have somewhat different answers to this question but, we think, they would essentially agree that

170

defeating patriarchy 'must begin with a basic reworking of women's consciousness so that each woman recognizes her own values and strength; rejects patriarchal pressures to see herself as weak, dependent and second-class' (Lengermann and Brantley-Niebrugge, 1992: 475). Men are perceived as colonisers and captors of both women's minds and bodies, and it is the agenda of second-wave feminists to unmask patriarchy's invasion of women's private life. Thus, the focus of radical feminism is the female body, through which women have historically been identified and oppressed as social machines of reproduction and child minding. One way for women to rid the shackles of patriarchy and overcome their own 'biological fate' is to gain (or reclaim) control over reproductive rights. Humm (1992: 53) observes that 'second wave feminism takes as its starting point the politics of reproduction'. In other words, women's control over reproduction (e.g. birth control, voluntary sterilisation, and abortion) would reduce their dependency on men and allow them a greater chance at self-actualisation. Furthermore, radical feminists argue that the current patriarchal system cannot be reformed (as suggested by liberal feminists) but would need to be dismantled and a new social system rebuilt form scratch, using women as the point of origin (Jarvie and Maguire, 1994). Birrell (2002: 65) writes that 'sport as we know it must be entirely dismantled so that a feminist alternative might be constructed'. That is, it makes little sense for women to try to fit into and achieve in a system that was originally created for men by men to perpetuate masculinity and male dominance.

According to radical feminists, regardless of progress made by liberal and Marxist feminists, women still have to play by man-made rules and meet male hegemonic expectations if they want to partake in sport and exercise. Given that radical feminism has paid extensive attention to the social control and male colonisation of the female body, let's refer back to the bodybuilding example yet again. Radical feminists would argue that despite crossing gendered borders by becoming a bodybuilder, women are still engulfed by man-made structures and expectations regarding their corporeal display. In other words, female bodybuilders, and other athletes too, have to be 'doing girl' to fit in and to be accepted by current structures. Women conforming to male-designed structures can be observed when female athletes apply makeup, undergo plastic surgery, wear revealing (often uncomfortable) clothing, and perform sport-specific tasks in high-heeled shoes to appear more feminine and conform to the traditional image of femininity envisioned and enforced by the male judging panel. Choi (2000) explains that it is not the most muscular female bodybuilder who wins competitions (which would be the main criterion for male bodybuilders), but it is the one who manages to achieve the best balance between appearing muscular while still retaining her femininity. Therefore, as long as patriarchal structures and practices are dominant in society, women will always be oppressed and marginalized, and the only way to redress this subjugation is, radical feminists would argue, by creating new ones in which women have central roles.

Post-modern feminism(s)

Despite the more inclusive approach adopted by radical feminists, they still seemed to represent women as a unified group, jointly aiming to overthrow patriarchy. However, as feminist thinkers, scholars, and activists of the second wave uncovered, explored, and voiced more and more issues, a pluralisation (emergence of a number of diverse ideas) of feminist theoretical perspectives began to appear. Theory pluralisation, in a field already theoretically assorted, led to the materialization of what is now called the third wave (1980s onward) of feminism. The chief characteristic of feminist approaches of this wave is the rejection of essentialist representations and monolithic concepts of women, gender, and femininity. That is, third-wave feminists critique, but also build upon, work produced in the second wave and 'attacks universalism and describes and celebrates the experiences of many 'different' women' (Humm, 1992: 193). Burman (1992: 45) explains: 'What we need is a feminist realism that does not resort to positivism, that ties discourse to politics, and that makes politics more than discursive'. In achieving such aims, feminists of the third wave have adopted a range of post-modern/post-structuralist concepts and approaches – including elements of queer theory, women-of-colour consciousness, post-colonial theory, ecofeminism, transgender politics, and deconstruction of the gender binary, to name but a few – to interpret women's wide-ranging positions and oppressions in contemporary society, including sport and exercise. Post-modern feminists, similar to post-modernist scholars in general, aim to capture the plurality of contemporary social phenomena with specific focus placed on women and their varied experiences affected by divergent forms of social stratification. Post-modern feminists turn against the ideas, promises, and achievements of modernity to challenge grand narratives and recognise the plural subtleties of contemporary social existence (for a more detailed discussion of post-modernity, see Chapter 9).

By rejecting modernist ideas and grand narratives (a comprehensive explanation of how society operates), post-modern feminists turned toward *deconstructing* features of patriarchy and related oppression. They pay specific attention to the male/female aspect of the Western binary conceptual system. Western binaries such as man/woman, body/mind, and nature/culture do not signify simply difference but a hierarchy, exposing latent power relations between, in this case, men and women. Differently put, by deconstructing and, in turn, revealing that gender difference is socially constructed and is perpetuated through our culture of binary oppositions, post-modern feminists exposed a culturally inherent power imbalance between men and women that is reinforced through domineering gender discourses (for a theoretical overview of ways of deconstructing heteronormativity discourses in sport studies, see Sykes, 2006). These discourses 'shape [among other things] sexual identities and sexual practises in profound ways' (Weedon, 1999: 24) that were not fully explored by previous feminist approaches. Hargreaves (2004: 189) explains that post-modern feminists 'have focused particularly on the body, sexuality and identity'. Of particular relevance has been Michel Foucault's theories regarding (bio-) power, surveillance, and discipline (see Chapter 9) to unfold the ways in which sport and exercise can act as a form of domination which locks women into a web of normalising practices (Markula, 2003). In exploring Foucault's relevance to sport and exercise, Pirkko Markula's work stands out, which extensively informed discussion on women's (lack of) empowerment in and through physical activity (Markula, 1995, 2001, 2003).

CRITIQUING FEMINISM

Feminism is in a somewhat unique position in terms of its critiques as it has been challenged both from the outside and from within. Feminist thinkers occupying one of the branches of feminist theory often point out the limitations of other perspectives by highlighting specific interest groups (e.g. class, race, sexual orientation) that have been neglected or marginalised (Birell, 2002). For instance, representatives of queer theory would point out the limitations of those feminist perspectives that, while detesting male hegemony, buy into the concept of heteronormativity (normalisation and dominance of heterosexuality). To trouble the dominance of heterosexuality and related ideologies, queer theorists would aim at 'avoiding normative and essentialising identities; resisting regimes of the 'normal'; violating compulsory sex/gender relations; dismantling binary gender relations; and undermining heteronormative hegemonic discourses' (Caudwell, 2006: 2). Evans (1997: 17) also described this dual struggle as follows:

> ...those of us teaching Women's Studies have been arguing with the... battalions of male chauvinism...[and] we have also faced... opposition... from other feminists who have voiced either their misgivings or outright hostility to the mere idea of Women's Studies.

To further illustrate the internal critique present in feminism, the limitations of liberal feminism are often revealed by outlining its ignorance of power, class, and race differences between women. When discussing the relation between gender and technology, Gill and Grint (1995: 7) argue that 'liberal feminism is clearly theoretically underdeveloped. Its critique of existing social relations does not bear sustained analysis, since gender is presented both as being profoundly important... and simultaneously as having had no impact on technologies or any other social products'. The overemphasis on gender and the negligence of key social categories such as nationality, age, and religion is 'a serious problem for those engaged in critical analysis of sport [and exercise] because gender is only one part of the interconnected matrix of relations' (Birell, 2002: 65). As a response to these limitations and internal critiques, 'monocausal and totalizing theories of patriarchy have largely been replaced by multifaceted explorations' (Kemp and Squires, 1997: 6), and contemporary feminist theory has demonstrated a move toward theoretical synthesis and a 'shift from woman to women to reflect the vast experiential diversity of women's lives' (Birell 2002: 65, italics in original).

Though feminist thinkers may extensively debate the future direction(s) of their own and competing theoretical approaches, by

174

establishing common moral and political positions, they all agree on the need for feminist analyses and discourse in society and sociology (Ramazanoğlu and Holland, 2002). External critiques take a view that is the polar opposite and argue, in different shape or form, against the need for any feminist perspective. The pinnacle of antagonism takes place between feminists and anti-feminists. Anti-feminists aim to annihilate feminism, as they see it as the ultimate cause of most of our social issues/troubles and argue that it paralyses social progress and development. For instance, the Anti-Feminism Worldwide web site (www.antifeminism-international.org) says that 'Feminism belongs to the dustbin of history'. Other arguments include the blaming of feminism and feminists for the break up of traditional social order and the prevalence of casual sex, pornography, homosexuality, and the loss of (traditional man-made) femininity through participating in masculinising sport activities. Birell (2002) mentions three main critiques toward feminism: (1) biological determinism, that is, men and women are different by 'design' (nature) and thus should have different social roles and expectations; (2) scientific credibility, meaning that feminist studies lack the quality and robustness of traditional (men-made) scientific approaches as they are value-laden, self-interest-driven, and subjectivist; and, finally, (3) the cumbersomeness of equal rights legislations (e.g. Title IX and Affirmative Action) that have created societies in which women enjoy more advantages than men.

In brief, let's look at the critiques mentioned by Birell (2002). Despite it being deemed obsolete, biological determinism (biologism) still seems to be referred to when discussing gender roles and relations in society. According to this account, due to distinct physiological differences, men and women should occupy different positions in any given culture that would aid and maintain the harmonious functioning of society (cf. Functionalism in Chapter 3). It is argued that gender-based differences can be detected in every society and that these natural factors were/are reflected in inequalities between genders (e.g. men hunt and women gather and look after offspring). To translate this perspective into sport and exercise, women and men should partake in different, gender-appropriate sports and physical activities that would reinforce their gendered social functions and positions. For instance, men should play football and rugby (sports requiring extensive physical contact) and lift weights to reinforce their biologically determined (superior) social position. Conversely, women should participate in gymnastics and synchronised swimming (sports requiring little to no physical contact) and attend aerobic classes to stay (or become) slim and toned as indicated by dominant media discourses (Markula, 2001). What seems to be often ignored by arguments adopting or borrowing from biologism is that social activities, roles, and perceptions are not biologically created but socially manufactured. Social perceptions of the physical human body, its needs and functions, change over time and, in turn, so do social meanings associated with it. Giddens (2006: 459) points out that the 'natural difference' theory is often embedded in research on animal behaviour 'rather than in anthropological or historical evidence about human behaviour', not to mention the fact, that with the emergence of sex-reassignment surgery and transexuality, it has become possible to change both sex and gender. Consequently, one can argue that not even one's biological sex is fixed for life and that women who have undergone sex-reassignment can assume male identities and roles in society.

REFLECTION

To provide a sport-related example on gender transformation, we refer to the case of Heidi Krieger, who was an East German shot putter and one of the victims of her country's centralised doping regime. Due to the excessive doping that she had received during her athletic career, she began to develop physical features that are considered masculine and, when finally giving up sport, was left with those masculine features. As a result, Krieger underwent sex-reassignment surgery in 1997 and became Andreas Krieger. Andreas still suffers from both physical and psychological scars incurred through sport but has assumed a different gender identity and is now married to Ute Krause – another sufferer of the East German sport production machinery. This example supports the argument that not even sex is fixed, and it is possible for both men and women to assume gender identities associated with the opposite sex.

The second critique is the lack of scientific robustness and objectivity of feminist studies. This assessment of feminism has come from dominant scientific approaches observing that feminists have failed to 'produce adequately rational, scientific or unbiased knowledge' (Ramazanoğlu and Holland, 2002: 3). Though it is naive to argue that

176

feminist perspectives and research embedded in these practices are objective, so is it to claim that research interpreting society from other theoretical positions is more so. For instance, to turn this argument on its head, critics of feminist thought when denouncing feminism as subjectivist, embroiled in self-motivated political agendas, themselves promote their own androcentric self-interest and political platform whereby they wish to maintain and/or restore their own (Western rational male) hegemony across society. In this sense, mainstream research has become 'male-stream' research and scientific practice (for more in-depth discussion, see Malson, 1998: 34-37). In other words, declaring that feminism is self-centred and self-serving and other theoretical approaches are not is as false as claiming that there is social research that is fully objective and exempt from political undercurrents and personal bias. In this sense, this critique is not unique to feminism and is suffered by most other less traditional approaches that can be perceived as genuine instances of a paradigm shift (see Evans, 1997) and, in turn, experience a clash with the Western scientific establishment regarding the way knowledge should be generated. Besides, feminism as a theoretical framework and an academic discipline has never fully enjoyed dominant status and been continuously forced to prove its credentials. Given that feminism is scrutinised from both the outside and the inside, feminist scholars are continuously kept on their theoretical and methodological 'toes'. It can, therefore, be argued that feminisms are theoretically and methodologically more robust and tested than some of the traditionally established theories. In fact, we would point out that one of the major strengths of feminist studies has been their struggle for becoming accepted and acknowledged through incessant dialogues inside and outside of academia.

The final point that we will discuss and is often brought up against feminism is the unfair advantages women have gained through the political movement that is, by and large, associated with the second wave of feminism. The unfair-advantage claim can be relatively easily rebutted by looking at gender equity statistics in various social spheres. For instance, 'the media seem stuck in a very traditional and stereotypical groove' (Ross and Byerly, 2004: 9) in which women still are frequently sexualised, portrayed through the lens of traditional femininity, and underrepresented in leadership positions. Grey (2006: 492) also points out that 'women make up slightly more than 50% of the world's population, yet average only 16% of the world's elected political posts'. Sreberny and van Zoonen (2000: 1) make a related observation regarding politics and femininity and argue that 'it is not uncommon to see politics and femininity constructed as each other's antithesis' and, thus, women being underrepresented. In a similar vein, sport and femininity have been considered as each other's antithesis and, although the gender balance in sports has become more even as more women have been participating in sports and exercise than before (Coakley and Pike, 2009), we have to be cautious when claming that equality has been reached.

A report on gender asymmetry in interuniversity (varsity) sports was released in late 2011 by the Centre of Sport Policy Studies (CSPS) in Canada. The CSPS's first gender equity report – that is, a biannual series tracking gender equity in participation opportunities and leadership positions – highlights both improvements and issues to address. Though there has been an increase in the number of women's sport teams and women's sport participation[5] at Canadian universities, it is noted that women are greatly underrepresented in leadership positions. To be precise, according to the CSPS's report, women occupy only 19 percent of head coach positions and only 17 percent of the athletic director positions. Coakley and Pike (2009: 273) note that 'only approximately one-third of the board members of the UK Sport Councils are female, and some national governing bodies... have no women on their boards'. International sport governing bodies are no exception; for example, the IOC has an all-male executive committee. By virtue of the preceding, we would argue that despite the increase in women's sport and exercise participation over the last thirty years[6], there is still a significant disparity in managerial and leadership potions between genders (See also Kay and Jeanes, 2009 and Shaw, 2006a, 2006b, 2006c). Consequently, to state that women have gained an (unfair) advantage over men in society due to feminist movements is unrealistic and ignorant of the aforementioned facts.

REFLECTION

You can investigate the degree to which women are still underrepresented in leadership positions by checking the number of female members of the national governing body of your sport activity and female coaches in your local area.

178

FURTHER READING

Despite the fact that feminism was a relative latecomer in sociology, there are numerous sources available that are relevant and useful to get better acquainted with this theoretical perspective and the issues it is concerned with. In terms of the general sociology of gender, Judith Butler is one of the most well known contemporary academics. Her most influential book is entitled *Gender Trouble* (1990), in which she questioned and deconstructed traditional/modernist conceptions of gender. Butler's ideas have shaped contemporary (post-modern) feminist thought and as such is a relevant source for further engagement with feminism. We would exercise a note of caution here, Butler has been extensively influenced by Foucault; thus, her work has the tendency to require an advanced knowledge of sociology and feminism. Also relevant but, perhaps, more accessible is the work of Judith Lorber (*Breaking the Bowls: Degendering and Feminist Change*, 2005; *Gender Inequality: Feminist Theories and Politics* (4th ed.), 2010). In the United Kingdom, Mary Evans, professor of Women's Studies, could be mentioned. Evans has written extensively on gender and related issues. She has also compiled introductory and more-advanced textbooks that provide useful overviews (e.g. *Gender and Social Theory*, 2003 and *Handbook of Gender and Women's Studies*, 2006).

In the area of sociology of sport and exercise, we must mention the pioneering work of Jennifer Hargreaves, who has widely written on women's (lack of) engagement with sport and exercise (e.g. *Sporting Females*, 1994). To provide a non-exhaustive list, other notable feminist academics in the field of sport and exercise are Susan Birrell; Mary McDonald (*Reading Sport: Critical Essays on Power and Representation*, 2000); Susan Bandy; Anne Darden (*Crossing Boundaries*, 1999); and Jayne Caudwell (*Sport, Sexualities and Queer / Theory*, 2006).

CHAPTER 9

POST-MODERN PERSPECTIVES

Post-modern theoretical thinking has not fully penetrated sociological explanations of sports and exercise. Despite its gradually growing popularity and significance, post-modern thought is still amiss in sport studies (Jarvie and Maguire, 1994; Rail, 1998; Andrews, 2000). Though there might be multiple reasons for post-modern thought's absence, we must consider the ways in which this perspective(s) has contributed and can contribute to our understanding of contemporary sports and exercise practices. Let's look at an example through which we will illustrate the need for post-modernist thinking.

Imagine that you are in the gym and cycling on an indoor bike. You prefer cycling indoors as you do not feel safe on the road by yourself in the evening, try to avoid negotiating heavy traffic and air pollution, or simply do not want to face the elements and want a more controlled environment. While on the bike, you have your mobile at hand through which you can check your e-mails, browse the web, listen to music, access various social networking sites, check sport results, catch up on current affairs and read a book. You are wearing hi-tech compression shorts, a pair of state-of-the-art trainers, and sipping on one of the popular sport drinks containing 'essential' electrolytes. (Have you ever wondered what these might be and how essential they are?) The indoor bike itself is equipped with a range of gadgetry: You can monitor your speed, distance cycled, duration of your exercise, calories burnt, cadence, and heart rate (given that you are wearing a cardio-tester belt). The bike is also fitted with an LCD screen so while cycling, listening to music, 'checking in' on a social networking site, you are watching one of the TV channels on offer.

For the sake of this example, let's say that you have selected one of the contemporary music channels, plugged in your headphones, and are now drawn into a music video clip. Without having a crystal ball, we can probably predict that you are watching 'attractive' men and women singing, dancing, and assuming sexually suggestive positions following the tune of the music. By *attractive* it is usually meant that women are slim and toned and wearing makeup and men are big and muscular (they can also be toned and more and more frequently wear makeup). The mirrors are plentiful in the gym, which allows you to compare your body to those featured on TV. Whether you are or are not satisfied with what you see and who you are, what is certain is that you (we perhaps all) are 'plugged in' and heavily influenced, in some shape or form, by the technological advances of post-modernity.

Features, consequences, and technological inventions of post-modernity are impossible to escape. They penetrate all aspects of social life, and sports and exercise are no exceptions. Technological inventions have been affecting the way we watch, perceive, and consume sport and the way we think about, do, and consume exercise. Social conditions triggered by post-modernity are fairly recent and, thus, one can argue that theoretical perspectives developed in pre-modern and modern times cannot sufficiently explain our 'runaway world'[1]. Giddens (1999: 1) argued that there are reasons to believe that 'we are living through a major period of historical transition' and that we 'face risk situations no one in previous history has had to confront' (1999: 3). New social challenges and issues (e.g. sedentary lifestyle and obesity) 'stretch' our thinking and require novel theoretical insights to explain them. Thinkers adopting post-modernity have attempted to

---

REFLECTION

Having read and thought about the preceding example illustrating some aspects of post-modernity, think about questions sociologists would ask in attempting to better understand the nature of post-modernity (i.e. what the foregoing example described). What issues do you think sociologists would need to consider? Furthermore, think about the ways in which you and people you know are plugged into and influenced by post-modern technological inventions on a daily basis.

interpret, respond to, and provide remedies for the malaise brought forth by post-modern social conditions. To understand post-modern conditions and how they have come about, we must trace their historical roots. Hence, in the following part of this chapter, after attempting to define what post-modernity is, we will outline the shift from modernity to post-modernity.[2]

POST-MODERNITY DEFINED

When you open a book that has 'post-modernity' in its title, it is probable that in the introduction you will read something such as 'It is a challenging enterprise (or mission impossible – see the preface to Lyon, 1994) to define post-modernity because it can stand (and has stood) for a multitude of things and can cover a wide range of phenomena' (Farganis, 2004). Evidently, post-modernity tries to capture the plurality of contemporary social phenomena where 'anything goes'. For instance, post-modernity has become part of a range of academic disciplines such as anthropology, philosophy, economic, and sociology (Smart, 1993). Besides being part of academic thought, post-modernity is pertinent in other social spheres. It is also a social movement that first grew in popularity in New York around the 1960s in the circles of young artists and writers forming a *contra* movement against the existing modern over-institutionalisation (Rail, 1998). Jencks (1986) argues that *post-modernity* is a controversial term that has challenged philosophy and practices of modern arts. 'Postmodernism, then, is not easily encapsulated in one phrase since it has been used in various disciplines' (Rail, 2002: 180). Hebdige (1988: 181) expresses the intricacy of defining postmodernism as follows: 'It becomes more and more difficult to...specify exactly what it is that "postmodernism" is supposed to refer to as the term gets stretched in all directions across different debates, different disciplinary and discursive boundaries'. Consequently, it is safe to say that post-modernity has been used by many theorists to express and interpret the complexity, plurality, and fluidity of contemporary social conditions (think of the previous exercise example).

Nevertheless, when hard pressed, some definitions can be located that give us a general idea of what post-modernity might be. For instance, Smart (1993: 12) defines post-modernism as 'a form of life, a form of reflection upon and a response to the accumulating signs of the limits and limitations of modernity'. Also, post-modernity refers to general social conditions of the economically developed societies that began in the twentieth century and accelerated in the 1970s and 1980s (Hebdige (1988). Post-modernity is often associated with post-industrialism and post-Marxist social order (Farganis, 2004). Simply put, to Giddens (1990), post-modernity is a form of life beyond modernity.

Based on the preceding and on general perceptions of what post-modernity is or has been considered to be, we see post-modernity as a turn against the ideas, promises, and achievements of modernity to challenge grand narratives and recognise the plural subtleties of contemporary social existence. Post-modernity is a reaction against an ordered view of the modern world and fixed ideas about the forms and meanings of (social) texts. In its reaction against modernist ideals and to create ways of better capturing reality (or realities), post-modern writings and arts emphasise employing devices such as *bricolage* (this term is also associated with cultural studies). Post-modernity has also led to a proliferation of critical theories, most notably deconstructionism, and the breaking down of disciplinary silos and the distinction between high and pop culture (Boyne and Rattansi, 1990). In addition, post-modernity is interconnected with globalisation and technological development in a way that global satellites and other broadcasting systems have created a post-modern environment that has modified local identities, cultures, and social practices (Ward, 1997). For post-modernists, the endless 'proliferation of products and images [across the globe] strongly figures in their "story" of the post modern' (Rail, 1998: xiii). That 'story' – like the exerciser on the indoor bike – of post-modernity is elusive, multidimensional, and idiosyncratic, which are probably the reasons why it is challenging to find a single, all-embracing definition.

REFLECTION

Think of the gym exerciser example detailed at the beginning of this chapter and explain how that (all or various aspects of it) fits in with the definition(s) of post-modernity. What are the features of post-modernity that have made that example a reality? What do you think post-modernity has done to sports and exercise?

FROM MODERNITY TO POST-MODERNITY[3]

There are sceptics who would protest against using post-modernity as an historically defining term (or, in fact, protest against using the term at all), and even David Lyon, who wrote a book entitled *Postmodernity*, makes the following prediction: 'The idea of postmodernity may yet turn out to be a figment of overheated academic imagination, popular hype, or disappointed radical hopes' (Lyon, 1994: 4). Though it is good practice to be critical of post-modernity (or, for that matter, any other social theory), questioning whether our contemporary era turns out to be only an extension of modernity, late-modernity or, indeed, post-modernity (or post-post-modernity; see Palmer, 1977) may not be as relevant as the qualitative socio-cultural, political, and economic changes societies (especially Occidental ones) have undergone in the last fifty to sixty years. In other words, regardless of what we may or may not label the most recent historical epoch, we have been experiencing new forms of art, cultural exchanges, consumption of products and services, and sports and exercise. Therefore, in this sub-section, we aim to provide a brief overview of the cultural shift from modernity to post-modernity and to present you with an historical outline that will give you an idea how this shift challenging modernity has taken place (see Table 9.1).

Modernity began to gradually supersede pre-modern, pre-industrial feudal societies around the sixteenth century, which were fundamentally embedded in agricultural production, manual manufacturing, and

Table 9.1 General features of pre-, post- and industrial societies (based on Bell, 1973)

	Pre-Industrial	Industrial	Post-Industrial
Domination	Farmers, fishermen, miners and un-skilled workers	Semi-skilled workers and engineers	Professionals and technical scientists
Challenges	To extract things from nature	To deal with/operate machinery more efficiently	To provide services based on knowledge difference
Power	Land owners and military hold power, which manifests in direct use of force	Business people exercise power via influencing politicians	Scientist and researcher come to fore as the dominant figures in seeking to balance technical and political forces

184

REFLECTION

Should you wish to further your knowledge about the links between modernity and post-modernity and industrialisation and post-industrialisation and their consequences and discontents, you will find plenty of useful sources (e.g. Bell, 1973; Featherstone, 1991; Bauman, 1997).

(mono- or multi-) deity-centred social practices. Political power and influence were associated with land (and/or religion), and production was directly reliant and dependent on nature and on people extracting produce from nature. Modernity parted with pre-modern times by featuring significant advances in the fields of science, technology, and politics. Instead of exclusively relying on magico-mythical guidance from a deity or deities or their earthly representatives, logical and rational explanations and directions began to be sought out. Rationalising nature and social practices emerged as the norm, and scientists were in search of the ultimate, objective truth (searching for the ultimate truth derives from the idea of positivism, associated with the work of Auguste Comte (1798–1857), which is still dominant in many natural sciences). Power became associated with industry, and business owners' political influence grew. There was also a shift from producing with/through nature to producing with/through machinery and an emerging need to build, maintain, and operate machinery. The gradually growing industry (especially the industrial revolution) and its need for semi-skilled workers eventually led to urbanisation and a fundamental shift from agricultural to an industry-based economy. These social processes gradually restructured the social, economic, and power arrangements of Western societies and remained dominant until the end of the first half of the twentieth century.

When and how post-modernity emerged is extensively debated (see Rose, 1991); however, in discussing post-modernity, we refer to an historical era that followed modernity, indicating a cultural shift in multiple social spheres. That is, 'to speak of postmodernity is to suggest an epochal shift or break from modernity involving the emergence of a new social totality with its own distinct organising principles' (Featherstone, 1991: 3). Post-modernity essentially is a way of coping with the general disappointment in modernist goals and desires. Post-

In what ways do you think the emergence of modernity, industrial-isation, and urbanisation have influenced the development of modern sports and leisure activities? You would probably need to think about when, where, and how sports were created and to contemplate the concept of rational recreation.

modern societies are dominated by professionals and scientists who hold specialist knowledges and are often called upon to provide advice on social situations involving politics, economy, and health. Scientists are becoming a permanent feature of the news and specialist programmes in the media.[4] For instance, you may have seen experts voicing their views on the harmful effects of tobacco, alcohol, recreational drugs, and the benefits of exercise and healthy dieting (see, 5-a-day health campaign by NSH; http://www.nhs.uk/livewell/5aday).

The service industry has also demonstrated a significant growth spurt. Bell (1973) observes that after the 1950s, the number of white-collar workers began to overtake the number of blue-collar ones, resulting in the majority of jobs now existing in the service industry in most Western countries. We, thus, rely on one another's services as society has become so complex that one cannot be familiar with each and every aspect of it. We call upon solicitors when we want to buy a house, we see financial advisors when intending to invest, we seek the help of personal trainers when we want to lose weight or tone muscles, and we can spend hours in a sport shop buying the most appropriate running shoes fitted and advised by an expert. They all posses specialist knowledge that we purchase and use to our ends.

Consequently, in post-modern societies, power is directly associated with scientific knowledge and information: knowledge that is generated by science (everything has to be 'clinically proven' – check how many times this phrase appears in advertisements) and information distributed by the mass media.[5] Interestingly, post-modernity also challenges previous priorities regarding science's obsession with finding the ultimate truth. This is based on the premise that if societies and social rules (even fundamental ones) are socially constructed by humans, those can be changed and interpreted in multiple ways. If

186

Another example of knowledge relevance is the proliferation of universities and the increasing number of university students. Students enrol in universities and pay for their learning (i.e. to gain knowledge in a specialised area). (That our society is highly specialised is reflected by the proliferation of university degrees. For instance, if you study at a sport and exercise department, you could be enrolled on sport psychology, sport studies, sports science, sport business, sport management, or sport development degree programmes.) Universities are the holders of knowledge, for which you as a student pay and, by completing your course, you earn specialist knowledge and the qualification to prove that knowledge (see also end note 4). That qualification then grants you access to becoming a sport psychologist, a personal trainer, or the manager of a sport facility. That is, universities provide a service that you pay for to use it to your own ends (e.g. to get a job, to improve your earning potential, or to further your education).

we accept that social rules and society per se can be interpreted and understood in multiple ways then there is no ultimate truth, ergo, no reason for searching for it. This is a hard-hitting criticism of previous, predominantly positivist/objectivist approaches to understanding society, calling for the deconstruction of previous knowledge (Rail, 2002).

Under modernist influences (e.g. positivism), it made sense to establish dualistic categories and social compartments through which, as and when necessary, people could be pigeonholed (categorization is evident in sports: e.g. male and female). It also made sense to create meta-narratives (all-encompassing or totalizing stories) that provided grand explanations as to how societies operate. Post-modernity eroded all these barriers and created new categories or simply merged already existing ones (e.g. metrosexuality, which refers to heterosexual men displaying feminine dispositions). With regard to sport, Rail (1991) notes that the dissolutions affecting post-modern sport appear mainly in dualities such as male versus female, work versus leisure, self versus body, and universal versus particular. She argues that the aforementioned social binaries are being dissolved through the conditions and demands

187

driven by post-modernity. For instance, with regard to the 'particular and universal' Rail (1991) observes that communication and mass media are responsible for diminishing the borderlines between national sport organisations and international sport organisations. As Rail notes:

> International sport federations are consolidating themselves and multiplying in number; international committees and multi-sport organisations are increasing in strength; and international games as well as world championships are growing in scale.
>
> (Rail, 1991: 747)

To some extent, Rail (1991) is correct; however, the recent case of Mokgadi Caster Semenya may indicate that we should reconsider the dissolution of modernist categories of male and female and, to some degree, global, and local. Semenya, born in South Africa in 1991, won the gold medal in the women's 800-m race at the 2009 World Athletic Championship. After the race, her sex was questioned, triggered by her outstanding performance on the track. Also, due to her features, which were considered masculine by many, people believed that she may have a physiological condition (or *disorder*, to use a modernist term) that might have given her an unfair advantage over other women (women who conform to a modernist category of the female gender; see Nyong'o, 2010). As a consequence of these claims, she was withdrawn from competition and underwent the so-called sex test (see Chapter 8). This caused uproar in South Africa and in the world of sport. The action of the International Amateur Athletic Federation (IAAF) was considered sexist, racist, and an attack on human rights. In July 2010, the IAAF cleared Semenya of the charges and reinstated her athletic status. The findings of the test were never officially released although numerous speculations were present in the media. What is to note with regard to Semenya's case is that regardless of us living the post-modernist dream (or nightmare) and witnessing the dissolution of gender, ethnic, and geo-social barriers, we still have some strong signs of modernist thinking present. We would argue that sport and exercise are social spheres where modernist technocratic thinking and practices are still dominant, which, perhaps, partially explains the lack of post-modernist thought in these areas.

Nevertheless, some of the concepts and ideas of the leading figures of deconstructing post-modernity (e.g. Michel Foucault, Jean Baudrillard,

188

In this sub-section, we very briefly outlined general features of modernity and post-modernity and the transition between them. It is, however, important to note that societies do not develop in such clear-cut fashion. Similar to others, we use these phrases (modern and pre-modern) as heuristic devices through which we aimed to demonstrate a process: socio-cultural change from modernity to post-modernity. Hence, do not think that one day people lived in modernity and the next morning when they woke up it was already post-modernity. On the contrary, social values are part of long-term social processes that move slowly and unevenly across societies (see also Chapter 7). Social practices and habits dominant in one era do not necessarily and fully disappear in the following one. For instance, pre-modernity was fundamentally reliant on agriculture, which remained part of both modernity and post-modernity. Of course, the degree to which we are reliant on agriculture is not the same as it was in pre-modern societies, but it has not vanished. The same could be argued about the ethos of amateurism, a modern invention of sporting philosophy. Amateurism was the dominant value system associated with modern sport, especially with the early phases. However, later on, professionalism gradually superseded amateurism. Even the International Olympic Committee (IOC), one of the fiercest supporters of the idea, decided to remove amateurism from its charter to meet the demands of post-modern times. Regardless of professionalism being the dominant value system in sports, amateurism has not been completely phased out. Amateur athletes are still out there running, cycling, and kicking the ball about. They partake in sports and physical activity for reasons different from those of professional athletes. A similar argument could be put forward regarding volunteer coaches who get and stay involved for reasons other than financial gain.

Jean-Francois Lyotard, Jacques Derrida, and Nancy Scheper-Hughes) have been utilized to make sense of our contemporary sporting and exercise habits. Two of these post-modernist thinkers, Michel Foucault and Jean Baudrillard, are discussed in the following sections. Both of them are presented here under the aegis of post-modernity despite the fact that many academics would debate their inclusion in this category (see Giulianotti, 2004b). In fact, Baudrillard himself had issues with the term *post-modern*, which, he thought, really meant nothing. Though acknowledging this debate, we decided to present a specific aspect of their work in this chapter, as they have links with post-modernist thinking that focuses on technological advances influencing society whereby new cultural formations can emerge and have emerged (see Ritzer, 2003).

FOUCAULT: DISCIPLINING THE BODY

Similar to other social thinkers before and after him, Foucault concentrated a significant part of his intellectual inquiry on understanding power and power relations in society (Smart, 2002). However, he was one of the first academics to include the body in his discussions on power (bio-power) whereby 'Foucault has put the body at the centre of research agendas in the social sciences and humanities' (Rail and Harvey, 1995: 169). That he was a forerunner with investigating the social entanglement of the body is evident by the fact that Foucault began his investigations in the 1970s – *Discipline and Punish* (1977) and *History of Sexuality* (vol. 1, 1978) – but claims were still made in the 1980s and 1990s by both Turner (1984/2008) and Shilling (1993) regarding the lack of social thought on the human body. Foucault demonstrated that the body is not neutral but is both historical and cultural and, thus, socially constructed. 'The body is shown to be located in a political field, invested with power relations which render it docile and productive' (Smart, 2002: 75). In this section of the chapter, we will focus on Foucault's view of disciplinary power in relation to the body.

In *Discipline and Punish*, Foucault provides an analysis of how the manifestation of power shifted from sovereign to administrative (from pre-modern to modern). In pre-modern times, power was totalising and associated with specific individuals or individual such as a king whose power and authority had to be made visible to be sustained. Instilling one's power (e.g. the king's power) into the public's mind often took place through gruesome open torture (see the famous torture scene in *Discipline and Punish*). The idea behind public tortures was to instill fear into everyone. 'Spectacles of torture...were

190

successful...to the extent that they made visible the king's power to the criminal and, more importantly, to the ritual's spectators' (Cole et al., 2004: 210).

In modern and post-modern societies, power has been transformed and has become relational,[6] not totalising. The public spectacle of torture disappeared, and other forms of punishments were implemented (Smart, 2002), targeting the 'soul' of the delinquent. This, however, does not mean that we have become less cruel. On the contrary, we have changed only our methods of 'torture' and have developed more sophisticated and efficient ways of disciplining. For instance, Ritzer (2003: 237) notes 'that it is almost impossible to torture an entire population, but rule-based control can be exercised over a population'. In tandem with rule-based control, we have created instruments of observation and surveillance. Foucault borrows from Jeremy Bentham to illustrate how contemporary surveillance systems work to keep us under control.

Bentham's prison system is called 'Panopticon' (all-seeing), which was designed 'to induce in the inmate a state of conscious and permanent visibility that assures the automatic functioning of power' (Foucault, 1979: 201). The arrangement of the Panopticon, with a central watch tower and cells concentrically surrounding it, ensures that the surveillance is permanent or, at least, it appears to be. Due to the location of the watch tower and to the preventive measures taken to disallow inmates to see inside, inmates do not know whether there are guards in the watch tower. Foucault notes that there is no need for guards as the possibility of being watched is sufficient to force people to behave.

> The perfection of power should tend to render its actual exercise unnecessary; that this architectural apparatus should be a machine for creating and sustaining a power relation independent of the person who exercises it; in short, that the inmates should be caught up in a power situation of which they are themselves the bearers.
>
> (Foucault, 1979: 201)

This theory has two basic features: visible and unverifiable. Visible means that the inmates will constantly have before them the central tower from which they are *potentially* observed. Unverifiable means that the inmate must never know whether they are being looked at in any one moment; but they must know that they *may always* be seen.

BIOGRAPHIC NOTE

Michel Paul Foucault (1926–1984), a key historian, philosopher, and critic of the twentieth century, was born in Poitiers, France. He was to become a surgeon, but he turned out to be a disappointment to his father, a surgeon himself, with his weak academic achievements. Later, Foucault improved his academics (he explained his academic progress as the consequence of his desire to attract the attention of good-looking boys) and was one of the best in passing his entrance exam to the eminent École Normale Supérieure. His time at École Normale Supérieure was stressful and, thus, he often visited a psychotherapist, which prompted him to study psychology. After completing his university studies, he taught across Europe but, in 1960, returned to France to complete his doctoral thesis and to become a professor of philosophy at the University of Cermont-Ferrand. In 1965, he moved to the University of Tunis to follow his lover, who had been moved to Tunisia as part of his military service. Although Foucault was still in Tunisia when the 1968 student riots broke out, he was indirectly influenced by it as the government created an experimental university, Paris-VIII, at Vincennes and appointed Foucault the first head of its philosophy department. Two years later, he was elected to France's most prestigious academic body, Collège de France, as professor of the History of Systems of Thought, which solidified his academic and public celebrity status.

Foucault investigated the development of Western civilization, focusing on attitudes toward sexuality, madness, illness, and knowledge (some common threads with Elias's work can be detected here; see Smith, 2001). Foucault had a specific obsession with sexuality and went to great lengths to experiment with his own. Openly gay, Foucault was attracted to the budding gay community of San Francisco. He was involved in sadomasochistic activities and impersonal sex, which he often called 'limit experiences' (Miller, 1993). He used his sexual 'limit experiences' to achieve intellectual breakthroughs and to gain personal and academic understanding of Western sexuality (Ritzer, 2003).

192

Foucault published numerous books including: *The Birth of the Clinic* (1963), *The Order of Things* (1966), *The Archaeology of Knowledge* (1969), *Discipline and Punish* (1977), *History of Sexuality, Volume* 1(1976) and *The Use of Pleasure* (1984) and *The Care of Self* (1984). Despite the broad sweep of his publications, a recurring theme in Foucault's work was the struggle of social agency (the individual) against the powers of society. In his writings, he focused on technologies of power and the reasons why individuals conform to the rules of society. This central idea was underpinned by his theories on the role of prisons in society. Foucault was heavily influenced by Nietzschean genealogy, to which he referred as:

> a rejection of imminent direction to history and society... [which] places much emphasis on struggle for power by different forces and on the lack of necessary order inherent in this. The methodological consequence of this attitude is that the historian should try to uncover the contingent and violent course that society has historically taken.
>
> (Barth, 2008: 279)

Foucault died of AIDS in Paris in 1984, one of the first public personalities in France who died of the disease, which was still relatively unknown at that time.

In other words, people are aware of the fact that they are continuously being watched by the authority, but they cannot identify who is watching them or when they are being watched.

Disciplinary power, a correctional form of power, is sustained via three means: hierarchical observation (a form of coercive observation allowing those in power to oversee others); normalising judgement (social norms are set by those in power and others and their actions/ bodies measured against those norms); and examination (involves both hierarchical observation and normalising judgement, i.e. observing what people do and how they conform to set norms). Through these practices, disciplinary power 'trains' (conditions) individuals into being both objects and instruments of its exercise (Foucault, 1979). Disciplinary power "trains' the moving, confused, useless multitudes of

Let's stop and think about how you may use panopticism in practice. To link the panopticon theory to a sport-related example, we will outline the global practices of the World Anti-Doping Agency (WADA). The WADA, established in 1999 as part of an IOC scheme to control illegal performance-enhancing substances, initiated the Whereabouts programme, first provisionally launched in 2004 and put into full effect in 2009. This programme requires selected elite athletes to constantly inform their International Sport Federation or WADA regarding their whereabouts (They have to be *visible*). The rationale behind this programme is that it is insufficient and ineffective to test athletes shortly before or after competition, as WADA believes that out-of-competition testing is 'the most powerful means of deterrence and detection of doping and are an important step in strengthening athlete and public confidence in doping-free sport'. Whether we accept, reject, or question the WADA's logic is inconsequential. What, however, is relevant is the WADA's global panopticon system through which elite athletes are kept under constant surveillance. The WADA's panopticism is difficult (not impossible) to escape as it is based on seemingly constant surveillance. Athletes under this system may or may not be tested before competition, but they all have the potential to receive an unannounced visit from the WADA (*unverifiability* of the system). Remember what Foucault (1979: 201) said: 'The perfection of power should tend to render its actual exercise unnecessary'. That is, the fear of the potential of being tested should keep athletes out of mischief. (information about the WADA can be found at: www.wada-ama.org).

bodies' (Foucault, 1979: 170). A specific form of disciplinary power that is focused on the body is bio-power. Bio-power is power over life that optimises the capabilities of the body enhancing its economic utility and ensuring its political docility (Smart, 2002).

Sport is the very example of disciplinary bio-power. It is a social field where bodies have high economic utility and are trained, regulated, and tested. Athletes' bodies are constantly trained and under surveillance by coaches, other athletes, and spectators. That is, sport and exercise are 'an ensemble of disciplining and normalising parties...that produce and put under surveillance multiple bodies' (Rail and Harvey, 1995: 173). Sports are also normalised by set rules established by national and/or international governing bodies. At competitions, athletes are observed, and their performances (their bodies) are measured against set standards and results achieved by other, previous athletes. Performance to be rewarded has to be of exceptional quality and within the rules. Foul play is punished (correctional power), and outstanding performance is rewarded (positive power).

Let's take bodybuilding as an example. Bodybuilders train and discipline their bodies on a daily basis. Everything they do is carefully calculated, such as when they get up, what they eat, when they train, and when they go to bed. (This probably is applicable to most elite athletes.) Those bodies are under constant surveillance in the gym by other bodybuilders and are constantly monitored (inside and outside of the gym) by their owners. At competitions, there is further observation by judges and audience, and bodies are measured against standards established by the International Federation of Bodybuilders. Those who, within the set regulations, outperform the others are rewarded; the rest are 'sentenced' to more gruelling weight lifting. During this process of training, measuring, and evaluating, bodies become docile and productive and, in turn, politically and economically useful (Smart, 2002). That power is relational is indicated by the fact that bodies have economic utility for both the individuals (owner of the body) and for the organising structures. Individuals and their bodies need the structures through which their bodies may be displayed and marketed, and structures need individuals (and their bodies) to market, display, and profit from. So, in a Foucauldian sense, power (bio-power in this case) is 'not an evil to be escaped, but a matter of strategic games, which can be played with more or less domination' (Smith Maguire, 2002: 296).

REFLECTION

'As a coach, I always believed that discipline was a good thing' – announces Denison (2007: 373) when analysing his own performance as a coach for long-distance runners. Do you think that discipline is a good thing when it comes to being an athlete or coaching athletes? Read Denison's (2007) article and discuss his view in comparison to yours.

BAUDRILLARD: HYPER-CONSUMPTION AND HYPER-REALITY

Baudrillard was extensively influenced by Marxist and neo-Marxist ideas, especially in the early years of his academic career. Later, he parted with Marxism as a political movement but kept some of its fundamental ideas such as examining society through an economic lens. Baudrillard (2006: 105) argued that 'concepts fundamental to Marxist analysis need to be questioned' as focusing on use and exchange values was outdated. Thus, what separated Baudrillard, even in his early years, from other Marxists was his focus on consumption instead of production and sign value instead of use value. He was pioneering the use of linguistics, commodity signs specifically, to interpreting contemporary society's consumption-related practices. 'The "classical" definition of productive forces is a restricted definition, and we enlarge our analysis in terms of productive forces to the entire field thus far blind to signification and communication' (Baudrillard, 2006: 71).

In post-modernity, not only products are produced but so also the desire to purchase them. In other words, capitalist societies are not only supplying goods but the demand for those as well. Featherstone (1991: 14) summarises: 'The expansion of capitalist production... necessitated the construction of new markets and the 'education' of publics to become consumers through advertising and other media'. However, we are selling not only products per se but cultural meanings associated with them. Those meanings are disseminated through society and become cultural codes. It is not only the physical product we buy but cultural meaning attached to it. Thus, the commodities we buy and possess and the activities we do are also cultural signs showcasing who we are and what we do. These signs make sense only through codes (a system that allows us to understand these cultural signs) that we interpret on a daily basis. These signs are, to name but a few, the clothes we wear, the cars we drive, the food we buy, and the spare-time activities we do. For instance, owning a Ford Fiesta or Ferrari has different signs attached to it through which we gauge an individual's social class and presume that the owner of the Ferrari would have more disposable income. This could also be observed with regard to road cycling (or mountain biking and motor biking) where having the appropriate and most expensive gear may indicate the individual's social class. It could be argued that not even the most

Use your sociological imagination and think of examples from your own life when you bought things not because you needed them but because you wanted them. Have you been influenced by commodity signs? Have you ever bought a product because you thought that your family/friends/team-mates would think more of you because of having ownership of it? Think of situations in which you bought a more expensive product simply because it was associated with a specific brand name that had higher social status.

expensive cycling gear is going to make a significant performance difference for an amateur weekend warrior, but that is not really the point in buying them. Also, owning a Ferrari will not necessarily allow us to get from A to B significantly faster than a Ford Fiesta would, as speed limits would apply to both cars, consequently producing similar travel times. Baudrillard argued that it was not necessarily the functionality or effectiveness of the products we buy them for. On the contrary, we buy them because we can, and we want others to know that we can. Hence, buying commodity is not simply about satisfying needs but communicating.

Ritzer (2003) observes that consumption is based on the fact that others will understand the cultural meaning of why and what we consume. (Think of Nike's 'Just Do It!' slogan or BMW's advertisement that explicitly states that the manufacturers of that car are not simply selling *a car* but *joy* as well.) So, if we can get from A to B in a Ford Fiesta but decide to buy a Ferrari, that indicates that there is a certain excess of desire over the object (Butler, 1999). In a consumer society, the focus is on consumption instead of production and, in turn, high levels of consumption are associated with a high level of success. Products of post-modernity have more purpose than simple functionality; they have cultural meaning embedded in them, which we decode and interpret. With regard to sport and exercise, we can think of ski holidays, golf, and paragliding as activities that signify higher social class due to the costs associated with these activities. Being able to afford these activities indicates how much disposable income we may have and allows us to socialise with people of the same ilk, which

BIOGRAPHIC NOTE

Jean Baudrillard (1929–2007), one of the most significant and controversial cultural critics of the twentieth century, was born in Reims, France. He was the first to attend university in his family, as his lineage was a long line of peasants and civil servants. At Sorbonne, he read German and literature, leading him toward a teaching career. Whilst teaching, Baudrillard was an active writer, contributing to literary work and translating numerous German works to French. Perhaps due to the translations he had done, he slowly turned his attention toward the discipline of sociology in which he wrote his doctoral thesis at the University of Paris, Nanterre. After successfully defending his doctoral thesis, Baudrillard took up a post at Nanterre where he spent his academic career. Initially, Baudrillard was heavily influenced by Marxian ideas and was politically active. However, what clearly separated his work from Marxists was his focus on consumption instead of production. Later in his life, he parted with Marxian ideas, quit academia, and devoted more time to writing.

Baudrillard, a prolific writer, published numerous books and articles on a wide range of topics from consumerism through gender relation to AIDS and the Gulf War. Rex Butler (1999), with Baudrillard's own endorsement, categorises Baudrillard's work into three distinctive epochs. First phase (approx. 1960–1976) was represented by observational, empirical evidence and heavily embedded in sociological interpretations. These works include *The System of Objects* (1968), *For a Critique of the Political Economy of the Sign* (1972), *The Mirror of Production* (1972), and *Symbolic Exchange and Death* (1976). The second phase (approx. 1976–1983) represents 'a period of frantic theoretical production' (Butler, 1999: 7) in which he broke away from empirical observation and paid more attention to theory (not exclusively sociological) and criticism. Works he produced in this phase include *Forget Foucault* (1977),[7] *In the Shadow of the Silent Majorities* (1978), *Simulacra and Simulations* (1981), and *Fatal Strategies* (1983). The final phase (1983 onward) introduces a different Baudrillard who ceases being both empirical and

198

theoretical. He gives up his teaching position in 1987 at Nanterre and finds a form of solace in a state of 'permanent sabbatical'. In this 'semi-retirement', he explores different forms of writing and produces commentaries on a wide range of topics and issues. His writings include *The Transparency of Evil* (1990), *The Gulf War Did Not Take Place* (1991), *The Illusion of the End* (1992), and *The Perfect Crime* (1994). As a consequence of the wide range of genres and issues Baudrillard covered during his life, his thinking has affected many social spheres from academia to pop culture. Ritzer (2003) notes that one of Baudriallrd's books even features, quite appropriately, in the movie *The Matrix*.

in turn makes us *appear*[8] more successful (cf. Chapter 4 on Marxism, especially the discussion on Bourdieu's gains in distinction). Ritzer (2003: 250) succinctly sums it up: 'People are what they consume; they define themselves and are defined by others, on that basis'. That is, we do not 'directly desire any specific object...[but] desire [it] only in a competitive relationship with others' (Butler, 1999: 27).

In post-modernity, our consumer needs (wants) are manipulated by commodity-signs that we receive and absorb through the mass media. We consume products not only because we need them but because we are tricked into buying (needing) them. We are overloaded with information through the media, which 'confront us with an endless flow of fascinating images and simulations' (Featherstone, 1991: 68). In this sense, our needs are not *real* but simulated by post-modern social conditions. Equally, our social surroundings and our interpretation of them are too simulated, creating *hyperreality*. Under hyperreal conditions, the boundaries between what is real or unreal are diminished; 'the real and the imaginary are confused' (Featherstone, 1991: 68). The concept of hyperreality refers to our inability to distinguish between real and fantasy and features in earlier works but was fully developed in Baudrillard's *Simulacra and Simulation* (1981/1994) and *Simulations* (1983). Often cited cases are his analyses of America, Disneyland, Las Vegas, music, and pornography.

For instance, when writing on pornography, Baudrillard claims that 'porn is precisely that which, through a surplus of "reality"...[is] more real than real' (2006: 251). In pornography, everything is visible in a way that it would not be under 'real' circumstances. Pornography is hypervisible and hyperexposed; 'your sex, you've never *seen* it function, not from so close' (Baudrillard, 2006: 25, italics in original). This example indicates that pornography, like other simulations of the real, is not necessarily unreal. Rather, the hyperexposure of sex through pornography makes sex more real than real. 'The simulacrum, therefore, is marked not by an unreality but instead by its *excess* of reality' (Merrin, 2005: 39, italics in original). *Excess of reality* or *more real than real itself* means that whatever we are experiencing, being hyperexposed to in hyperreality is qualitatively better than reality. In hyperreality, everything is nicer, more organised, more beautiful and truer. Ritzer (2003: 256) observes, 'The pornographic film star with her implants, additional cosmetic surgeries, tattoos, body make up, and other alterations can be viewed as a simulated temptress'. Similarly, Baudrillard's examination of Disney World is that it is supposed to be a mirror image of America and American society. However, the real America is much different from Disney's creation where everything is clean and orderly and employees are polite. The gap between real and unreal is blurred and, thus, hyperreality (e.g. Disney Land) 'emerges as a copy for which there is no original' (Jarvie and Maguire, 1994: 222).

With regard to sport, Andrews's (1997) study of the American National Basketball Association (NBA) and its players' roles and functions in the mass media adopted a theoretical framework linked to hyperreality. Andrews states that sport and athletes in the post-

Giulianotti (2004b) points out that Baudrillard envisioned that sport would also be extensively influence by media-generated simulations. He believed that, at some point in post-modernity, games will be played in empty stadia as fans and supporters will be staying at home (or, perhaps, in pubs) where they would have access to highly sophisticated media technologies through which they can control what they want to see. Also, the mass media would provide 'superfluous streams of useless information transmitted in pornographic detail: the multiple camera angles…, the reams of physiological data on players, the seamless and confusing blend of live and recorded event.' (Giulianotti, 2004b: 234). Consequently, the argument is that as the hyperreal televised sport becomes better quality and more desirable than being live in the stadia, it itself will become real.

Another example of hyperreality is the way bodies are portrayed in the media. Through very carefully orchestrated imagery and use of advance computer technology, bodies are airbrushed and, thus, simulated. As a result of this simulation, we are faced with bodies that are literally unobtainable without chemical, imagery, and/or surgical enhancement. Nevertheless, these bodies are presented as real (more real than the real as they are bigger, more muscular, and better shaped than real bodies are) and, thus, desirable. Bodies that exist in a hyperreal context and are portrayed as ideal (lean and muscular) have also become commodity signs, signs of health, attractiveness, discipline, well-being, and wealth. Having or not having 'the right' body (or even the 'right' attitude toward the body) conveys social meanings (codes) that we interpret like any other commodity signs. (Think back to the exerciser example at the beginning of this chapter and, for some personal accounts of body obsession, see Fussell, 1991 and Friedman, 2009.)

modern era have had new functions which manifest themselves in the way the media represent sport events. Andrews (1997: 75) notes that the goal of the organisers of the NBA was to turn it 'into one of the most popular commodity-signs that had usurped the material economic commodity as the dynamic force in structuring principles of everyday American existence'. This goal has been reached through the reproduction (simulation) of the functions and images of NBA players from a subsidiary sport league to a 'hyperreal circus'. 'The NBA is first and foremost an entertainment company that manufactures a phantasmagorical world of commodity-signed narratives and identities: triumphs and tragedies, success and failures, heroes and villains' (Andrews, 1997: 78). Therefore, sport should not only be seen as an overly organised form of physical activity but is rather a complex entertaining, money-making realm that, via post-modernity, moved from the local to the global level.

The features of post-modernity are placing 'athlete-images' or 'commodity-signs' in the global public eye (Silk and Andrews, 2001) and have opened doors to the largest market ever as 'there are 250 million potential NBA fans in the US, and there are 5 billion outside the US' (Comte, 1993: 43, cited in Andrews, 1997: 79). Baudrillard's post-modernist standpoint can make an important contribution to the understanding of a television and imagery-advertising dominated culture, as 'it is possible to characterise the promotional circus engaged by the NBA as an attempt to manipulate popular need and consumption by subjecting the audience to the anticipated verification of their behaviour' (Andrews, 1997: 80).

CRITIQUING POST-MODERNISM

Post-modernist views of sport and exercise have shed new light upon social issues and introduced sociological debates from a different angle. Post-modernity has significantly influenced sport-society discussions, though concentrating mainly on recent times. Post-modernists attribute social changes to features of (post-)modernity such as industrialisation, computerisation, technologisation, and scientisation. However, this today-centred feature of post-modernist explanation of social phenomena perhaps carries the problem of reductionism in terms of neglecting long-term historical processes as a part of socio-cultural interpretations. Jarvie and Maguire observe, 'Postmodernism tends to collapse important questions of periodisation and history and as such any account which fails seriously to take account of social and cultural history must ultimately be prone to the charge of presenting a detached representation of reality' (1994: 223).

202

Although it is obvious that both Foucault (e.g. sexuality) and Baudrillard (e.g. signs) carried out historical analyses, which to some extent refutes the critique of being ahistorical, historians voiced their concerns regarding hasty conclusions based on inadequate and insufficient evidence. Even if we accept this critique and that, for example, Foucault's arguments might have been flawed due to the inadequacy of evidence, his methodologies still have merit and significance and can be reproduced with a broader and more adequate set of (archival and/or textual) evidence.

Critical observations toward the work of both Foucault and Baudrillard have come from feminist writers who accused them of not representing women, not speaking for women (Rail and Harvey, 1995). This is especially true of Baudrillard, who made suggestions regarding women being offered up as sacrifices in the American desert (Giulianotti, 2004b). Nevertheless, feminists have embraced post-modernity and related theories (e.g. Hargreaves, 2004), which they have used effectively to voice their concerns with contemporary issues surrounding sport, exercise, and sexuality (see Chapter 8 on Feminism).

Another critique of post-modernist perspectives, especially of Foucault and Baudrillard, is that they paint a negative, pessimistic picture of contemporary society. According to Baudrillard, we are constantly and inescapably influenced by the media, and we live in societies that are mere simulations and have little to do with what once was real. Foucault's perception of power could also be perceived pessimistically as an ever-present constant disciplinary force from which no one can escape. Regardless of where we go, we are being constantly observed by authorities or their representatives. To escape this panopticon, we may find solace in spaces uncontaminated by hierarchical observation. However, escaping surveillance and retreating to spaces of relative freedom may, in fact, mean a form of confinement in which the body is incarcerated. We think that it is too soon to tell whether post-modernity has provided us with a pessimistic or, perhaps, realistic outlook on itself.

FURTHER READING

An edited book by Genevieve Rail (1998), entitled *Sport and Postmodern Times*, introduces and applies a range of key concepts associated with post-modernism and provides interpretations of sport and exercise through post-modernist lenses. A general but detailed and often-cited, work on Foucault is written by James Miller (1993) and provides an analytical insight into Foucault's life and thinking. Barry Smart's (2002) introduction to Foucauldian work and thinking is also a useful source for getting further acquainted with the concepts of the post-structuralist master. With regard to a general overview on Baudrillard, we would recommend the work of Butler (1999) and Lane (2008). For post-modernist views on sport and exercise, research carried out by David L. Andrews, Cheryl L. Cole, Genevieve Rail, Michael Silk, Richard Pringle, and Jennifer Smith Maguire would be recommended as further reading.

CHAPTER 10

A GUIDE TO THE CRAFT OF SOCIOLOGY

INITIAL STUMBLING BLOCKS

When you first encounter sociology in a university environment, it is not simply the discipline that poses a challenge. There will be other novel expectations facing you. You will notice or have already noticed that one of these expectations is to become and be an independent learner and thinker. The sooner you mange to develop into one, the easier your life is going to be at university. Initially, you may be thinking: 'How hard can it be to become an independent learner/thinker? Being independent means that I can do whatever I want, doesn't it?' Though we can see and appreciate your logic, being an independent learner is a slightly different animal and is probably more demanding than you may have thought. First of all, remember that regardless of who you are and where you are, you will always be, more or less, regulated by social structures (e.g. see our discussion on Foucault's concept of power in Chapter 9). Hence, you cannot do 'whatever you want'. Your freedom and independence are relational (i.e. you are free to act within the already established rules). In other words, to gain your 'freedom' and 'independence', first you need to learn about external constraints – in this case, the rules of engagement at your university. Learning about the system and expectations will help you see where you are socially positioned and what you can and cannot do in that particular social milieu in that given time (see discussion on personal troubles versus social issues in Chapter 2). That is, learning the rules and expectations will set you free(er) and will allow you to more effectively negotiate your way through your degree. For instance, knowing that you have access to interlibrary loan services but that sources ordered through that service may take up to one week to arrive would help you increase the quality of your project and manage your time. However, not knowing about interlibrary loans and how much time it may take for your order to arrive could greatly disadvantage you. So, read student handbooks, module guides/outlines, and assignment briefs very carefully, as those are both your 'prison guards' and the key to independence!

The other reason why you may find it demanding to become an independent learner is because you may never have been required to be one. It is not unusual to see our students missing this part of their pre-university education. Ken Robinson rightly posed the question: Do schools kill creativity? His speech, which he delivered at a conference in Canada in 2006, is both revealing and thought-provoking as regards how schools tend to operate.[1] He argues that schools have the potential to kill human creativity (and independent thinking with it) by shaping pupils' minds in a uniform way without acknowledging individual abilities and talents. So, if you have always been told what to do and when and how to do it – which is a general concern for people involved in sport – there is a considerable possibility that your creativity and potential for independent thought might have been oppressed. This passive-oppressive outlook, what Freire (1970) called 'the concept of banking education, leads to 'digestive' education, promoted by 'ready-to-wear' approaches serving to obviate thinking. Thinking is the essence of an independent learner. Robinson insightfully pointed out that we cannot predict the future and, thus, cannot know what will be useful knowledge or skills in ten, twenty, or thirty years' time. Nevertheless, what we know for certain is that there will be problems to be solved, some of which will require unorthodox, outside-the-box thinking. Consequently, becoming and being an independent and creative learner and thinker, we argue, should be the main purposes of education regardless of its level and discipline.

Unfortunately, developing critical and independent thinkers is not always on top of the education agenda, which often seems to be concerned with delivering pre-set curricula (Illich, 1970). So, it is no surprise that, at university, when you are 'unexpectedly' asked to be independent, take initiative, explore, analyse, critique, synthesise, and generate ideas, you may find yourself between a rock and a hard place, so to speak. Differently put, it is not only the subject area you might be struggling with but the ways in which you are required to learn about it. You will be directed to copious amounts of readings, which you will have to 'process' so you can follow lectures, partake in seminar discussions, develop assignments, and come up with dissertation ideas. Most of these readings you will have to locate in the university's library, then read and analyse them. The knowledge, ideas, observations, and questions will grow out of this process or craft. You will have to do some groundwork to develop your craft. This groundwork may not be glamorous, but this is the very foundation on which your university education and success will rest.

Bearing in mind the issue of engaging sociological imagination (SI) and developing the craft of sociology faced by many students in higher education, in this chapter, we outline a practical guide to *doing* sociology. We aim to give you pointers on and describe a process, our process of doing sociology based on Mills' original idea. Our intention is to help you work on your craft of doing sociology and find and reawaken your SI, thereby enabling you to become a more independent, effective, and creative student. What follows is only a *guide* and not principles set in stone. Hence, we advise that you adjust and remould this craft to suit you and your own learning. Although we will chiefly consider sociology and sociology modules in this chapter, we think that the general practice set out below could be applicable to other disciplines and modules as well.

THE CRAFT OF DOING SOCIOLOGY

In the last chapter of *The Sociological Imagination*, Mills outlines how he goes 'about his craft' (1959/2000: 195). This has particular value to newcomers to sociology. Loy and Booth (2004: 71) observe that only a 'precious few [textbooks]... offer explicit explanations on the craft of sociology'. Although it may initially seem mechanical or overly structured and, to some degree, naive, the intellectual craft of doing sociology, as outlined by Mills, is a useful guide for students of sociology at all levels (us included). In the following lines, we will introduce and elaborate on what we consider the key concepts of contemporary sociological craft for university students. Most of the concepts to be introduced can be found in Mills' book and neatly structured by Loy and Booth (2004). We, however, added and perhaps tweaked a few of them to be more in line with contemporary issues raised by our students and observed by us.

SI is a practice – a practice of doing sociology. We firmly believe in what Goffman once said: 'Sociology is something that you do, not something you [only] read' (cited in Birrell and Donnelly, 2004: 49). This entire book is embedded in the idea of not only reading but doing sociology and actively engaging with social theories. In our view, sociological craft is an active process that requires familiarity with and practice in six main areas: *reading, writing/note taking, filing, recognising connections, using personal experiences,* and *balancing theory and evidence.* We must note that you should not consider these areas of practice as mutually exclusive. On the contrary, they are greatly interlinked and have the potential to complement each other. Let's begin with reading and coming to terms with the jargon (socspeak).

Reading

One of the challenges our students seem to face when it comes to sociology is the amount and nature of reading. Lectures and seminars are informed by sociology sources and research and, as part of your preparation, you must read. One of the principal mistakes you can make is not keeping up with the reading and when the assessment deadline approaches you are playing catch-up. In theory, you could go through the assigned sources in a couple of weeks, but that would be a rushed job, not allowing time for reflection and for using and developing your SI. Besides, it is likely that you have to prepare for multiple assessments simultaneously, and you are not going to be able to give due attention to readings and areas you previously neglected. A simple solution to this issue is that you learn to manage your time effectively and read every week and develop this into a habit. Remember: you are supposed to *read* for a degree!

In sociology modules at university, most of what you learn, or will learn, will be new to you. Not necessarily the phenomena such as sexism, racism, and social class but the terminology surrounding them. When we pose the £1 million-question at seminars – Why didn't you read the assigned article? – what you tend to say is concerned with the nature of the sources, that is, the language is too complicated as the text is full of long, unknown words. It is correct, reading sociology can be a daunting task because of the technical terminology that is often employed. Mills (1959/2000: 217), rightly so, was against the overuse of jargon and wrote: 'I know you will agree that you should present your work in as clear and simple language as your subject and your thought about it permit'. It was pioneering of Mills to put a call out for more accessible sociology, as it had been riddled with jargon.[2] Based on what you might have read so far in other sources, you are probably thinking that Mills' call for adopting simpler language in sociology has not entirely been successful. You are partially correct, and even Mills (1959/2000: 217) admits that 'a turgid and polysyllabic prose does seem to prevail in the social sciences'. Regardless of what Mills and other sociologists like him have tried to achieve, this discipline is (and others too are) loaded with jargon, some of which you must learn to be able to manoeuvre your way through books and articles. In this book, we have made an attempt to be sensitive to this issue and, while still using terminology, provide ample explanations and a glossary to enable you to look up concepts you are unfamiliar with or still learning. There are other useful sources that could help you break the jargon; these are sociology dictionaries (e.g. *Collins Dictionary of Sociology* by David and Julia Jary, 2000) and specific sport studies dictionaries (e.g. *The Sage Dictionary of Sport Studies* by Dominic Malcolm, 2008). These reference books will prove useful throughout your undergraduate studies and are invaluable to have at hand when you are reading and having seminar discussions.[3] We would consider them as essential investments for university students.

Writing and note taking

Developing the habit of regular reading and using this book's glossary and other relevant dictionaries to decode jargon or refresh your knowledge are good practices that will help you come to terms with the foundation of sociology (or with any other discipline you apply this approach to). Another skill that you should simultaneously develop is writing. Similar to reading, you should make an effort to write on a regular basis. This might be in the form of note taking when attending lectures and seminars, when reading assigned sources, or jotting down ideas for assignments or for your dissertation. With the technology readily available, you have a range of choices to take notes with and record your own or others' thoughts. You can use your portable computer, your mobile phone, or PDA to note down key concepts and their meanings and/or your ideas. Or, alternatively, you can always use the age-old, but tried and tested, paper-and-pencil method. Most lecturers also provide PowerPoint notes that you can download and use as a guide to key concepts and definitions when reading and preparing your assignment.

It does not matter which way(s) of recording you adopt as long as you develop that into a habit. You will see that there are multiple advantages to nurturing this skill. For instance, we suppose, you do not want to admit to your lecturer in a tutorial that: 'I have read this good idea or concept somewhere but cannot find the article' or 'One of the lecturers suggested an idea for my assignment but I cannot remember.' Neither do you want to spend ages in the library to locate a source that would have taken minutes to find if you had written down the exact reference to it. These frustrating and embarrassing moments can easily be avoided with the simple practice of note taking. Whether you employ the traditional paper-and-pencil technique or the more technologically advanced portable computer approach, you will find that the advantages of note taking are

- less likely to lose ideas;

- less likely to lose relevant sources (write down full references of books and articles, including relevant page numbers for direct quotations);

- more likely to develop critical insights as you can easily access and revisit your notes and contrast different views;

- more likely to retain information as you remain engaged with the material while taking notes; and

- using your own words/definitions and examples (i.e. drawing upon previous experience will help you understand and remember new key ideas whereby you connect old and new knowledge for more effective learning).

When you have developed reading and writing into a habit and you take ample and useful notes during lectures, seminars, and while reading, you are on track with your craft and coming to terms with sociology.

The approach that we have outlined so far with regard to coming to terms with sociology can be applied to other academic disciplines. You will find that the initial effort invested in reading, note taking, and learning will make your life easier in the long run. When you have created a solid foundation of skills and ideas, your engagement with more advanced materials will be easier, more effective and, thus, more enjoyable.

Filing

Mills also suggests the filing of your ideas and creating a filing system. For Mills, it was pretty much the good old way of filing hard copies of paper that nowadays may be considered cumbersome and difficult to search through. Nevertheless, the idea of having a filing system is a good one and so is keeping hard copies as backup. Nowadays, most of us keep files electronically on our computer, so we suggest that you learn to arrange your files on your computer in a logical order. You may not see the relevance of a filing system when you are in the first year of your university education. However, as you progress through the years, you will be bombarded with more and more information. Let's consider how much information it really is.

During your university studies, you will be introduced to thousands of new concepts; you will read numerous articles, will enroll on more than a dozen modules, and will attend hundreds of lectures and seminars. By doing so, you will take notes, print out assigned articles, check out relevant source materials from libraries, and buy books online. In other words, you will search through and accumulate an enormous amount of information in the form of both hard and electronic sources. You cannot fully retain this large amount of information, but you will need to remember most of it as you are progressing through your studies and enrolling on new, more advanced modules. So, for instance, in your second year, your sociology lecturer is discussing Marxism and uses terms such as surplus value, proletariat, and bourgeoisie (you will find these terms in this book's glossary), which you covered in the previous year. You have not completely forgotten what they mean but are not fully confident about your knowledge. What do you do next? You need

Always, always back up your electronic files! It is a good idea to buy an external hard drive and regularly save your files from your own computer onto the external hard drive. You can also send e-mails with relevant documents attached as a further backup. We have seen too many times that students could not submit their essays because their computer's hard drive became corrupted. Be smart, learn from the mistakes of others!

to revisit your previous studies. This is exactly the situation in which your filing system will become very handy! So, what we are suggesting is that you create folders by year and within them create folders by module. In your module folder, you can create further subfolders based on lecture themes, theories, or assignments. We would suggest that in your module folder, you should keep the module guide or module handbook, required reading list, references of sources you have read, all the electronic notes and materials provided by the lecturer, and your notes and completed assignments. Essentially, you need a filing system that you are familiar with, is easy to operate, and is helpful. After a couple of clicks on your computer, you will find the first-year sociology module folder and in it the folder on Marxism, in which you would still have your notes from last year, so you can easily and quickly look up the meaning of the concepts mentioned by your lecturer.

If you know where to find your sociology notes from last year on your computer, it is a five-to-ten-minute job to refresh your knowledge. However, if you have not taken notes and do not know how to locate the information you are after, you may have to begin from scratch. To avoid frustration and unnecessary work, our advice to you is to keep regular and organised notes and think of learning as a process, not a phase dictated by modules.This reduces the unwelcome effect of what is known as the *vaccination theory* of education (Postman and Weingartner, 1969). The theory stipulates that due to current educational structures, students have the tendency to see institutional education not as a process per se but as a set of fragmented 'hurdles' or modules they need to overcome to progress from one stage to another. As a corollary, students may also believe that after making successful headway in a module, they will not need to revisit academic areas

212

previously covered. That is, you may believe that what you learn in your first-year sociology module will bear no relevance to your second- and third-year modules. We would argue that to think of modules as isolated monads of knowledge is faulty and is a false economy.

Recognising connections

In most degree programmes, modules are both horizontally and vertically connected. This, for instance, means that your first-year sociology module is (horizontally) connected to your sport history, sport development, and/or sport management modules. Moreover, your second-year sociology module builds on (vertical connection) the material that is covered in the first-year sociology module, and the third-year module will anticipate knowledge acquired in your second year (again, this is not exclusive to sociology modules!). Therefore, knowledge and skills gained in one module can be and should be employed in other areas/modules. You might have come across the term *transferable skills*, which a module develops aside from disciplinary knowledge, such as essay writing, discussion, and presentation skills. These are called *transferable skills*, as they can be applied in other modules and, most of the time, in real job-related situations.[4] However, it is not only skills that can be used across a range of modules and scenarios but knowledge. Another, more imaginative aspect of having a well-functioning and easily accessed filing system is the combination of seemingly separate ideas, the cross-pollination of disciplines/theories. Mills (1959/2000: 211) argued that:

> The sociological imagination can also be cultivated; certainly it seldom occurs without a great deal of routine work. There is an unexpected quality about it, perhaps because its essence is the combination of ideas that no one expected were combinable... There is a playfulness of mind ... of such combining as well as a truly fierce drive to make sense of the world.

Let's try to make sense of what Mills means here and in what ways it is applicable to you and your studies.

Although we all have a certain degree of SI, like muscles, it requires ample exercise, otherwise it will atrophy. By developing the habit

The interconnectedness of modules is not unique to sociology. The same can be and has been observed (see Molnar and Bryson, 2009) with regard to research methods modules. The methods, ideas, and processes you learn in research methods are connected to almost all areas you may later study. For instance, a large chunk of your dissertation is driven by your knowledge of research methods. If you conduct your dissertation in the area of sociology, you find that research methods and sociology modules are connected and come together in the pinnacle of your university studies, which is your dissertation (Again, this is applicable to the relationship between research methods and other modules as well.) To see these connections, first and foremost you need to know/remember individual areas of study and then and only then you may be able to engage your SI to find the connection of ideas, concepts, and processes that you will be able to capitalise on. That is, having done the groundwork and established a solid academic foundation, you can engage in a higher level of intellectual enterprise.

of regular reading and writing, your SI is getting some 'exercise', which improves its effectiveness and hones its sharpness. You cannot expect to come up with an idea, a good idea, without training your SI. This training is what Mills calls 'routine work'. It is not always exciting (in fact, sometimes quite the opposite) to read through and take notes on a great many articles and books to find a usable idea for your assignment or dissertation. Unfortunately, without doing this groundwork, ideas hardly ever emerge. Even if they do surface, without knowing what is out there, you cannot be certain whether your idea is good or valid. Lecturers are familiar with this process and, when you come to a tutorial with an idea that is vague or 'a shot in the dark', they will tell you to read around it and will probably point you to appropriate sources. By doing this, they want you to exercise your inquisitive powers and engage your SI (or psychological imagination or historical imagination or whatever module you are taking).

When you leave the tutorial (and given that you have taken notes, which you should have), your next stage is the library to look up the recommended sources. After procuring them, your task is to begin reading and taking notes. Fortunately, you have already developed these skills, and you breeze through this task. Based on your reading, you come up with one specific idea that you think would work as a topic for your assignment, so you arrange another tutorial to discuss it. You have your notes and idea with you and are communicating them to your lecture, who is impressed by the amount of work you have done but believes that the actual idea requires further refinement. She or he suggests,

> Look, gender is a good topic, but women's underrepresentation in the media with regard to sport has been, by and large, exhausted. If you are deeply interested in the connection between women and media, I would suggest that you try to go beyond the obvious and find a different angle. Why don't you look at some other sources or other modules and issues discussed in them and try to re-think your idea.

This is the stage when your studious filing will again become extensively useful. If you have been keeping files on all past and current modules, it will be a fairly simple and painless exercise to go through the main concepts and issues discussed. And when you find an idea that will take your research or assignment to the required level, because you have filed your notes on your readings as well, it will be simple to locate key sources to read or revisit. Through this process (i.e. the routine work), you engage your SI in a creative playful way. At this more advanced stage, you try to find ideas, concepts, theories that you think you can fuse together to create something creative, something you did not expect. By disregarding traditional and artificially set modular and/or disciplinary boundaries, you have made an advanced step toward using your SI and developing your craft of doing sociology; this process, however, does not stop here. As Berger (1966: 29-30) put it: 'The sociologist, in his[her] quest for understanding, moves through the world...without respect for the usual lines of demarcation'.

Using personal experiences

So far, we have emphasised the generation of ideas and engagement of your SI, important parts of the craft of doing sociology, through reading, writing, filing, and recognising connections. The next phase of using your SI is connecting your personal experiences to your studies. Mills was very keen on establishing this connection and the constant interplay between personal and professional life. He (1959/2000: 195) wrote that 'the most admirable thinkers of the scholarly community you decided to join do not split their work from their lives. They seem to take both too seriously to allow such dissociation, and they want to use each for the enrichment of the other'. This is the practice we both subscribe to and have used time and again to generate research ideas by *reflecting* upon personal experience which we then sociologically investigated (for examples, see Molnar, 2010, and Kelly, in press).[5] By virtue of the preceding, the question you should be asking is, How can I use my SI to connect my personal experiences with my academic work? Let's take a close look at this aspect of using your SI.

Given that you have accumulated a decent sociological knowledge base regarding general issues in society and, specifically, around sport and exercise, you now must revisit these social issues (e.g. racial, gender, and class-based discrimination; lack of level playing field; social exclusion based on disability) in relation to your personal experiences. That is, after having taken stock of these issues, you begin to examine your personal life, past and present sport- and exercise-related experiences (experiences from other areas of your life can also be used but should be in line with your modules and degree programme). In essence, what you need to do is *reflect on* your previous or still existing personal troubles and, with the help of your sociological knowledge, indentify those that were/are not simply troubles but also social issues (regarding personal troubles and social issues, refer back to Chapter 2). When you have identified a few potential issues, you map those against your existing sociological knowledge and available research to check which one could be or should be further investigated. In doing so, you begin to create a sociological frame for your personal experience, which will help you make sense of it. This might sound a little complex, so let's proceed to a few examples to illustrate how it works.

Whilst taking sociology modules, you have hopefully been exposed to a wide range of social issues such as inequality based on social class, gender, race, geographic location, and the like. These issues are your reference points when you revisit your past and present personal experiences. Ideas can come from any part of your personal life (e.g. your sporting life, your exercise experience, or your family relations).

You map your experiences against class, gender, race, and other issues and check which one fits the bill – so to speak. For example, you may have never had the chance to play tennis, as you did not have access to it and your parents could not afford to take you or did not have the time to do so. In this case, you may want to ponder on the relevance of social class regarding sport participation and access (or lack of it) to specific sports and the ways in which your social class has affected you and others of the same ilk. You may also have wanted to engage in football and/or rugby, but there existed no such teams for women in your vicinity and, again, your parents could not afford to take you or did not have the time to do so. Now, you should be looking into multiple issues such as social class (could not afford to travel) and gender (there were sport teams nearby but only for men). Another scenario could be that you play in a women's rugby team but, because of the heavy training and constant pounding on your body, you have developed what is considered by some as masculine features. Playing rugby, coupled with a muscular body, has given people a preconception regarding your sexual orientation. You found this frustrating and eventually leave the sport. Again, multiple issues to consider here: first, social stereotypes with regard to sports and gender. Rugby is still often considered a male-specific sport, and women partaking in it may have to face social disapproval. Due to the nature of the sport, which involves extensive physical contact and demand, players develop muscular bodies, which is perfectly acceptable for men, but women may have to struggle for acceptance. As women playing rugby have the tendency to break with social norms regarding traditional femininity, their sexual orientation is also often in question, and they might be considered to be lesbians by some. By now, you can probably see that faced with so many challenges, an athlete would have to have strong dedication to this sport to stay the course of public spite, which is causing her personal troubles. Therefore, another issue you could consider is the involuntary career termination of athletes. Given the aforementioned external pressures a female rugby player may have to face whilst involved in the sport, it is no surprise that some of them may decide to prematurely end their involvement. This example would give you a few potential avenues to investigate: What happens to female athletes whilst involved in rugby? How did they cope with the issues/troubles faced and, if they decided to leave the sport, how did they live through the transition? These questions are only examples, and there are many more of them to consider and investigate. Your limit is your imagination!

As you can see, your and everyone's personal life is entangled in numerous social issues that you can sociologically investigate. To identify social issues you might have faced in the past or are still involved in, you need to use your sociological knowledge and engage in the process of reflection. By reflection, we mean an active process through which you understand previous and existing knowledge/experiences by employing and integrating new knowledge/experiences (Brown et al., 1999). That is, in this case, you use your newly acquired sociological knowledge to make sense of and analyse your past experiences. This 'playful' discovery of the interplay between different sets of knowledge and experience is part of you engaging your SI, more specifically, it is the *recognising connections* part. Reflection, if it is done properly, requires time. It is impossible to identify the exact amount of time required for reflection to be done properly, as it depends on the individual and the situation. However, we can say for certain that it cannot be rushed. This you should factor into your timetable to ensure that you have sufficient temporal space set aside for reflection.

Reflection can be in the form of having time to revisit your notes and/or to read and reread assignments before submission. Rereading your assignments is a useful and rewarding practice that we always recommend to our students. We know very well that when you are focused on your writing, what seemed perfectly logical yesterday does not necessarily make sense today. Hence, revisiting and reflecting on your ideas and their written manifestations is always good practice. Ensure that you have time to do it! Reflection and being reflective do not stop with revisiting written work and making connections between personal and professional experiences. They are also involved in the interpretation of personal and professional experiences through the engagement of sociological theories.

Theory – evidence balance

So far you have learned about what Mills called reading, writing, making connections, and finding/developing ideas for your assignment or research project: the groundwork of sociology. The next stage of your craft is collecting (primary and/or secondary) evidence that you will sociologically interpret. We will not spend time here on various types of data collection practices, as you will learn many of those in research methods modules and can review them in a number of good quality research methodology books (e.g. see Silverman, 2005; Robson, 2002). Instead, we will focus on the importance of considering your evidence in light of sociological theories. This entire book is dedicated to the importance of sociological theories and, in the previous chapters, theory by theory, we introduced the ways in which they can be used to make sense of sports and exercise in society. To consider the issue of balance is fundamental, as both in the formulation and execution of assignments and research, you will be confronted with the relationship between theory and evidence. You, therefore, must engage in the constant process of theory formation and empirical inquiry. This constant interplay between the thought processing directed jointly by theoretical insight and empirical particulars should be part of your sociological craft. This balance-related process is the acquisition of an uninterrupted two-way traffic between two layers of knowledge: that of general ideas, theories, or models and that of observations and perceptions of specific events (Mennell and Goudsblom, 1998). Essentially, we argue that sociology and theories that have grown out of it have contemporary currency and are useful tools to explain why we do what we do.

Mills was heavily critical of sociology that was unilateral in terms of involving only theory or evidence. He believed that being both exclusively theoretical and empirical had their shortcomings. In his book on SI, Mills (1959/2000: 33) argues that grand theory is overly abstract in its language and its thinking, which prevents grand theorists to 'get down from their higher generalities to problems in their historical and structural contexts'. By being overly abstract, grand theories and theorists have the characteristic of 'seemingly arbitrary and certainly endless elaboration of distinctions which neither enlarge our understanding nor make our experience more sensible' (1959/2000: 33). In this case, the theory becomes more important than what it aims to explain and debunk. When theorising becomes more of 'an arid game of Concepts than an effort to define systematically... the problems at hand' (Mills, 1959/2000: 34), the value of that theory must be put under rigorous questioning. To paraphrase, we should not create theories solely for the sake of creating theories, which then would have little practical value and relevance to understating social issues. Instead, theories should be helpful guides through which we can structure and interpret our observations.

In the previous chapters, we provided a wide range of examples as to how you can use sociological theories to analyse and explain sport- and exercise-related social phenomena. Therefore, it is unnecessary to repeat here what we have already explained in other sections of this book. We would, however, like to remind you that although it is essential to use sociological theories in your interpretation of social issues, it is vital that you select what most appropriately explains what you have observed. You do not have to 'stick to' one particular theory. On the contrary:

> 'You [should] try to think in terms of a variety of view points and in this way to let your mind become a moving prism catching light from as many angles as possible'.
>
> (Mills, 1959/2000: 214)

Mills was also critical of those social scientists who were infinitely entrapped by evidence and the collection of that. Mills believed that being overly empiricist and mimicking the methods and thought processes frequented in natural sciences did little good to social investigation. He went as far as saying that 'much 'empirical research' is bound to be thin and uninteresting' (1959/2000: 205). To avoid falling prey to abstract empiricism, we then must ensure that data collected have clear links to theoretical constructs and that such studies 'must be efficient, neat and, if possible, ingenious' (1959/2000: 205): that is, well designed. As Mills was not overly keen on collecting empirical evidence as 'it is a great deal of trouble' (1959/2000: 205), his view on the need for empirical data is debatable. We would argue that if it is essential to collect primary data, we should not shy away from it simply because it might be a troublesome exercise. We cannot always solely rely on data collected by others. There might be cases when data are unavailable, outdated, or biased, which should prompt us to pursue empirical data collection. Moreover, we would argue that it is not only empirical research that has to be well designed. In fact, all sociology-related projects should have their aims and research designs robustly rationalised whether they be module assignments, dissertations, or doctoral theses.

In general terms, along with Mills, we suggest that good sociological inquiry will have considered the theory–evidence balance. You should not be satisfied with investigations that are driven exclusively by tenets of either grand theory or abstract empiricism. The need for data collection should emerge from theoretical engagement, and empirical evidence should, in turn, permit further theoretical and conceptual work. In other words, the theory–evidence balance rests on the continuous interplay between what you think and what you find. Consequently, good sociological craft would be both empirically solid and theoretically engaged. Only in this way – by striking a balance – can social reality adequately be understood and explained and the gap be reduced between sociologists 'who would observe without thinking and those who would think without observing' (Mills, 1959/2000: 214).

CONCLUDING THOUGHTS

In this chapter, we combined our sociological knowledge and personal teaching-related experiences and engaged our SI to provide you with a practical guide to doing sociology. In writing this chapter and, in fact, the entire book, we consulted our students to help us create a text that they would find useful. Bearing in mind their comments, we provided ample examples and outlined, we think, a useful process of developing the craft of sociology. In this concluding section, what is still left for us to do is to reiterate the point that all the previously discussed aspects of SI and craft of doing sociology must be envisioned as interlinking pieces of the puzzle of your intellectual development. Thus, you must pay attention to the concerted improvement of all of them to achieve your academic potential and cultivate a critical and inquisitive mindset. This critical and imaginative mindset, coupled with the ground skills of reading, writing, filing, and making connections may turn out to be your most valuable asset (cultural capital) when faced with unexpected problems and challenges real life will throw at you. Then and only then you may realise the value of the hard work you invested into your learning at university[6] and that the power of sociology 'lies in the fact that its perspective makes us see in a new light the very world in which we have lived all our lives' (Berger, 1966: 32–33).

GLOSSARY OF SELECTED TERMS

Ahistorical – Any interpretation and/or account that is lacking historical insight or sensibility.

Agency – Active, individual human beings in social environments who have the capacity to act but whose actions are enabled and constrained by social **structures**.

Alienation – A term that originated from Karl Marx and refers to the loss of control social agents experience over social situations and their destiny. For Marx, alienation was directly associated with loss of control over one's labour and product of labour.

Anticipatory Socialization – Usually applies to new or un-established group members of a subculture to describe their trying to confirm stereotypical behaviour in their attempt to fit in. Inexperienced football fans may, for example, go out of their way to show that they know all the words to their club's songs, that they have the latest replica clothing, or that they hate their rivals more than anyone else. These actions are similar to **dramatic realization** except that they usually occur with novice/un-established group members.

Articulation – The temporary 'putting together' of different social elements to express and represent particular meanings and relationships between them. Articulation is often used in cultural studies to expose the social, cultural, or political powers that appear natural. For example, the Olympics, nation-state, and elite sporting prowess are usually articulated (put together) to provide a particular reading of Olympism grounded in nationalism and elitism.

222

Back Region/Backstage – The opposite to Goffman's concept of **front region**. The region where people can act and behave in private, away from public eyes, and can possibly let their guard down. For example, the coaches' office may act as back region if only the coaches are present and they feel free to express themselves in the knowledge that they are their own exclusive audience. However, it is to note that, even if only coaches are present, some form of staged performance is still occurring and, thus, the extent to which the coaches' office is a true back region is questionable. Perhaps the only true back region is where individuals are alone. Goffman stressed that some of the most informative social behaviours were witnessed at the threshold point between front and back regions where people would suddenly adapt their behaviour (and appearance) to stage another performance (e.g. going from the locker room to the sports arena).

Base-Supersturcture Model – In Marxist analysis, a society consists of two sections: base and superstructure. The base chiefly considers economic forces and relations associated with production. Superstructure consists of cultural institutions, political power, law, sports, and so on. By incorporating superstructure into social analysis, this model also indicates that despite viewing society from an economic vantage point, Marx did pay a great deal of attention to the creation and use of social values and ideology.

Bourgeoisie – In the classical Marxist sense, in societies with capitalist mode of production, it refers to the class that owns the means of production and raw materials and is the employer of wage labourers (i.e. **proletariat**). In a contemporary setting, bourgeoisie is often used to describe the lifestyle of the middle classes.

Bricolage – Refers to the process of creating new or transforming objects/symbols by the combining and/or arranging of things that were previously unrelated or unmerged.

Carceral Society – A concept often associated with the work of Michel Foucault and, in that context, means a society that holds and maintains power and control over its citizens by keeping them under constant surveillance through the means of modern technology. In essence, it is a society that is modelled on prison tactics to maintain order.

Civilising Process – Associated with Norbert Elias and provides an explanation as to how manners and our tolerance for violence changed during the course of history. The general argument is that as time moved on and social circumstances changed, we reduced our tolerance for violence and, thus, became more civilised. However, this process of increasing levels of civilisation does not take place in a liner fashion, and societies often revert back to earlier, less civilised phases, which are called de-civilising spurts.

Class – A form of social stratification that reflects a hierarchy between individuals and groups in society based on financial differentials (e.g. disposable income).

Class Consciousness – Frequently associated with Marx and Marxism. The term refers to one's consciousness of one's social class or economic standing in society. By being class–conscious, one can recognise social interests and barriers that one shares with others of the same social class. In Marxism, class consciousness is often associated with people's need to either create class consciousness or act upon their class consciousness.

Collective Effervescence – When extraordinary and intense emotion is collectively felt and expressed in groups, where it both generates a sense of shared experience and simultaneously fuels the collective feeling even more as a result.

Cultural Capital – Associated with the work of Pierre Bourdieu and means cultural assets one might possess beyond economic means. Cultural capital may manifest in the form of knowledge, ideas, and/ or education through which one can achieve and maintain power and social status.

Cultural Relativism – Opposes and offers a remedy to **ethnocentrism** by stating that cultures and social practices embedded in them should not be judged based on the values of another culture. Hence, each culture must be understood and interpreted on its own terms, not judged in relation to others.

Culturalists – The post-WW II cultural commentators who stressed the ordinary, everyday nature and potential of culture. They viewed culture as less a 'thing' to see and more a set of relational experiences, beliefs, practices, and outcomes that were the lived realities of people's lives. Culturalists were instrumental in the shift from Marxism to cultural studies.

Deconstructionism – Frequently associated with post-modern/post-structuralist thinkers, specifically with the work of Jacques Derrida. As Derrida was reluctant to provide a definition of what he meant by deconstruction, there are many competing interpretations of this process. However, we believe that the term generally refers to the rejection of traditional knowledge and understanding. That is, deconstructionists would argue that society cannot be portrayed or understood through traditional dichotomies (binary conceptual systems; e.g. male/female, local/global, work/leisure) and that the legitimacy of those pre-established binaries must be challenged, through which marginalised interest groups can be empowered.

Dialectic Model of Logic – A three-stage process for guiding our thoughts and actions into conflicts that ultimately lead to a resolution. The stages of this process are thesis (giving rise to a proposition) – anti-thesis (contradicting the thesis) – synthesis (reconciling the conflict between thesis and anti-thesis by forming a new position).

Division of Labour – Durkheim used this term to describe the increasingly complex organization of society, including people's working habits and structures governing human interaction.

Dramatic Realisation – The conscious behaviour and appearance of individuals who infuse their activity with signs that dramatically portray and confirm their group identity to others. For example, the rock climber may conspicuously 'litter' her or his phrases with specialist rock-climbing terminology or ensure she or he has and dons the latest kit to confirm to others she or he belongs.

Dramaturgy – The type of impression management Goffman (1959) utilized in his *The Presentation of Self in Everyday Life* book whereby the metaphor of a staged drama is used to explain social interaction between different people in a variety of settings.

225

Epistemology – A branch of philosophy that is concerned with knowledge and knowing (i.e. the ways in which we can generate knowledge of reality). Generally speaking, epistemology revolves around the following questions: What is knowledge, and how is knowledge generated?

Established/Outsiders – Associated with a study carried out by John Scotson and Norbert Elias in Leicester in the early 1960s. The study predominantly focused on the relationship and interaction between two social groups (Zones 2 and 3) of the same economic standing. The only significant difference was the length of time the inhabitants of Zone 2 (established) and 3 (outsiders) had spent in the district under investigation. The main finding of the study was that the established group showed prejudice toward the outsiders, who represented a threat to their identity, as inferiors and, thus, the established groups morally separated themselves from the outsiders, believing in their own 'natural' moral superiority.

Ethnocentric – An old-fashioned way of perceiving and interpreting other peoples' culture. Ethnocentrism is usually judgemental and demeaning toward other cultural formations with the view to attribute superiority and more importance to one's own culture.

Exchange-value – Linked to Marx and Marxism and refers to the value for which a product can be exchanged (sold) on the market. Exchange-value is connected to **use-value** – the amount of the former is not determined by the latter but the forces of the market. Marx argued that, unlike **use-value**, exchange-value is unnatural to humankind and is brought on by capitalism, leading to distorted societies that are captivated by commodity fetishism.

Exploitation – Frequently associated with Marxist and critical theory and refers to the appropriation of **surplus value** (i.e. the predominantly financial gap between the ruling class and other social classes), which allows the ruling class to take unfair advantage of people of other social classes. In the classical Marxist sense, the **bourgeoisie** exploited the **proletariat** because the latter were in a disadvantaged position due to the former having full ownership and control over the means of production and, thus, surplus value.

False Consciousness – A Marxian concept that indicates that capitalist societies are deceiving social classes, especially the working class(es), by camouflaging the true relationship between the ruling class and other social classes. Consequently, the lower classes are kept under careful ideological control, of which they are mostly completely unaware.

Figurations – Derived from Norbert Elias and refer to the nexus of interdependencies between people: the chains of functions and the axes of tensions that can be identified in any social context. Figurations are not stable or unchangeable social structures, they are socially produced and reproduced and constantly change during the course of history.

Figurational Sociology (see **Process Sociology**)

Front Region/Frontstage – Originating in Goffman's dramaturgy work, the front region is where people act out their preferred public face in full knowledge that they are in the public eye. This usually involves behaving according to socially structured conventions/ expectations. The front region can range from an operating theatre to a public gym. The surgeon and nurses in the operating theatre and exercisers and personal trainers in the gym would, therefore, be acting and present in these front regions.

Gains in Distinction – Developed by Pierre Bourdieu, who extended economic-based analyses to consider class connections to practices such as eating habits and attitudes toward the body. People belonging to one class seek to show their superiority to their closest neighbouring class groups by accumulating social, cultural, and educational capital (power) over their nearest class rival, thus maintaining their differential status. Accumulating such power (capital) is compounded by having, and being seen to have, good taste that allowed one to separate oneself from class rivals.

Globalisation – A series of developments that have led to a virtual compression of time and space on a worldwide scale. There has been considerable debate as to when globalisation began and what its root causes were. Disagreement also centres on the implications of the process of globalisation. At one extreme, it is argued that globalisation will result in the creation of a single global community with a shared culture, thereby obliterating national, regional, and local differences (homogeneity). The counter-argument pertains that in response to global forces, people will seek comfort in particularistic traditions and identities (local resistance). Somewhere between these oppositions is the argument that, whilst difference is undeniably being diminished, variety has been greatly increased in most parts of the world.

Habitus – Taken-for-granted ways of acting in social situations. Habitus is the foundation of our personality structure that we acquire during socialisation processes and social interactions and is used to explain individual preferences and behaviours.

Hegemony – An indirect and subtle form of domination through which the ruling class and/or country employs means of (cultural) power other than military force to gain advantage or maintain their position over subordinate countries/social groups. Hegemonic power is well implemented when the suppressed are unaware of the oppression and actually believe the status quo to be in their best interests.

Historical Materialism – Primarily considers human history through the modes of production, which in capitalist societies is driven by material/market forces. These material forces then are perceived to be chiefly responsible for producing and reproducing societies, social values, and social practices.

Homines Aperti (open people) – A way of understanding social relations and interdependencies. 'Open people' are those who recognise the ever-changing interdependency chains of human societies (social figurations) and can imagine themselves as a part of them.

Homo Clausus (closed human) – A way of understanding social relations and interdependencies. Such human beings are prone to believe that their actual selves somehow exist inside of them and that an invisible barrier separates their inside from everything existing outside. From this perspective, the ever-changing and complex social connections (or figurations) and interdependencies are not fully recognised.

228

Homophobia – An intense and irrational fear of or intolerance toward lesbians, gays, bisexual (biphobia), and transgender (transphobia) people. Homophobic behaviours often manifest in prejudice and discrimination and can lead to violence toward people whose sexual orientation is perceived to be non-heterosexual.

Hyper-reality – Under post-modern social conditions, the boundaries between what is real and unreal are blurred; thus, hyper-reality refers to our inability to distinguish between real and fantasy. In hyper-reality, everything is nicer, more organised, and more beautiful. Hyper-reality is an excess of reality, meaning whatever we are experiencing, being hyperexposed to in hyperreality, is qualitatively better than reality.

Ideology – A system of ideas that forms the foundation of any social and/or political action. Ideology is frequently used to indicate ideas that underpin and legitimise the domination of one social stratum over another (e.g. gender ideology).

Impression Management – The ways in which people seek to control and manage the impressions they make on others. It usually involves ensuring that one avoids faux pas or embarrassing themselves and others in the daily interaction of everyday life.

Industrialisation – A process in human history that significantly altered social production and relations. Prior to industrialisation, agriculture was the main mode of production and was gradually transformed by emerging industries in some of the Western European countries in the 1800s. Industrialisation and technological development also led to a shift from manual labour to machine-operated production and to the gravitation of people from rural areas to towns and cities, which triggered a range of **urbanisation** processes. Gaining more control over nature and establishing more regular working hours opened a more systematic and rational world view and thinking that became gradually infused with capitalist values.

Industrial Revolution – A trend begun in Britain with effects that gradually spread across the globe. It refers to specific phases during the process of **industrialisation** and is associated with the invention and implementation of technology. Generally speaking, industrial revolution in the 1800s is argued to have been chiefly triggered by considerable improvements made in the iron and textile industries and by the invention of the steam engine. The industrial revolution had social and economic corollaries that manifested in sustained economic and population growth.

Interaction Order – A general term Goffman used to describe face-to-face interaction between two or more individuals in which behaviour is inscribed by a number of protocols, as expressed in his works on impression management. Goffman used four main metaphorical terms to capture the interaction order: drama, game, ritual, and frame (Chapter 6, *Symbolic interaction perspectives* deals mainly with drama.)

Means of Production – Refers to the physical infrastructure that is required in the production of goods and includes instruments of labour (machinery, factories, tools, and other facilities) and subjects of labour (raw materials and natural resources). In the classical Marxist analysis of society, both instruments and subjects of labour are owned by the **bourgeoisie**.

Mechanical Solidarity – A term that originates from Durkheim's work to describe primordial societies that were held together by groups sharing similar tasks and goals. Thus, in those societies, there was little division of labour, and group solidarity is maintained by and within a series of simple relations.

Modernity – A historical era characterised by the move from agricultural to industrial societies. It also refers to the ideas and ways of living and creating that arose and stayed dominant in post-feudal societies. Modernity can be described through the emerging social domination of rationality, science, and technology. It has, however, been argued that modernity, as an historical era, has come to be replaced by **post-modernity**.

Neo-Marxism – A sociological trend that emerged in response to the critiques **orthodox or classical Marxism** received due to being perceived as economically deterministic. Neo-Marxists began recognising that, although being inextricably linked to economics, wealth, and modes of production (and consumption), societies were much more complex than outlined by classical Marxists, with ideology and power being central components. Rather than cultural institutions reflecting capitalist society, they were claimed to be paradigms of it – reinforcing and reproducing the social forms and institutions that shaped and manipulated the activity in the first place.

Organic Solidarity – A term that originates from Durkheim's work to describe modern societies that are held together by increasingly divergent groups responsible for different tasks. Thus, in modern (and post-modern) societies, there is a substantial division of labour so people must cooperate in increasingly complex and specific relations to ensure that their society is maintained.

Orthodox (Classical) Marxism – Concerned with the role of cultural institutions in analysing industrial societies. According to this perspective, economic relationships form the base upon which institutions and the ideas generated within them are balanced. Thus, the material reality of producing the basic human needs of food and shelter influences or governs the social activities of a society.

Panopticon Theory – Originally developed by Jeremy Bentham as an effective prison system, the panopticon (all seeing) design has a central watch tower and cells concentrically surrounding it and ensures that the surveillance is permanent or, at least, appears to be. Due to the location of the watch tower and to the preventive measures taken to disallow inmates to see inside, inmates do not know whether there are guards in the watch tower. Consequently, there is no need for guards, as the possibility of being watched is sufficient to force people to behave. The panopticon theory relates to post-modern instruments of constant and unverifiable surveillance whereby contemporary societies are controlled.

Parliamentarisation – A key feature of the **Civilising Process** and an indicator of the increased level of civilisation that, perhaps, led to less violent ways of settling debates and social issues.

Patriarchy – A social system in which men hold power and exercise economic, cultural, and political dominance over women and younger males. Traditionally, sport has been a social arena dominated by masculine values (which have been passed onto young male participants) and served the perpetuation of patriarchy. Consequently, women taking part in sport have been considered as trespassers on male territory.

Positivism – A scientific paradigm frequently associated with **modernity** and the rationalisation of society. Positivism claims that social phenomena and actions have meanings external to social actors and, thus, can be objectively observed and interpreted. That is, scientific observations that aim to interpret and capture social reality can do so accurately and reliably and are not influenced by one's own preferences and prejudices.

Post-modernity – A turn against the ideas, promises, and achievements of **modernity** to challenge grand narratives and recognise the plural subtleties of contemporary social existence. Post-modernity is a reaction against an ordered view of the modern world and fixed ideas about the forms and meanings of (social) texts. In its reaction against modernist ideals and to create ways of better capturing reality (or realities), post-modern thinking emphasises the breaking down of disciplinary silos and the distinction between high and pop culture.

Process-Sociology (Figurational Sociology) – A sociological perspective developed by Norbert Elias and concerned with the sociological analysis of long-term socio-historical processes and the effect of those on the complexity and nature of social **figurations**.

Proletariat – Used to identify the lower classes, especially the working class. From a Marxist perspective, proletariat are exploited by the **bourgeoisie** who own the means of production, whereas the proletariat own only their labour force, which they sell to the bourgeoisie for a wage.

Schemes of Perception and Appreciation – Used by Pierre Bourdieu to express the interplay between structure and agency by examining the ways different groups experience and interpret the same phenomenon according to the groups' differing histories, values, and experiences. Their perception and appreciation are linked to their cultural history and may, therefore, differ from group to group.

Semiotics – The study of signs that explores the roles of signs and sign systems in communication. Language plays a central part of semiotic analyses and is perceived as a key system that constitutes a culture. However, it is not only the spoken language that can and has been the subject of semiotics; scholars have also investigated the language of dance, fashion, cock fights, and physical appearance.

Sexism – Attitudes and actions of an individual or a group toward others manifesting in various forms of discrimination on the grounds of their gender. In sport, a type of sexism is the preferential treatment of men over women by giving men more opportunities, better facilities, higher status, and higher rewards.

Signifying System – A system of attributing meanings to objects and experiences. Signifying systems consist of both descriptive literal (denotative) and culturally interpreted (connotative) levels of analysis. A man who shoots another man is literally a killer (denotative) but may be viewed as either a terrorist or soldier (connotative) according to the culturally specific circumstances. These meanings (signs) become normalised into a signifying system.

Simulacrum – Term meaning likeness or similarity, but Baudrillard used it to express excess of reality or describe features of society that are more real than real itself. According to Baudrillard's understanding, the simulacrum is not even a copy of the real, but it becomes truth (real) in its own right. This argument claims that whatever we are experiencing, being hyperexposed to in hyper-reality is qualitatively better than reality. In hyper-reality, everything is nicer, more organised, more beautiful, and truer. In other words, under hyper-real conditions, the boundaries between what is real or unreal are blurred.

Social Capital – The non-material resources, such as social status, trust, and social networks that have the capacity to empower the individual who possess them and/or part of them. Social capital can be converted into financial capital via being part of powerful social networks (i.e. it is not necessarily what you know but whom you know.).

233

Sociological Imagination – Concerned with understanding one's position and role(s) in society. By actively employing this concept, one's level of social and self-awareness can be significantly increased. Enhancing self-awareness can be achieved by adopting self-reflective, self-investigative practices. The sociological self-discovery achieved through self-reflection can be effectively used exploring the connections between personal troubles and social issues (i.e. between **agency** and social **structures)**.

Sportisation – A long-term historical process that began to emerge around the mid-eighteenth century, is inexorably linked to globalization processes, and refers to the emergence, development, and regional and global diffusion of modern sports. Initially explained by Norbert Elias and later further developed by Joseph Maguire, the sportisation process is perceived to have five phases ranging from the 1750s to present times.

Status – The achieved or ascribed prestige or esteem an individual or a group is given by other members of society. For instance, male sports generally have higher social status than women's sports based on the common belief (ascribed status) that male sports are of higher standard. Status can be both positive and negative. Individuals and groups with extremely low social status may be discriminated against, treated as outcasts, and **stigmatised** because of the social perception they receive. For example, female athletes with masculine physical features may have their sexual orientation questioned and stigmatised as lesbians or transgendered.

Stigma – Harsh social disapproval of someone's social, psychological or physical attributes. Stigma may be triggered by physical deformity, nationality, ethnicity, religion, or sexual orientation or any combination of the aforementioned categories. In sport, gender- and race-related stigmas are still common.

Strongly Valued Goods – Can be defined as values and morals (goods) that we should possess or at least desire, even if we do not possess them. By not having and/or desiring such goods, we may be perceived by others as inferior or irregular. For example, patriotism is viewed by many as a moral good we all ought to value and, if we do not, we reveal a moral failing.

234

Structures – Social structures are created by humans for humans to regulate social existence. Social structures regulate and glue society together. They are both constraining and enabling. Our life is essentially a constant negotiation between us (**agency**) and social structures. Social structures include, for example, education, politics, economy, and sports.

Structuralists – The cultural commentators who stress the structural barriers to working class emancipation. For example, Louis Althusser (1918–1990), a structuralist himself, viewed the structural elements of society such as schools, religion, and civic society as powerfully guiding (or over-determining) people's views on social life and providing them with a false consciousness. Structuralists have strong links to orthodox Marxism.

Subsistence Wage – The lowest possible wage on which a worker and his or her family can survive.

Surplus Value – Part of the capitalist mode of production explained from a Marxist perspective and essentially the profit appropriated in the capitalist mode of production. For Marx, surplus value is achievable only through the exploitation of the labour force. That is, surplus value derives from the difference between wages paid to labourers and the price of the commodity they produce. Surplus value accrues when a commodity is sold beyond its production costs, which is the very essence of capitalism.

Sympathetic Introspection – A form of reflexivity whereby researchers or anyone wishing to understand someone else try to put themselves in the other's position, to see the world from their perspective.

Threshold of Repugnance – Often associated with **process-sociology** and linked to the **civilizing process**. As people become more civilized/Westernised over the centuries, their threshold of repugnance in relation to violence and public displays of bodily functions decreases. The threshold at which we become repulsed lowers; therefore, we are less able and willing to witness violence and other such (socially considered) uncivilised acts.

Urban Regime Theory – Questions and critiques the extent to which civic investments (e.g. staging major sporting events) genuinely benefit a city, a community, or a country. This theory highlights that planning, bidding for, and hosting mega events is not an apolitical enterprise and, thus, there are always winners and losers as a consequence of such investments. In true Marxist tradition, the 'benefits' to 'the community' are claimed to really be benefits to only some members of the community at the expense of others within the same social and geographic area.

Urbanisation – The process responsible for the growth and development of cities and towns. It is directly associated with modernisation and industrialisation, which triggered the development of cities and the movement of labour force from rural areas to urbanised ones.

Use-Value – Part of the capitalist mode of production explained from a Marxist perspective. Use-value is the degree of usefulness (utility) of a service or product in society (i.e. the degree to which a product satisfies a human need). Though use-value is the precondition of **exchange-value**, the amount of the latter is not solely determined by the use-value.

Valorisation – The process through which commercialisation and professionalization (i.e. capitalism-driven social relations) extended over sport and leisure activities (e.g. exercise). It refers to the value-related transmutation of sport from **use-value** into **exchange-value** and then into **surplus-value**.

Vocabulary of Fronts – A Goffman term to explain the socially constructed patterns of expectation we might have about particular situations (and people involved in them) that prevent us from needing to approach every single situation anew as though we had no knowledge of its context. Vocabulary of fronts emerges from past experience and sometimes stereotypes. For example, we might expect a physical education teacher to wear a tracksuit and have a whistle around her or his neck, but we would not expect the mathematics teacher to dress the same way. Each time we enter a new situation, we are familiar with the vocabulary of fronts that may face us such as the place, the actors, and the activities.

NOTES

1 INTRODUCTION

1 See NHS fitness guidelines in this regard at http://www.nhs.uk/Livewell/fitness/Pages/physical-activity-guidelines-for-adults.aspx

2 To attain a student-centred approach, we 'enlisted' some of our students to review most of the chapters included in this book. Their useful comments helped shape our interpretation of social theories and use of examples in this book. We thank them for their efforts and insightful comments.

2 C. WRIGHT MILLS AND THE SOCIOLOGICAL IMAGINATION

1 For an explanation regarding the difference between social and sociological issues, see Willis (1996).

2 Mills often uses the word *man* or *men* to describe the actions of human beings in general. Although his writing style can be considered sexist in today's terms, he refers to both men and women in his sociological treatise.

3 In the *Afterword* to the Fortieth Anniversary Edition of *The Sociological Imagination*, Todd Gitlin (2000: 229) succinctly describe Mills' combative nature: 'He was a radical disabused of radical traditions, a sociologist disgruntled with the course of sociology, an intellectual frequently skeptical of intellectuals, a defender of popular action as well as a craftsman, a despairing optimist, a vigorous pessimist...'

4 For Mills to be critical of American democracy and the power elite leading the country in the middle of the Cold War and McCarthyism was outright dangerous. During McCarthyism and the so-called Second Red Scare (an era of heightened fear of communist influences in the United States), a high number of American citizens' loyalty to their country was publicly questioned by government and private industry panels. These 'trials' were often deeply humiliating and mostly relied on either inconclusive or

questionable evidence. Regardless, to be cited to such a panel had severe consequences to the individual, and many suffered loss of employment and even imprisonment.

5 Leonard (1996) argues that approximately 99 percent of American athletes do not make the transition from high school to college sports.

6 These questions are borrowed from Willis (1996) but employed here in a somewhat different way. We split critical sensibility into ontological and epistemological aspects. We ontologically separate social from natural sciences and epistemologically question what we know and how we know it. As this is an introductory book on social theory, we do not wish to get further into a philosophical discussion on various scientific paradigms but, if you are interested in developing your understanding of this area, we would recommend the following sources: Guba (1990), Williams and May (2000), and Baert (2005).

7 See National Health Service statistics on obesity at http://www.ic.nhs.uk/statistics-and-data-collections/health-and-lifestyles/obesity/statistics-on-obesity-physical-activity-and-diet-england-2011.

8 Although infrequently noted, Mills was critical of orthodox Marxism and recognised its limitations. In his posthumously published work, *The Marxist* (1962), he suggested that Marxist theories should be reexamined. For instance, Mills did not believe that it was going to be a united working class to become an important agency in implementing radical societal change. He attributed more potential to the intelligentsia to play a crucial role in initiating such change (see Eldridge, 1983).

3 FUNCTIONALIST PERSPECTIVES

1 Given that much of Functionalist theory developed in the United States during the 1940s and 1950s, Anglo-American society is actually 'the society' that is best conceptualized in Functionalist models.

2 In October 2001, President George W. Bush implemented the 'Patriot Act' in direct response to the 9/11 atrocities the previous month.

4 MARXIST PERSPECTIVES

1 West Ham and Portsmouth were not included due to their debt being so large they failed to gain UEFA licences that year (see *The Guardian*, 23 February 2010 and *The Telegraph*, 4 June 2009).

2 Marxism is sometimes referred to as conflict theory due to its focus on economic (and other) conflict arising between human groups within society.

3 Hegelian dialectic models are three-stage processes for guiding our thoughts and actions into conflicts, which ultimately lead to a predetermined solution. The stages of this process are thesis – anti-thesis – synthesis.

238

4 Althusser's famous essay, 'Ideological State Apparatuses', was heavily criticised for being overly deterministic, providing a view of education and other such spheres as mere sites of ideological indoctrination of the masses by the powerful elites.

5 Although during his life Marx was financially depended on Engels, Engels was the junior partner in the intellectual venture forged between Marx and himself. Engels went as far as admitting that Marx was the intellectual giant in their partnership, and he could not have achieved what Marx did (see Ritzer, 1992).

6 Marxists might describe the very phrase 'credit crunch' as a mystification-inspiring term that (by design or default) camouflages the true issues, which, in reality, are actually the cumulative effects of years of corporate class greed and insurance mismanagement, inflated property valuation, and excessive and risk-laden loan lending.

7 In 2008, these losses totalled £24.1 billion. Mr Goodwin left the company on 1 January 2009 with his pension package. Marxists would acknowledge the high-profile government, media, and public concern about this at the time. However, Marxists would remind us of the power – legislative and ideological – that ultimately enabled it, despite such voluminous, yet, impotent, opposition.

8 Greece, France, Republic of Ireland, Germany, and other nation states have acted similarly.

9 Another example of assuming capitalist interests to be universal was exposed when the UK Conservative–Liberal Democrat coalition government, elected in 2010, appointed millionaire ex-banker David Laws as Chief Secretary to the Treasury. Unobvious to many was the irony of appointing an ex-banker to oversee the cutting of the £156 billion deficit in the public purse, when it had been the irresponsible practices by bankers that had been held responsible for much of the 'credit crunch' in the first place. Mr. Laws subsequently resigned after details emerged of his illegitimate claims for accommodation expenses totalling £40,000 of taxpayers' money.

10 In Western societies, especially during the Cold War era, Marx was often portrayed as a fanatic, blood-thirsty reactionary who wanted to overthrow both the economic and political systems through an organic revolution to create, what he believed would be, the ultimate society. This negative propaganda against Marx and his ideas is highly flawed. Although, Marx did call for revolution and the restructuring of capitalist societies, he never believed that this process should necessarily be bloody. Essentially, Marx was a humanist and, as such, envisioned the transformation from capitalism to socialism to take place peacefully (Ritzer, 1992).

5 CULTURAL STUDIES PERSPECTIVES

1 Hare coursing involves dogs, usually whippets or greyhounds, chasing hares across fields in a test of the dogs' speed and agility. It often results in the death of the hare.

2 From the end of World War One until the mid-1990s, the Conservative Party was the governing party sixteen times compared to seven for Labour.
3 In 2011 and in 2012, two horses died as a result of the race and though some years no horse dies, it is a relatively common occurrence.
4 In the second edition, Stephen Lukes (2005) acknowledges the influence Gramsci had on his original 1974 book on power.
5 See *The Guardian*, 22/9/07.
6 As of 2011, these include homecoming parades, newly invented memorial services specifically for servicemen (and women) killed after WWII, the creation of the Millies (a military version of the Oscars), the X-Factor television show having a 'song for heroes', and the creation of an annual Armed Forces Day.
7 This coincided with England's preparations for the World Cup, where the team were preparing for their first match in the competition and took place a matter of days before the Saville Report into Bloody Sunday was published. The Report's findings led to the Prime Minister publicly apologising on behalf of the United Kingdom and armed forces for its 'unjustified' and 'unjustifiable' killings of fourteen innocent and unarmed civil rights marchers in Derry (North of Ireland) in 1972. The report unequivocally blamed the British soldiers for the killings and for subsequently lying about the events.
8 The actual use of the term *drug* reveals an ideological position and, to cultural studies theorists, illuminates the power to define and label behaviour/acts with loaded terms that serve to position the reader in a particular way.
9 Princess Anne is the patron of the SRU and is perhaps its most celebrated supporter. Since the early 1990s and coinciding with a rise in Scottish political nationalism that resulted in the 1999 reopening of the Scottish parliament, the SRU adopted the nationalistic anthem 'Flower of Scotland'. In the media coverage of Scotland's matches, the Princess is often captured lustily singing the anthem.

6 SYMBOLIC INTERACTION PERSPECTIVES

1 For example, sport and exercise psychology and/or motor control books often encourage coaches to use models of learning that fail to consider such symbolic interaction factors. These models include Fitts and Posner's (1967) three-stage model that views learning as a sequential process or Schmidt's (1975) schema theory that posits that learning occurs by sensory recall based on previous experiences of the movements required.
2 The Chicago School refers to the works and scholars that developed urban anthropology and ethnography at Chicago University during the twentieth century and has since become associated with the sociology

department's work on deviance and its development of symbolic interaction.

3 Here we begin to see the potential for symbolic interaction to be combined with more critical approaches such as cultural studies.

4 Bench clearing describes the practice in baseball and ice hockey of fellow players leaving the players' benches to enter the field of play or rink to join in a physical fight with opponents. Equivalents occur in rugby union.

5 Pierre Bourdieu, who was once dubbed 'the French Goffman', was clearly influenced by Goffman, and he used 'schemes of perception and appreciation' to describe a similar concept.

6 Here we see the influence Parsons had on Goffman's writings. Parsons had earlier described 'status roles' as roles people occupied, which involved reciprocal degrees of expectations in terms of the behaviour one should perform and could expect in return.

7 Although being a Scottish football club based in the capital city of Edinburgh, Hibernian was formed by Irish Catholic immigrants and has had, to varying degrees, Irish Catholic linkages throughout its history.

8 Up until the late 1990s English football fans had a reputation for drunkenness and violence during a period in which Scotland football fans improved their reputation to such an extent that fans of the Scotland national team became known for generating a carnival and good-natured atmosphere.

9 Coakley and Pike (2009) use the broader term 'interactionist theory' rather than symbolic interactionist, but the differences are negligible for our purposes.

7 PROCESS SOCIOLOGY

1 Note that the civilising process should not be envisioned as a linear line that indicates a continuous growth of civilisation and, in turn, decline in the level of violence. Elias and his colleagues pointed out clearly that the civilising process is often interrupted by de-civilising spurts that halt the increase of civilisation and increase the level of violence (e.g. the 'wars' the United States and United Kingdom have been fighting in Iraq, Afghanistan, and Libya).

2 We think it is relevant to point out that our tolerance for violence has not decreased across all spheres of society, which could be a critique of process sociology. In fact, we feel it important to point out that, ironically, while we focus on the inhuman nature of hounds killing foxes for the sake of killing, we have ongoing 'wars' in Afghanistan and Libya where both invader and indigenous troops are killed on a regular basis.

3 11 May 2011, Yahoo Sport reported that an Aussie Rules player was sent off for having a dangerous haircut. Nathan van Someren, Simpson Tigers, was deemed too dangerous to play by an umpire in the match against Otway Districts, who claimed that Someren's Mohawk haircut could have

poked another player in the eye. This is an example par excellence of how practices once considered normal, acceptable, and not dangerous can and do change over time as rules and social practices are reconsidered. In this particular case, the Victorian league admitted that the umpire had been a little overly zealous in applying a rule meant to protect players from opponents wearing jewelry or other items that could cause injury. (http://uk.eurosport.yahoo.com/blogs/world-of-sport/article/46544/)

4 This quotation by Elias regarding understanding what sociology is can be problematic as it may give the impression that understanding sociology per se is the 'prize' awaiting us at the end of our social inquiries. Conversely, we argue that our task should not exclusively be trying to understand sociology but rather to use sociology to understand society and ourselves in the dense network of social figurations. In essence, sociology is a tool, a means to an end, but not an end in itself.

5 Alan Klein writes the following in the preface to Maguire's (2005) work:

> Joseph Maguire deserves to be called the pioneering figure in the study of sport globalisation. He's been at it for more than fifteen years, and has developed a corpus of work that has to be admired by all of us...It doesn't matter where – on the theoretical spectrum – you fall, Maguire's work has become the benchmark for where the rest of us take off.

6 With regard to finding alternative sources and views on the historical origins and development of globalisation, see Giddens (1990), Held et al. (1999), and Therborn (2000).

7 Another strength of recognising and exploring the commingling of globalisation and sportisation is that it rejects the passivity of sports that simply mirror but do not influence society and thereby advocates that we should collectively view sports in contemporary society as an organic part of everyday life. James Riordan (2007: 275) writes that 'there are moments in history when sport, instead of simply reflecting the economic and political structure[s] of society, may significantly contribute to changing [them]'.

8 FEMINIST PERSPECTIVES

1 It may not be too surprising that this explicit show of heterosexual femininity occurs given that it remains a common narrative reproduced in many mainstream media forms. For example, British Olympic cyclist Vikki Pendleton is one of many female athletes who is often portrayed in this way. One such example occurred when she was interviewed by the BBC and the male interviewer, ex-Olympic rower Matthew Pinsent, accompanied her on her 'routine' visit to the beauty parlor to get her nails painted and culminated with Pinsent asking her a series of questions designed to reveal how she 'maintained her feminine girly side' (See BBC1 *Inside Sport*, 8 April, 2008).

242

2 For the sake of this example, you are portrayed as a heterosexual women, but it does not mean that you have to be or that all male or female bodybuilders are.

3 This is, of course, an outdated position, given the now-recognized responsibilities and challenges when raising children. However, biologism may be at least partly linked to socialization processes whereby, in many capitalist societies, activities that do not earn money (or other materially based goods) are framed as less valuable, less intellectual, less skillful, and even less challenging. In our opinion, this seriously underestimates the skills and requirements of raising children in a safe and successful manner.

4 Although we date the first wave of feminism between 1860s and 1930s, the historical roots of feminist writings and movement go as far back as the 1600s. Moreover, Ritzer (1992) aptly observes that whenever women were oppressed, there was always some form of feminism present and, thus, one could argue that feminism is as old as male dominated societies.

5 According to the report, there are almost as many varsity teams for women (425) as there are for men (431) at Canadian universities, which reflects respectable gender equilibrium.

6 This increase in participation does not mean that we have reached gender equality. On the contrary, The Active People Survey 2009–10 indicates that there are still more than 1.4 million more men taking part in sport over the same period as compared to women.

9 POST-MODERN PERSPECTIVES

1 Anthony Giddens (1999) used this phrase to describe contemporary social conditions.

2 As mentioned in other chapters, historical insight or historical sensibility (see Mills, 1959) is an essential part of any good sociological analysis. In other words, to fully understand the 'why' we must consider the 'when' and 'for how long'.

3 To further complicate matters, post-modernity, post-modernism, and post-structuralism are often interchangeably used in academic sources, although we must point out that some theorists would argue that these terms have their own and distinctive theoretical lineage (see Ward, 1997; and Andrews, 2000). For the sake of simplicity, we will use 'post-modernity' throughout this chapter to denote theoretical perspectives discussed.

4 Whilst running on a treadmill on a Sunday morning and watching BBC One's *The Important Question* programme, one of us witnessed the following scene. In that episode (27/03/11), there was a discussion regarding whether creationism should be taught in schools and whether it was a considerable alternative to the theory of evolution. The discussion panel consisted of a range of individuals, but scientists seemed to

dominate the discussion. As the discussion became heated due to a clash of opinions, one of the participants made an attempt to capitalise on science's social status by saying: 'Listen to me! I am involved in research about this.' Later on, before answering a question, she also made the following statement: 'I have two degrees in biology.' Her proclamations could be interpreted as the public recognition and credibility of scientific knowledge that is often demonstrated by having academic degree(s) and being involved in research.

5 This does not necessarily mean that information presented in the mass media is always based on credible scientific knowledge or that scientists when expressing their views are only motivated by the idea of knowledge transfer. On the contrary, information presented in the mass media can be – and is often – bogus (remember the WMD fiasco in Iraq), and scientists can be influenced by personal and political views or motivated by financial gains when expressing their opinion. In other words, following post-modernist thought, there is no ultimate truth but various (sometimes reasonable, sometimes unreasonable) accounts of truth.

6 We have provided only a basic introduction to Foucault's theory of power. For Foucault, power is not associated with a specific individual, group, or class. Rather, 'power circulates through a network of individuals; it is omnipresent; it is in everyone; it is immanent' (Rail and Harvey, 1995: 166). For a more detailed and sport-related account, see Smith Maguire (2002).

7 Interesting to note that despite the tension between Baudrillard and Foucault, they had common theoretical grounds. For instance, both of them rejected the terms *post-modernity/post-structuralism* and were influenced by Nietzsche's thoughts.

8 The word *appear* is italicised, as appearing successful and being successful are not the same. For a short while, we can disguise the true limitation of our disposable income by taking out loans and using credit cards to buy the things we want (not the things we need). Such a social venture often has disastrous outcomes (e.g. ruined credit reports and accumulation of high interest rates).

10 A GUIDE TO THE CRAFT OF SOCIOLOGY

1 Ken Robinson's speech can be view on the Internet at: http://blog.ted.com/2006/06/27/sir_ken_robinso/

2 In the second chapter of *The Sociological Imagination*, Mills demonstrated that it is possible to simplify the language of social sciences without losing meaning. It is worth reading his 'translations' of Talcott Parsons's work on social systems.

3 In addition to sociology-specific dictionaries, it is also helpful to have a general English dictionary at hand. *Oxford* and *Collins* are tested editions that can serve you well throughout your university studies. However,

if you are not overly fond of hard copies, most publishers also provide electronic dictionaries that you can install and use on your computer. Or, if you are really into your technology, you can download a mobile phone application that will do exactly the same. It does not matter whichever way works for you as long as you use a dictionary.

4 In a real job situation, you can draw on what you have learned at university. For instance, you will be able to file reports, present ideas, and debate and question potential avenues for progress. You may even find that your filing and organisation skills will become important assets in the eyes of your line manager.

5 Another example of engaging SI and using personal experiences to enrich professional work is done by the late Alan Ingham (with Alison Dewar, 1999), a pioneering figure in the sociology of sport, whose observations as a father attending his son's ice hockey training formed the foundation of a book chapter.

6 Philip Bourgois (1995), in his ethnographic study on the drug dealings in East Harlem, New York, depicts a vivid picture of some of the struggles of his participants who tried to evade the life of a drug dealer by attempting to acquire and keep legitimate jobs but failed to do so as they invariably lacked the necessary social capital. Bourgois writes (1995: 142):

> The 'common sense' of the white-collar work is foreign to them [participants from East Harlem]; they do not, for example, understand the logic in filing triplicate copies of memos or for postdating invoices. When they attempt to improvise or show initiative, they fail miserably and instead appear inefficient – or even hostile – for failing to follow 'clearly specified' instructions.

Though they lack social capital required in the legal world, they have plenty of social capital in running successful underground ventures. Generally speaking, knowledge and experience gained by dealing drugs is non-transferable to legal jobs they could potentially procure and, in turn, they are set up for structural failure as soon as they try to go 'legit'. The moral of this story, aside from not to be a drug dealer unless it is legitimate, is that developing skills in not always sufficient; you must ensure that you develop the skills you will most likely need in your future personal and professional environment. (Note: Please disregard this piece of advice if you are the next Albert Einstein or Bill Gates.)

REFERENCES

The Active People Survey (2009-10). *Women's Sport Participation*. Available at http://www.wsff.org.uk/publications/fact-sheets/active-people-survey-2009-10-womens-sport-participation

Abrahamson, M. (1978). *Functionalism*. Englewood Cliffs, NJ: Prentice-Hall.

Adams, C. J. (2000). *The Sexual Politics of Meat: A Feminist-Vegetarian Critical Theory*. New York: Continuum.

Adorno, T.W. (1981). *Prisms*. Cambridge, MA: MIT Press.

Althusser, L. (1971). *Lenin and Philosophy and Other Essays*. London: New Left Books.

Anderson, B. (1983). *Imagined Communities: Reflections on the Origin and Spread of Nationalism*. London: Verso.

Andrews, D. L. (1997). The (Trans) National Basketball Association: American Commodity-Sign Culture and Global-Local Conjuncturalism. In A. Cvetkovich & D. Kellner (Eds.), *Articulating the Global and the Local: Globalization and Cultural Studies* (pp: 72–101). Boulder, CO: Westview Press.

Andrews, D. L. (2000). Posting Up: French Post-structuralism and the Critical Analysis of Contemporary Sporting Culture. In J. Coakley & E. Dunning (Eds.), *Handbook of Sport Studies* (pp: 106–137). London: Sage.

Andrews, D. L. (2002). Coming to Terms with Cultural Studies. *Journal of Sport and Social Issues*, 26(1): 110–117.

Andrews, D. L., & Loy, J. W. (1993). British Cultural Studies and Sport: Past Encounters and Future Possibilities. *Quest*, 45: 255–276.

Armstrong, K. L. (2007). Self, Situations and Sport Consumption: An Exploratory Study of Symbolic Interactionism. *Journal of Sport Behavior*, 30(2): 111–129.

Baert, P. (2005). *Philosophy of the Social Sciences*. Cambridge: Polity Press.

Bairner, A. (2001). *Sport, Nationalism, and Globalisation: European and American Perspectives*. Albany: State University of New York Press.

Bairner, A. (2006). The Leicester School and the Study of Football Hooliganism. *Sport in Society*, 9(4): 583–598.

Bairner, A., & Molnar, G. (Eds.) (2010). *The Politics of the Olympics: A Survey*. London: Routledge.

246

Bale, J. (2000). Sports as Power: Running as Resistance? In J. P. Sharp, P. Routledge, C. Philo, & R. Paddison (Eds.), *Entanglements of Power* (pp. 148–163). New York: Routledge.

Bandy, S. (2010a). Gender. In S. W. Pope & J. Nauright (Eds.), *Routledge Companion to Sport History* (pp: 129–147). New York: Routledge.

Bandy, S. (2010b). Politics of Gender through the Olympics. In A. Bairner & G. Molnar (Eds.), *The Politics of the Olympics: A Survey* (pp: 41–57). London: Routledge.

Bandy, S. J. & Darden, A. S. (eds)(1999). *Crossing Boundaries*. Champaign, IL: Human Kinetics.

Barker, C. (2008). *Cultural Studies: Theory and Practice* (3rd ed.). London: Sage.

Barth, L. (2008). Michel Foucault. In R. Stones (Ed.), *Key Sociological Thinkers* (2nd ed., pp: 278–292). Basingstoke, UK: Palgrave.

Baudrillard, J. (1983). *Simulations*. Cambridge, MA: MIT Press.

Baudrillard, J. (1994). *Simulacra and Simulations*. Ann Arbor, MI: University of Michigan Press.

Baudrillard, J. (2006). *Utopia Deferred: Writing for Utopie (1967–1978)*. New York: Semiotext(e).

Bauman, Z. (1997). *Postmodernity and Its Discontents*. Cambridge, UK: Polity Press.

Beal, B. (1995). Disqualifying the Official: An Exploration of Social Resistance through the Subculture of Skateboarding. *Sociology of Sport Journal*, 12(3): 252–267.

Beal, B. (2004). Symbolic Interactionism and Cultural Studies: Doing Critical Ethnography. In J. Maguire & K. Young (Eds.), *Theory, Sport and Society* (pp. 353–374). London: Elsevier Science.

Beames, S. K., & Pike, E. C. J. (2008). Goffman Goes Rock Climbing: Using Creative Fiction to Explore the Presentation of Self in Outdoor Education. *Australian Journal of Outdoor Education*, 12(2): 3–11.

Beamish, R. (2002). Karl Marx's Enduring Legacy for the Sociology of Sport. In J. Maguire & K. Young (Eds.), *Theory, Sport and Society* (pp. 25–39). Oxford: Elsevier Science Lt.

Beamish, R. (2009). Marxism, Alienation and Coubertin's Olympic Project. In B. Carrington & I. McDonald (Eds.), *Marxism, Cultural Studies and Sport* (pp. 88–105). Abingdon, Oxon: Routledge.

Becker, H. S. (1963). *Outsiders: Studies in the Sociology of Deviance*. New York: The Free Press.

Beddoe, D. (1998). *Discovering Women's History: A Practical Guide to Researching the Lives of Women since 1800*. London: Longman.

Bell, D. (1973). *The Coming of Post-Industrial Society: A Venture in Social Forecasting*. London: Heinemann.

Berger, P. L. (1966). *Invitation to Sociology: A Humanistic Perspective*. Harmondsworth, UK: Penguin.

Berry, B. (2010). Making It Big: Visible Symbols of Success, Physical Appearance, and Sport Figures. In E. Smith (Ed.), *Sociology of Sport and Social Theory* (pp. 187–200). Leeds, UK: Human Kinetics.

Beynon, J., & Dunkerely, D. (Eds.) (2000). *Globalization: The Reader*. London: The Athlone Press.

Birrell, S. (1981). Sport as Ritual. *Social Forces*, 60(2): 354–376.

Birrell, S. (2002). Feminist Theories for Sport. In J. Coakley & E. Dunning (Eds.), *Handbook of Sport Studies* (pp. 61–77). London: Sage.

Birrell, S., & Donnelly, P. (2004). Reclaiming Goffman: Erving Goffman's Influence on the Sociology of Sport. In R. Giulianotti (Ed.), *Sport and Modern Social Theorists* (pp. 49–64). Basingstoke, UK: Palgrave Macmillan.

Birrell, S. & McDonald, M. G. (eds)(2000). *Reading Sport: Critical Essays on Power and Representation*. Boston, MA: Northeastern University Press.

Bourdieu, P. (1984). *Distinction: A Social Critique of the Judgement of Taste*. London: Routledge.

Bourgois, P. (1995). *In Search of Respect: Selling Crack in El Barrio*. Cambridge, UK: Cambridge University Press.

Boutilier, M. A., & SanGiovanni, L. F. (1994). Politics, Public Policy and Title IX: Some Limitations of Liberal Feminism. In S. Birrell & C. L. Cole (Eds.), *Women, Sport and Culture* (pp. 97–109). Champaign, IL: Human Kinetics.

Bowes, P. (2011). LA Cricket: Club Helps Tame Compton's Mean Streets. *BBC online news US & Canada*. 10 February. Available at:http://www.bbc.co.uk/news/world-us-canada-12382224

Boyne, R., & Rattansi, A. (1990). *Postmodernism and Society*. Basingstoke, UK: Macmillan Education.

Brohm, J.-M. (1978). *Sport: A Prison of Measured Time*. London: Ink Links.

Brown, M., Fry, H., & Marshall, S. (1999). Reflective Practice. In H. Fry, S. Ketteridge, & S. Marshall (Eds.), *A Handbook for Teaching & Learning in Higher Education* (2nd ed., pp. 215–225). London: Routledge.

Burkitt, I. (1991). Social Selves: Theories of the Social Formation of Personality. *Current Sociology*, 39(3): 1–225.

Burman, E. (1992). Feminism and Discourse in Developmental Psychology: Power, Subjectivity and Interpretation. *Feminism & Psychology*, 2(1): 45–59.

Butler, J. (1990). *Gender Trouble: Feminism and the Subversion of Identity*. London: Routledge.

Butler, R. (1999). *Jean Baudrillard: The Defence of the Real*. London: Sage.

Butt, J., & Molnar, G. (2009). Involuntary Career Termination in Sport: A Case Study of the Process of Structurally Induced Failure. *Sport in Society*, 12(2): 236–252.

Butterworth, M., & Moskal, S. D. (2009). American Football, Flags, and 'Fun': The Bell Helicopter Armed Forces Bowl and the Rhetorical Production of Militarism. *Communication, Culture and Critique*, 2(4): 411–433.

Calhoun, C., Gerteis, J., Moody, J., Pfaff, S., Schmidt, K., & Virk, I. (2002). *Classical Sociological Theory*. Oxford: Blackwell.

Carrington, B. (2009). Sport without Final Guarantees: Cultural Studies/Marxism/Sport. In B. Carrington & I. McDonald (Eds.), *Marxism, Cultural Studies and Sport* (pp. 15–31). Abingdon, Oxon: Routledge.

Carrington, B., & McDonald, I. (Eds.)(2009). *Marxism, Cultural Studies and Sport*. Abingdon, Oxon: Routledge.

Carroll, R. (1980). Football Hooliganism in England. *International Review for the Sociology of Sport*, 15(2): 77–92.

Carroll, J. (1986). Sport: Virtue and Grace. *Theory, Culture & Society*, 3(1): 91–98.

Caudwell, J. (Ed.) (2006). *Sport, Sexualities and Queer/Theory*. London: Routledge.

Centre of Sport Policy Studies. (2011). *Gender Equity in Canadian Interuniversity Sport: A Biannual Report*. Available at https://physical.utoronto.ca/Libraries/CSPS_PDFs/CIS_Gender_Equity_Report_2011.sflb.ashx

Choi, P. Y. L. (2000). *Femininity and the Physically Active Woman*. London: Routledge.

Coakley, J., & Pike, E. (2009). *Sport in Society: Issues and Controversies*. London: McGraw-Hill.

Cohen, G. A. (1978). *Karl Marx's Theory of History: A Defence*. Oxford: Oxford University Press.

Cole, C. L., Giardina, M. D., & Andrews, D. L. (2004). Michel Foucault: Studies of Power and Sport. In R. Giulianotti (Ed.), *Sport and Modern Social Theorists* (pp. 207–223). London: Palgrave.

Collins, R. (1981). Crises and Declines in Credential Systems. In R. Collins (Ed.), *Sociology Since Mid-Century: Essays in Theory Cumulation* (pp. 191–215). New York: Academic Press.

Craig, P., & Beedie, P. (2008). *Sport Sociology*. Exeter: Learning Matters.

Crehan, K. (2002). *Gramsci, Culture and Anthropology*. London: University of California Press.

Creighton, J. (2011). Women's Boxing Split as Governing Body Suggests Skirts. *BBC Sport*. Available at http://news.bbc.co.uk/sport1/hi/boxing/15452596.stm

Cuff, E. C., Sharrock, W. W., & Francis, D. W. (1998). *Perspectives in Sociology* (4th ed.). London: Routledge.

Curry, T. (1991). Fraternal Bonding in the Locker Room: A Profeminist Analysis of Talk about Competition and Women. *Sociology of Sport Journal*, 8(2): 119–135.

Davis, K., & Moore, W. E. (1945). Some Principles of Stratification. *American Sociological Review*, 10(2): 242–249.

Davis, K., Evans, M. & Lorber, J. (eds)(2006). *Handbook of Gender and Women's Studies*. London: Sage.

De Frantz, A. (1997). The Changing Role of Women in the Olympic Games. *Olympic Review*, 26(15): 18–21.

Delaney, T., & Madigan, T. (2009). *The Sociology of Sports: An Introduction*. London: McFarland and Co.

Denison, J. (2007). Social Theory for Coaches: A Foucauldian Reading of One Athlete's Poor Performance. *International Journal of Sport Science and Coaching*, 2(4): 369–383.

De Oca, J. M. (2007). The 'Muscle Gap': Physical Education and US Fears of a Depleted Masculinity, 1954–1963. In S. Wagg & D. L. Andrews (Eds.), *East Plays West: Spot and the Cold War* (pp. 123–148). London: Routledge.

Dine, P., & Crosson, S. (Eds.) (2010). *Sport, Representation and Evolving Identities in Europe.* Witney, UK: Peter Lang.

Donnelly, P. (2000). Interpretive Approaches to the Sociology of Sport. In J. Coakley & E. Dunning (Eds.), *Handbook of Sport Studies* (pp. 77–91). London: Sage.

Donnelly, P. (2002). George Herbert Mead and an Interpretive Sociology of Sport. In J. Maguire & K. Young (Eds.), *Theory, Sport and Society* (pp. 83–102). London: Elsevier Science.

Duncan, M. C., & Messner, M. A. (2005). *Gender in Televised Sports: News and Highlights Shows, 1989–2004.* Los Angeles: Amateur Athletic Foundation.

Dunning, E. (1994). Sport as a Male Preserve: Notes on the Social Sources of Masculine Identity and Its Transformations. In S. Birrell & C. L. Cole (Eds.), *Women, Sport and Culture* (pp. 163–179). Champaign, IL: Human Kinetics.

Dunning, E. (1999). *Sport Matters: Sociological Studies of Sport, Violence and Civilisation.* London: Routledge.

Dunning, E. (2002). Figurational Contributions to the Sociological Study of Sport. In J. Maguire & K. Young (Eds.), *Theory, Sport and Society* (pp. 211–238). Oxford: Elsevier Science.

Durkheim, E. (1893/1984). *The Division of Labour in Society* (revised ed.). London: Macmillan.

Durkheim, E. (1895/1982). *The Rules of the Sociological Method* (revised ed.). London: Macmillan.

Durkheim, E. (1897/1952). *Suicide: A Study in Sociology* (revised ed.). London: Routledge.

Durkheim, E. (1912/1915). *The Elementary Forms of the Religious Life* (revised ed.). London: George Allen & Unwin.

Edwards, H. (1973). *Sociology of Sport.* Homewood, IL: Dorsey Press.

Eldridge, J. (1983). *C. Wright Mills.* Sussex: Ellis Horwood Ltd.

Elias, N. (1939/2000). *The Civilising Process* (revised ed.). Oxford: Blackwell.

Elias, N. (1978). *What is Sociology?* New York: Columbia University Press.

Elias, N. (1983). The Retreat of Sociologist into the Present. *Theory, Culture and Society,* 4: 223–417.

Elias, N. (1969/1983). *The Court Society.* Oxford: Blackwell.

Elias, N. (1986). Introduction. In N. Elias & E. Dunning (Eds.), *Quest for Excitement: Sport and Leisure in the Civilising Process* (pp. 19–62). Oxford: Blackwell.

Elias, N., & Dunning, E. (Eds.) (1986). *Quest for Excitement: Sport and Leisure in the Civilising Process.* Oxford: Blackwell.

Engels, F. (1884/1972). *The Origins of the Family, Private Property and the State.* London: Penguin Press.

Evans, M. (1997). In Praise of Theory: The Case of Women's Studies. In S. Kemp & J. Squires (Eds.), *Feminisms* (pp. 17–22). Oxford: Oxford University Press.

Evans, M. (2003). *Gender and Social Theory.* Buckingham: Open University Press.

Falcous, M., & Silk, M. (2005). Manufacturing Consent: Mediated Sporting Spectacle and the Cultural Politics of the 'War on Terror'. *International Journal of Media and Cultural Politics*, 1(1): 59–65.

Falcous, M., & Silk, M. (2006). Global Regimes, Local Agendas: Sport, Resistance and the Mediation of Dissent. *International Review for the Sociology of Sport*, 41(3-4): 317–338.

Farganis, J. (2004). *Readings in Social Theory* (4th ed.). New York: McGraw-Hill.

Feather, J. (2008). *The Information Society: A Study of Continuity and Change* (5th ed.). London: Facet Publishing.

Featherstone, M. (1991). *Consumer Culture & Postmodernism*. London: Sage.

Fitts, P. M., & Posner, M. I. (1967). *Human Performance*. Oxford: Brooks and Cole.

Foucault, M. (1978). *History of Sexuality: An Introduction* (vol. 1). New York: Pantheon Books.

Foucault, M. (1979). *Discipline and Punish: The Birth of the Prison*. London: Penguin Books.

Freire, P. (1970). *Pedagogy of the Oppressed* (revised ed.). London: Penguin Books.

Friedman, P. (2009). *Diary of an Exercise Addict*. Guilford, CT: The Globe Pequot Press.

Fuller, S. (2006). *The New Sociological Imagination*. London: Sage.

Fussell, S. W. (1991). *Muscle: Confessions of an Unlikely Bodybuilder*. New York: Avon Books.

Gale, Z. (1990). Foreword. In C. P. Gilman, *The Living of Charlotte Perkins Gilman: An Autobiography* (pp. xxvii–lii). Madison: University of Wisconsin Press.

Geertz, C. (1973/2000). Deep Play: Notes on the Balinese Cockfight. In C. Geertz (Ed.), *The Interpretation of Cultures* (pp. 412–453). New York: Basic Books.

Giddens, A. (1979). *Central Problems in Social Theory*. London: Macmillan.

Giddens, A. (1986). *Sociology: A Brief but Critical Introduction* (2nd ed.). London: Macmillan.

Giddens, A. (1990). *The Consequences of Modernity*. Cambridge: Polity Press.

Giddens, A. (1999). *Runaway World: How Globalisation is Reshaping Our Lives*. London: Profile Books.

Giddens, A. (2006). *Sociology* (5th ed.). Cambridge: Polity.

Gill, R., & Grint, K. (Eds.)(1995). *The Gender-Technology Relation: Contemporary Theory and Research*. London: Taylor and Francis.

Gilman, C. P. (1898). *Women and Economics: The Economic Relation between Men and Women as a Factor in Social Evolution*. Boston: Small, Maynard & Co.

Gilman, C. P. (1990). *The Living of Charlotte Perkins Gilman: An Autobiography*. Madison: University of Wisconsin Press.

Gilman, C. P. (1997). *The Yellow Wallpaper and Other Stories*. New York: Dover Publications.

Gilman, S. L. (2008). *Fat: A Cultural History of Obesity*. Cambridge, UK: Polity.

Gitlin, T. (2000) Afterword. In C. W. Mills (Ed.), *The Sociological Imagination* (40th Anniversary ed.). Oxford: Oxford University Press.

Giulianotti, R. (1991). Scotland's Tartan Army in Italy: The Case for the Carnivalesque. *The Sociological Review*, 39(3): 503–527.

Giulianotti, R. (2004a). Civilising Games: Norbert Elias and the Sociology of Sport. In R. Giulianotti (Ed.), *Sport and Modern Social Theorists* (pp. 145–160). London: Palgrave.

Giulianotti, R. (2004b). The Fate of Hyperreality: Jean Baudrillard and the Sociology of Sport. In R. Giulianotti (Ed.), *Sport and Modern Social Theorists* (pp. 225–239). London: Palgrave.

Goffman, E. (1956/1967). The Nature of Deference and Demeanour. In E. Goffman (Ed.), *Interaction Ritual: Essays on Face-to-Face Behaviour* (pp. 47–95). New York: Pantheon.

Goffman, E. (1959). *The Presentation of Self in Everyday Life*. London: Penguin.

Goffman, E. (1961). *Asylums: Essays on the Social Situation of Mental Patients and Other Inmates*. New York: Doubleday, Anchor.

Goffman, E. (1974). *Frame Analysis*. Cambridge, MA: Harvard University.

Goffman, E. (1979). *Gender Advertisements*. New York: Harper and Row.

Goffman, E. (1981). *Forms of Talk*. Philadelphia: University of Pennsylvania.

Gramsci, A. (1971). *Selections from the Prison Notebooks*. In Q. Hoare & G. Nowell-Smith (Eds.), London: Lawrence and Wishart.

Greendorfer, S. (1983). Shaping the Female Athlete: The Impact of the Family. In M. Boutilier & L. SanGiovanni (Eds.), *The Sporting Woman* (pp. 135–155). Champaign, IL: Human Kinetics.

Grey, S. (2006). Numbers and Beyond: The Relevance of Critical Mass in Gender Research. *Politics & Gender*, 2(4): 492–502.

Griffin, P. (1998). *Strong Women, Deep Closets: Lesbians and Homophobia in Sport*. Champaign, IL: Human Kinetics.

Grossberg, L. (1997). Cultural Studies, Modern Logics, and Theories of Globalisation. In A. McRobbie (Ed.), *Back to Reality? Social Experience and Cultural Studies* (pp. 7–35). Manchester, UK: Manchester University Press.

Gruneau, R. (1983). *Class, Sports, and Social Development*. Leeds, UK: Human Kinetics.

Gruneau, R. (1988). Modernisation or Hegemony: Two Views on Sport and Social Development. In J. Harvey & H. Cantelon (Eds.), *Not Just a Game: Essays in Canadian Sport Sociology* (pp. 9–32). Ottawa, ON: University of Ottawa Press.

Gruneau, R. (1993). The Critique of Sport in Modernity: Theorising Power, Culture, and the Politics of the Body. In E. Dunning, J. Maguire, & R. E. Pearton (Eds.), *The Sports Process: A Comparative and Developmental Approach* (pp. 85–109). Leeds: Human Kinetics.

Gruneau, R. (1999). *Class, Sports, and Social Development* (new ed.). Leeds, UK: Human Kinetics.

Gruneau, R. (2006). 'Amateurism' as a Sociological Problem: Some Reflections Inspired by Eric Dunning. *Sport in Society*, 9(4): 559–582.

Guba, E. G. (Ed.) (1990). *The Paradigm Dialog*. London: Sage.

Guttmann, A. (2002). *Olympics: History of the Modern Games* (2nd ed.). Champaign, IL: University of Illinois Press.

Hall, S. (1980). Cultural Studies and the Centre: Some Problematics and Problems. In S. Hall, D. Hobson, A. Lowe, & P. Willis (Eds.), *Culture, Media, Language* (pp. 15–47). London: Hutchinson.

Hall, S. (1981). Notes on Deconstructing the 'Popular'. In R. Samuel (Ed.), *People's History and Socialist Theory* (pp. 227–240). London: Routledge.

Hall, S. (1992). Cultural Studies and Its Theoretical Legacies. In L. Grossberg, C. Nelson, & P. Treichler (Eds.), *Cultural Studies* (pp. 277–294). London: Routledge.

Hamilton, P. (1983). Editor's Foreword. In J. Eldridge (Ed.), *Key Sociologists: C. Wright Mills* (pp. 7–9). Chichester, UK: Ellis Horwood Ltd.

Hargreaves, J. (1982). Theorising Sport: An Introduction. In J. Hargreaves (Ed.), *Sport, Culture and Ideology* (pp. 1–29). London: Routledge.

Hargreaves, J. (1986). *Sport, Power and Culture*. Cambridge: Polity.

Hargreaves, J. (1994). *Sporting Females: Critical Issues in the History and Sociology of Women's Sports*. London: Routledge.

Hargreaves, J. (2004). Querying Sport Feminism: Personal or Political? In R. Giulianotti (Ed.), *Sport and Modern Social Theorists* (pp. 187–205). Basingstoke: Palgrave.

Hargreaves, J., & McDonald, I. (2000). Cultural Studies and the Sociology of Sport. In J. Coakley & E. Dunning (Eds.), *Handbook of Sport Studies* (pp. 48–60). Thousand Oaks, CA: Sage.

Hebdige, D. (1988). *Hiding in the Light: On Images and Things*. London: Routledge.

Held, D., McGrew, A., Goldblatt, D., & Perraton, J. (Eds.)(1999). *Global Transformations: Politics, Economics and Culture*. Cambridge: Polity Press.

Hoggart, R. (1957). *The Uses of Literacy*. London: Penguin.

Horowitz, I. L. (Ed.) (1963). *Power, Politics and People: The Collected Essays of C. Wright Mills*. New York: Oxford University Press.

Howell, J. W., Andrews, D. L., & Jackson, S. J. (2002). Cultural and Sport Studies: An Interventionist Practice. In J. Maguire & K. Young (Eds.), *Theory, Sport and Society* (pp. 151–177). Oxford: Elsevier Science Ltd.

Hughes, R., & Coakley, J. (1991). Positive Deviance among Athletes: The Implications of Over-conformity to the Sport Ethic. *Sociology of Sport Journal*, 8(4): 307–325.

Humm, M. (Ed.) (1992). *Feminisms: A Reader*. London: Harvester.

Illich, I. (1970). *Deschooling Society*. London: Marion Boyars Publishers.

Ingham, A. G. (1975). Occupational Subcultures in the Work World of Sport. In D. Ball & J. Loy (Eds.), *Sport and Social Order* (pp. 333–389). Reading, MA: Addison-Wesley.

Ingham, A. G. (1982). Sport, Hegemony and the Logic of Capitalism: Response to Hargreaves and Beamish. In H. Cantelon & R. Gruneau (Eds.), *Sport, Culture and the Modern State* (pp. 198–208). Toronto, ON: University of Toronto Press.

Ingham, A. G. (2004). The Sportification Process: A Biographical Analysis Framed by the Work of Marx, Weber, Durkheim and Freud. In R. Giulianotti (Ed.), *Sport and Modern Social Theorists* (pp. 11–32). London: Palgrave.

Ingham, A. G., & Dewar, A. (1999). Through the Eyes of Youth: 'Deep Play' in PeeWee Ice Hockey. In J. Coakley & P. Donnelly (Eds.), *Inside Sports* (pp. 17–27). London: Routledge.

Ingham, A.G., & Loy, J. W. (Eds.) (1993). *Sport in Social Development: Traditions, Transitions and Transformations.* Champaign, IL.: Human Kinetics.

James, C. L. R. (1963). *Beyond a Boundary.* London: Stanley Paul and Co.

Jarvie, G. (1991). *The Highland Games: The Making of the Myth.* Edinburgh: Edinburgh University Press.

Jarvie, G., & Maguire, J. (1994). *Sport and Leisure in Social Thought.* London: Routledge.

Jary, D., & Jary, J. (2000). *Collins Dictionary: Sociology* (3rd ed.). Glasgow: Harper Collins Publisher.

Jencks, C. (1986). *What is Post-Modernism?* New York: St. Martin's Press.

Johnson, T., Dandeker, C., & Ashworth, C. (1992). *The Structure of Social Theory: Dilemmas and Strategies.* London: Macmillan Press Ltd.

Jones, O. (2011). *Chavs: The Demonization of the Working Class.* London: Verso.

Kanemasu, Y., & Molnar, G. (in press). Collective Identity and Contested Allegiance: A Case of Migrant Professional Fijian Rugby Players. *Sport in Society.*

Kay, T., & Jeanes, R. (2009). Sport and Gender Inequity. In B. Houlihan (Ed.), *Sport and Society: A Student Introduction* (2nd ed., pp. 130–154). London: Sage.

Kelly, J. (2007). Hibernian Football Club: The Forgotten Irish? *Sport in Society,* 10(3): 514–536.

Kelly, J. (2008). Flowers of Scotland? Rugby Union, National Identities and Class Distinction: *Stadion. International Journal of the History of Sport,* 34(1): 83–99.

Kelly, J. (2011). 'Sectarianism' and Scottish Football: Critical Reflections on Dominant Discourse and Press Commentary. *International Review for the Sociology of Sport,* 46(4): 418–435.

Kelly, J. (in press). Popular Culture, Sport and the 'Hero'-fication of British Militarism. *Sociology.*

Kemp, S., & Squires, J. (Eds.) (1997). *Feminisms.* Oxford: Oxford University Press.

Krieken, R. van (1998). *Key Sociologists: Norbert Elias.* London: Routledge.

Krieken, R. van (2009). Norbert Elias and Process Sociology. In G. Ritzer & B. Smart (Eds.), *Handbook of Social Theory* (pp. 353–367). London: Sage.

Lane, A. J. (1990). Introduction. In C. P. Gilman (Ed.), *The Living of Charlotte Perkins Gilman: An Autobiography* (pp. xi–xxiv). Madison: University of Wisconsin Press.

Lane, J. R. (2008). *Jean Baudrillard* (2nd ed). Oxon: Routledge.

Larrain, J. (1983). *Marxism and Ideology.* London: Macmillan Press.

Layder, D. (2006). *Understanding Social Theory* (2nd ed.). London: Sage.

254

Lengermann, P. M., & Brantley-Niebrugge, J. (1992). Contemporary Feminist Theory. In G. Ritzer (Ed.), *Sociological Theory* (3rd ed., pp. 447–496). London: McGraw-Hill.

Lengermann, P. M., & Brantley-Niebrugge, J. (2009). Classical Feminist Social Theory. In G. Ritzer & B. Smart (Eds.), *Handbook of Social Theory* (pp. 125–137). London: Sage.

Leonard, W. (1996). The Odds of Transiting from One Level of Sports Participation to Another. *Sociology of Sport Journal*, 13(3): 288–299.

Lever, J. (1978). Sex Differences in The Complexity of Children's Play and Games. *American Sociological Review*, 43(August): 471–483.

Lewandowski, J. (2007). Boxing: The Sweet Science of Constraints. *Journal of the Philosophy of Sport*, 34(1): 26–38.

Lorber, J. (2005). *Breaking the Bowls: Degendering and Feminist Change*. New York: W. W. Norton & Co.

Lorber, J. (2010). *Gender Inequality: Feminist Theories and Politics* (4th ed). New York: Oxford University Press.

Loy, J., & Booth, D. (2000). Functionalism, Sport and Society. In J. Coakley & E. Dunning (Eds.), *Handbook of Sports Studies* (pp. 8–28). London: Sage.

Loy, J., & Booth, D. (2004). Consciousness, Craft, Commitment: The Sociological Imagination of C. Wright Mills. In R. Giulianotti (Ed.), *Sport and Modern Social Theorists* (pp. 65–80). Basingstoke, UK: Palgrave.

Luciano, L. (2001). *Looking Good: Male Body Image in Modern America*. New York: Hill and Wang.

Lukes, S. (1974/2005). *Power: A Radical View* (2nd ed.). Basingstoke, UK: Palgrave Macmillan.

Luschen, G. (1990). On Theory of Science for the Sociology of Sport: New Structuralism, Action, Intention and Practical Meaning. *International Review for the Sociology of Sport*, 25(1): 69–83.

Lyon, D. (1994). *Postmodernity*. Buckingham UK: Open University Press.

Maguire, J. (1990). More than a Sporting 'Touchdown': The Making of American Football in England, 1982–1990. *Sociology of Sport Journal*, 7(3): 213–237.

Maguire, J. (1991). The Media-Sport Production Complex: The Case of American Football in Western European Societies. *European Journal of Communication*, 6(3): 315–335.

Maguire, J. (1993). Globalisation, Sport Development and the Media/Sport Production Complex. *Sport Science Review*, 2: 29–47.

Maguire, J. (1994). Preliminary Observations on Globalisation and the Migration of Sport Labour. *Sociological Review*, 42(3): 452–480.

Maguire, J. (1999). *Global Sport: Identities, Societies, Civilisations*. Cambridge, UK: Polity Press.

Maguire, J. (2004). Globalisation and the Making of Modern Sport. *Sportwissenschaft*, 34(1): 7–20.

Maguire, J. (Ed.) (2005). *Power and Global Sport: Zones of Prestige, Emulation and Resistance*. London: Routledge.

Maguire, J., & Stead, D. (1996). Far Pavilions? Cricket Migrants, Foreign Sojourns and Contested Identities. *International Review for the Sociology of Sport*, 31(1): 1–24.

Maguire, J., & Stead, D. (1998). Border Crossings: Soccer Labour Force Migration and the European Union. *International Review for the Sociology of Sport*, 33(1): 59–73.

Maguire, J., & Tuck, J. (1998). Global Sport and Patriot Games: Rugby Union and National Identity in the United Kingdom Since 1945. In D. Mayall & M. Cronin (Eds.), *Sporting Nationalism: Identity, Ethnicity, Immigration and Assimilation* (pp. 103–126). London: Frank Cass.

Maguire, J., Jarvie, G., Mansfield, L., & Bradley, J. (2002). *Sports Worlds: A Sociological Perspective*. Champaign, IL: Human Kinetics.

Maguire, J., & Tuck, J. (2005). National Identity, Rugby Union and Notions of Ireland and the Irish. *Irish Journal of Sociology*, 14(1): 86–109.

Malcolm, D. (2008). *The Sage Dictionary of Sports Studies*. London: Sage.

Malcolm, D., & Waddington, I. (Eds.) (2007). *Matters of Sport: Essays in Honour of Eric Dunning*. London: Routledge.

Malson, H. (1998). *The Thin Woman: Feminism, Post-structuralism and the Social Psychology of Anorexia Nervosa*. London: Routledge.

Mansfield, L. (2009). Fitness Cultures and Environmental (In)Justice? *International Review for the Sociology of Sport*, 44(4): 345–362.

Marcus. G. E., & Fischer, M. J. (1986). *Anthropology as Cultural Critique: An Experimental Moment in the Human Sciences*. London: University of Chicago Press.

Markula, P. (1995). Firm but Shapely, Fit but Sexy, Strong but Thin: The Postmodern Aerobicizing Female Bodies. *Sociology of Sport Journal*, 12(4): 424–453.

Markula, P. (2001). Beyond the Perfect Body: Women's Body Image Distortion in Fitness Magazine Discourse. *Journal of Sport and Social Issues*, 25(2): 158–179.

Markula, P. (2003). The Technologies of the Self: Sport, Feminism, and Foucault. *Sociology of Sport Journal*, 20(2): 87–107.

Marx, K. (1844/1988). *The Economic and Philosophical Manuscripts*. New York: Prometheus Books.

Marx, K. (1858/1993). *Grundrisse* (revised ed.). London: Penguin.

Marx, K. (1859/1977). *A Contribution to a Critique of Political Economy*. Moscow: Progress Publishers.

Marx, K. (1867/1990). *Capital: A Critique of Political Economy* (vol. 1, revised ed.). London: Penguin.

Marx, K. (1970). *A Critique of Hegel's Philosophy of Right*. Cambridge: Cambridge University Press.

Marx, K., & Engels, F. (1947). *The German Ideology*. New York: International Publishers.

Marx, K., & Engels, F. (1848/2005). *The Communist Manifesto*. London: Bookmarks Publications.

Marx, K., & Engels, F. (1890/1975). *Selected Correspondence*. Moscow: Progress Publishers.

McDonald, M. G., & Birrell, S. (1999). Reading Sport Critically: A Methodology for Interrogating Power. *Sociology of Sport Journal*, 16(4): 283–300.

McGrath, S. A., & Chananie-Hill, R. A. (2009). 'Big Freaky-Looking Women': Normalizing Gender Transgression through Bodybuilding. *Sociology of Sport Journal*, 26(2): 235–254.

McLennan, G. (2011). *Story of Sociology: A First Companion to Social Theory*. London: Bloomsbury.

Mennell, S. (1992). *Norbert Elias: An Introduction*. Dublin: University College Dublin Press.

Mennell, S., & Goudsblom, J. (Eds.) (1998). *On Civilisation, Power and Knowledge: Selected Writings*. Chicago: University of Chicago Press.

Merrin, W. (2005). *Baudrillard and the Media*. Cambridge, UK: Polity.

Messner, M. A., & Cooky, C. (2010). *Gender in Televised Sports: News and Highlights Shows, 1989–2009*. Los Angeles: Center for Feminist Research, University of Southern California.

Miller, J. (1993). *The Passion of Michel Foucault*. London: HarperCollins.

Mills, C. W. (1951). *White Collar: The American Middle Classes*. Oxford: Oxford University Press.

Mills, C. W. (1956). *The Power Elite*. Oxford: Oxford University Press.

Mills, C. W. (1959/2000). *The Sociological Imagination* (40th anniversary ed.). Oxford: Oxford University Press.

Mills, C. W. (1962). *The Marxist*. Middlesex: Penguin Books.

Mills, C. W. (1963). The Big City: Private Troubles and Public Issues. In I. L. Horowitz (Ed.), *Power, Politics and People: The Collected Essays of C. Wright Mills* (pp. 395–402). New York: Oxford University Press.

Mitchell, G., Obradovich, S., Herring, S., Tromborg, C., & Burns, A. L. (1992). Reproducing Gender in Public Places: Adults' Attention to Toddlers in Three Public Locales. *Sex Roles*, 26: 323–33.

Molnar, G. (2007). Hungarian Football: A Socio-Historical Perspective. *Sport in History*, 27(2): 293–318.

Molnar, G. (2010). Re-discovering Hungarianness: The Case of Elite Hungarian Footballers. In P. Dine & S. Crosson (Eds.), *Sport, Representation and Evolving Identities in Europe* (pp. 239–262). Witney, UK: Peter Lang.

Molnar, G., & Bryson, J. (2009). Enhancing Processual Learning: Some Observations on Teaching Research Skills. *The Journal of Pedagogical Research and Scholarship*, 1(2): 26–33.

Molnar, G., Doczi, T., & Gál, A. (2011). Socio-cultural Organisation of Hungarian Football: An Overview. In H. Gammelsæter & B. Senaux (Eds.), *Football across Europe: An Institutional Perspective* (pp. 253–267). London: Routledge.

Monaghan, L. F. (2008). *Men and the War on Obesity: A Sociological Study*. London: Routledge.

Morgan, W. J. (1994). *Leftist Theories of Sport: A Critique and Reconstruction*. Chicago: University of Illinois.

Morrison, K. (1995). *Marx, Durkheim, Weber: Formations of Modern Social Thought*. London: Sage.

Munch, R. (1987). Parsonian Theory Today: In Search of a New Synthesis. In A. Giddens & J. Turner (Eds.), *Social Theory Today* (pp. 116–155). Cambridge: Polity Press.

257

Murphy, P., & Sheard, K. (2006). Boxing Blind: Unplanned Processes in the Development of Modern Boxing. *Sport in Society*, 9(4): 542–558.

Nelson, C., Triechler, P., & Grossberg, L. (1992). Cultural Studies: An Introduction. In L. Grossberg, C. Nelson, & P. Triechler (Eds.), *Cultural Studies* (pp. 1–16). New York: Routledge.

Nitsch, J. R. (1985). The Action-Theoretical Perspective. *International Review for the Sociology of Sport*, 20(4): 263–282.

Nyong'o, T. (2010). The Unforgivable Transgression of Being Caster Semenya. *Women & Performance: A Journal of Feminist Theory*, 20(1): 95–100.

Oliver, A. (2012). Cost of Olympics to Spiral to £24bn ... TEN TIMES Higher than 2005 Estimate (and is It Any Wonder When We're Forking Out £335,000 for a Single Sculpture) *Mail Online*, 27 January. Available at http://www.dailymail.co.uk/news/article-2092077/London-2012-Olympics-cost-spiral-24bn--10-TIMES-higher-2005-e

Palmer, R. E. (1977). Postmodernity and Hermeneutics. *Boundary*, 2(5): 363–393.

Parsons, T. (1937/1967). *The Structure of Social Action* (revised ed.). London: Free Press.

Parsons, T. (1951). *The Social System*. New York: Free Press.

Parsons, T., & Shils, E. (1951). *Toward a General Theory of Action*. Cambridge, MA: Harvard University Press.

Polley, M. (2007). *Sports History: A Practical Guide*. Basingstoke, UK: Palgrave.

Postman, N., & Weingartner, C. (1969). *Teaching as a Subversive Activity*. New York: Dell Publishing.

Puig, N., & Vilanova, A. (2011). Positive Functions of Emotions in Achievement Sports. *Research Quarterly for Exercise and Sport*, 82(2): 334–344.

Rail, G. (1991). The Dissolution of Polarities as a Megatrend in Postmodern Sport. In F. Landry, M. Landry, & M. Yerles (Eds.), *Sport...The Third Millennium: Proceedings of the International Symposium, Quebec City* (pp. 745–751). Sainte-Foy: Les Presses de L'universite Laval.

Rail, G. (Ed.) (1998). *Sport and Postmodern Times*. Albany: State University of New York Press.

Rail, G. (2002). Postmodernism and Sport Studies. In J. Maguire & K. Young (Eds.), *Theory, Sport & Society* (pp. 179–207). Oxford: Elsevier Science Ltd.

Rail, G., & Harvey, J. (1995). Body at Work: Michel Foucault and the Sociology of Sport. *Sociology of Sport Journal*, 12(2): 164–179.

Ramazanoğlu, C., & Holland, J. (Eds.) (2002). *Feminist Methodology: Challenges and Choices*. London: Sage.

Rigauer, B. (2000). Marxist Theories. In J. Coakley & E. Dunning (Eds.), *Handbook of Sports Studies* (pp. 28–47). London: Sage.

Riordan, J. (2007). Sport After the Cold War: Implications for Russia and Eastern Europe. In S. Wagg & D. L. Andrews (Eds.), *East Plays West: Sport and the Cold War* (pp. 272–288). London: Routledge.

Ritzer, G. (1992). *Sociological Theory* (3rd ed.). London: McGraw-Hill.

Ritzer, G. (2003). *Contemporary Sociological Theory and Its Classical Roots: The Basics*. London: McGraw-Hill.

Robertson, R. (1992). *Globalization: Social Theory and Global Culture*. London: Sage Publications.

258

Robson, C. (2002). *Real World Research* (2nd ed.). London: Sage.

Roche, M. (2000). *Mega Events and Modernity: Olympics and Expos in the Growth of Global Culture*. London: Routledge.

Rose, A. M. (1991). *The Post-Modern & The Post-Industrial: A Critical Analysis*. Cambridge: Cambridge University Press.

Ross, K., & Byerly, C. M. (Eds.) (2004). *Women and Media: International Perspectives*. Oxford: Blackwell.

Roussel, P., Griffet, J,. & Duret, P. (2003).The Decline of Female Bodybuilding in France. *Sociology of Sport Journal*, 20(1): 40–59.

Sage. G. (1998). *Power and Ideology in American Sport: A Critical Perspective* (2nd ed.). Leeds: Human Kinetics.

Sassoon, S. (1979). *Memoirs of a Fox-hunting Man*. London: Faber & Faber.

Scherer, J., & Jackson, S. J. (2008). Cultural Studies and the Circuit of Culture: Advertising, Promotional Culture and the New Zealand All Blacks. *Cultural Studies – Critical Methodologies*, 8: 507–526.

Scherer, J., & Koch, J. (2010). Living with War: Sport, Citizenship and the Cultural Politics of Post-9/11 Canadian Identity. *Sociology of Sport Journal*, 27(1): 1–29.

Schimmel, K. S. (2010). Political Economy: Sport and Urban Development. In E. Smith (Ed.), *Sociology of Sport and Social Theory* (pp. 55–66). Leeds, UK: Human Kinetics.

Schmidt, R.A. (1975) A Schema Theory of Discrete Motor Learning. *Psychological Review*, 82(4): 225–260.

Schmitt, R. (1993). Enhancing Frame Analysis: Five Laminating Functions of Language in the 1987 NFL Strike. *Sociology of Sport Journal*, 10(2): 135–147.

Shaw, S. (2006a). Women in Sport Management: The Current State of Play and Visions for the Future. In C. C. Aitchison (Ed.), *Sport and Gender Identities: Masculinities, Femininities and Sexualities* (pp. 74–89). London: Routledge.

Shaw, S. (2006b). Gender Suppression in New Zealand Regional Sports Trusts. *Women in Management Review*, 21(7): 554–566.

Shaw, S. (2006c). Scratching the Back of 'Mr X': Analyzing Gendered Social Processes in Sport Organizations. *Journal of Sport Management*, 20(4): 510–534.

Shilling, C. (1993). *The Body and Social Theory*. London: Sage.

Silk, M., & Andrews, D. L. (2001). Beyond a Boundary? Sport, Transnational Advertising and the Remaining of National Culture. *Journal of Sport and Social Issues*, 25(2): 180–201.

Silk, M. & Falcous, M. (2005). One Day in September/A Week in February: Mobilizing American (Sporting) Nationalism. *Sociology of Sport Journal*, 22(4): 447–471.

Silverman, D. (2005). *Doing Qualitative Research: A Practical Handbook*. London: Sage.

Smart, B. (1993). *Postmodernity*. London: Routledge.

Smart, B. (2002). *Michel Foucault* (revised ed.). London: Routledge.

Smith, D. (1974). The Ideological Practice of Sociology. *Catalyst*, 8: 39–54.

Smith, D. (2001). *Norbert Elias and Modern Social Theory*. London: Sage.

Smith, G. (2006). *Erving Goffman*. Abingdon, Oxon: Routledge.

Smith, P. (2001). Student Protest: the NUS Lobby Wasn't Enough for Us. *The Guardian*. 10 November, Available at http://www.guardian.co.uk/commentisfree/2010/nov/10/student-protests-nus-lobby-anarchists

Smith, R. T. (2008). Pain in the Act: The Meanings of Pain among Professional Wrestlers. *Qualitative Sociology*, 31(2):129–148.

Smith Maguire, J. (2002). Michel Foucault: Sport, Power, Technologies and Governmentality. In J. Maguire & K. Young (Eds.), *Theory, Sport & Society* (pp. 293–314). Oxford: JAI Press.

Sparkes, A. C. (2007). Embodiment, Academics, and the Audit Culture: A Story Seeking Consideration. *Qualitative Research*, 7(4): 521–550.

Sreberny, A. & van Zoonen, L. (2000). Gender, Politics and Communication: An Introduction. In A. Sreberny & L. van Zoonen (Eds.), *Gender, Politics and Communication* (pp. 1–19). Cresskill, NJ: Hampton Press.

Stone, C. N. (1989). *Regime Politics: Governing Atlanta, 1946–1988*. Lawrence: University Press of Kansas.

Sugden, J., & Tomlinson, A. (1998). *FIFA and the Contest for World Football: Who Rules the People's Game?* Cambridge: Polity.

Sugden, J., & Tomlinson, A. (2002). Theory and Method for a Critical Sociology of Sport. In J. Sugden & A. Tomlinson (Eds.), *Power Games: A Critical Sociology of Sport* (pp. 3–21). London: Routledge.

Sykes, H. (2006). Queering Theories of Sexuality in Sport Studies. In J. Caudwell (Ed.), *Sport, Sexualities and Queer/Theory* (pp. 13–32). London: Routledge.

Taylor, C. (1989). *Sources of the Self: The Making of the Modern Identity*. Cambridge, UK: Cambridge University Press.

Taylor, S. R. (2007). Pastoral Support: The Key to Student Retention in Higher Education? *Journal of Pedagogical Research and Scholarship*, 1(1): 32–38.

Taylor, T. (1988). Sport and World Politics: Functionalism and the State System. *International Journal*, 43(4): 531–553.

Theberge, N., & Donnelly, P. (2004). *Sport and the Sociological Imagination*. College Station, TX: Texas A & M University Press.

Therborn, G. (2000). Globalisations: Dimensions, Historical Waves, Regional Effects, Normative Governance. *International Sociology*, 15(2): 151–170.

Thompson, E. P. (1963). *The Making of the English Working Class*. New York: Vintage.

Tischner, I., & Malson, H. (2011). 'You Can't Be Supersized?' Exploring Femininities, Body Size and Control within the Obesity Terrain. In E. Rich, L. F. Monaghan, & L. Aphramor (Eds.), *Debating Obesity: Critical Perspectives* (pp. 90–114). London: Palgrave.

Tischner, I., & Malson, H. (in press). Understanding the 'Too Fat' Body and the 'Too Thin' Body: A Critical Psychological Perspective. In N. Rumsey & D. Harcourt (Eds.), *Oxford Handbook of the Psychology of Appearance*. Oxford: Oxford University Press.

Turner, B. S. (1984/2008). *The Body and Society: Explorations in Social Theory*. London: Sage.

Ussher, J. M. (1997). *Fantasies of Femininity: Reframing the Boundaries of Sex.* London: Routledge.

UEFA. (2010). Europe's Club Football Landscape Surveyed. 24 February. Available at http://www.uefa.com/uefa/footballfirst/protectingthegame/clublicensing/news/newsid=1453119.html

Wacquant, L. D. (1989). Toward a Reflexive Sociology: A Workshop with Pierre Bourdieu. *Sociological Theory,* 7(1): 26–63.

Wacquant, L. D. (1992). The Social Logic of Boxing in Black Chicago: Towards a Sociology of Pugilism. *Sociology of Sport Journal,* 9(3): 221–254.

Wagg, S., & Andrews, D. L. (Eds.) (2007). *East Plays West: Sport and the Cold War.* London: Routledge.

Wallace, S. (2009). Agents Cost Premier League Clubs £70 million a Year. *The Independent,* 1 December. Available at http://www.independent.co.uk/sport/football/news-and-comment/agents-cost-premier-league-clubs-16370m-a-year-1831694.html

Ward, G. (1997). *Teach Yourself Postmodernism.* London: Hodder & Stoughton.

Weedon, C. (1999). *Feminism, Theory and the Politics of Difference.* London: Blackwell.

Weiss, O. (2001). Identity Reinforcement in Sport: Revisiting the Symbolic Interactionist Legacy. *International Review for the Sociology of Sport,* 36(4): 393–405.

Wesely, J. K. (2001). Negotiating Gender: Bodybuilding and the Natural/Unnatural Continuum. *Sociology of Sport Journal,* 18(2): 162–180.

Wilkes, C. (1990). Bourdieu's Class. In R. Harker, C. Mahar, & C. Wilkes (Eds.), *An Introduction to the Work of Pierre Bourdieu* (pp. 109–131). Basingstoke, UK: MacMillan.

Williams, M., & May, T. (2000). *Introduction to the Philosophy of Social Research.* London: Routledge.

Williams, R. (1958). *Culture and Society.* London: Chatto and Windus.

Williams, R. (1977). *Marxism and Literature.* Oxford: Oxford University Press.

Willis, E. (1996). *The Sociological Quest: An Introduction to The Study of Social Life* (3rd ed.). New Brunswick, NJ: Rutgers University Press.

Willis, P. (1982). Women in Sport in Ideology. In J. Hargreaves (Ed.), *Sport, Culture and Ideology* (pp. 117–135). London: Routledge.

INDEX

266